A Democratic Foreign Policy

"In *A Democratic Foreign Policy*, Ned Lebow develops the tragic view framework to analyze how and why states behave. Drawing on the author's half a century of distinguished scholarship, this book offers an original contribution to foreign policy literature. Lebow uses the idea of 'credible commitment' to formulate a strategy for dealing with the central challenge posed by the rise of China. In so doing Lebow effectively refutes the claim that power transitions inevitably lead to conflict. *A Democratic Foreign Policy* will constitute a valuable part of the debate over the next two years about what has gone wrong in twenty-first century US foreign policy and what needs to be changed."

—Fred Chernoff, *Harvey Picker Professor of International Relations, Colgate University, USA*

"In this insightful book, Ned Lebow suggests a modification of the muscular, hegemonic approach to foreign policy followed by both Republicans and Democrats since the beginning of the Cold War. This macho approach has led to frequent military actions, which often have not been in the country's best interest. Given today's realities, the cure that Lebow suggests is a more thoughtful, restrained, and affordable foreign policy more in line with national needs and values, and less dependent on overwhelming economic and military power. This is a discussion well worth having."

—J.M. Houlahan, *Foreign Service Officer (ret.)*

"Those seeking a sensible alternative to an American foreign policy suffused with triumphalism, unilateralism, and mercantilism need look no further. With his customary wit, incisiveness, command of history, and appreciation of the tragic element in politics, Ned Lebow provides a superb one."

—Rajan Menon, *Anne and Bernard Spitzer Professor of International Relations, City University of New York, USA*

Richard Ned Lebow

A Democratic Foreign Policy

Regaining American Influence Abroad

Richard Ned Lebow
King's College, London, UK

Pembroke College, University of Cambridge, Cambridge, UK

Dartmouth College, Hanover, NH, USA

ISBN 978-3-030-21518-7   ISBN 978-3-030-21519-4   (eBook)
https://doi.org/10.1007/978-3-030-21519-4

Cover illustration: Preto Perola / shutterstock.com

This Palgrave Macmillan imprint is published by the registered company Springer Nature Switzerland AG
The registered company address is: Gewerbestrasse 11, 6330 Cham, Switzerland

To my recently discovered Beck-Solomon family

Preface

In 2020 the American people will elect a new president, and if common sense and decency prevail it will be a Democrat. Donald Trump will become history, although the damage he has inflicted on the country will take a long time to undo. The Democratic Party has moved to the left, that is, away from the center-right position of Hilary Clinton and the party professionals. A president committed to change at home and abroad—and we hope with a majority in both houses of Congress—will have the kind of opportunities that were denied to Barack Obama. Opportunities are not enough. A new president must have a vision of what he or she wants to do and undo—a vision to which many senators, representatives, and the electorate are receptive. This is readily achievable in domestic affairs, where there is already much support for goals such as racial equality, more equitable tax structures, better urban infrastructure, more open access to citizenship, protection of national parks and monuments, and serious efforts to address pollution and climate change.

It is a more difficult project in foreign affairs. With any luck, the Alt Right, nativist nationalism, and mercantilist approaches to international trade will return to the shadow world they inhabited before 2014. This will leave the approach to foreign policy represented by what I call the national security establishment free of any serious competitors. This establishment reflects a near-consensus among the majority of people involved in foreign policy in and out of government (the media, think tanks, and the academy) that America is a hegemonic power, has a global responsibility for preserving the world's territorial and economic order, and that others welcome its dominant role. They also believe that power confers hegemony and demands not only a dominant economy but military spending at a level that guarantees American superiority and, with it, the ability to intervene anywhere in the world. These beliefs are bipartisan and have shaped the foreign and defense policies of Democratic and Republican administrations since the early days of the Cold War and the presidency of Harry S. Truman.

To be sure there are policy differences among those who subscribe to this view of the world when it comes to specific policies. Most recently they are divided on questions such as troop levels in Afghanistan, intervention in Syria—favored by Hilary Clinton and opposed by Obama—intervention by proxy in Yemen, and how closely the US should be associated with Saudi Arabia in the aftermath of its leader-authorized assassination of a dissident in their embassy in Istanbul. These are differences in degree, not of kind, and are largely tactical. Nobody in the establishment is suggesting that we consider deep cuts in the military budget, undertake a total withdrawal from Afghanistan, or a fundamental reorientation of our long-standing and deep commitment to Saudi Arabia.

There are alternative foundations for foreign policy: Marxism and libertarian-isolationism. They have no mainstream traction. Each has some valid insights. Marxism errs in its unquestioning belief in the economic determinants of policy of all kinds, but it is useful in highlighting some of the connections between business and foreign policy. Libertarian-isolationism is single-minded in its focus on terminating foreign commitments, but properly maintains that military interventions have not generally been in the country's interest.

In this book I propose an alternative vision of foreign policy, one based on a tragic understanding of life and politics. It is rooted in an understanding that the world is opaque, that we have at best limited ability to control and manipulate it, and that our efforts to do so often backfire. It further recognizes that conflict is inevitable because of clashing value systems and interests, but that too firm a commitment to these values and interests and unwillingness to compromise and exercise restraint can only intensify conflict. Tragedy also foregrounds the hubris of powerful actors and how overreaching and overconfidence in family life, domestic politics, and the international arena can lead to catastrophe. It teaches us that great powers are their own worst enemies. They act in ways to enhance their power but undermine it.

A tragic understanding of life and politics provides an intellectual, emotional, and psychological framework for thinking about politics. It offers no insights into the day-to-day formulation of foreign policy. For this we need some understanding of the national interest, and much of my book is about how we can think intelligently about our interests. I am clear at the outset that there is no such thing as *the* national interest. There are multiple conceptions of the national interest because it or they are reflections of our values and the projects to which we are committed. These are all subjective in nature and often a matter of difference or controversy within society. The national interest is political in nature just as the struggle among competing formulation of the national interest for audiences and primacy is a political process.

I use tragedy as a vantage point to critique the dominant understanding of security and the means by which it is secured: emphasis on power and especially military might, deterrence and compellence, American control of international institutions, the search for special privileges, and a reputation for being tough. I show just how questionable these mechanisms are and how they are often counterproductive to American security. I then step back and consider the national interest. What matters to most Americans? What values do they cherish? To what projects do they give rise or support? How can foreign policy best be made responsive to them? I describe values widely shared by Americans but certainly claim no right or authority to identify these values or how they should be realized. I do believe that a careful elaboration of values and how they relate to interests is a useful exercise and has the potential to stimulate meaningful debate in lieu of the kinds of sound bites and point scoring that now dominates political discussion.

My book draws on almost 60 years of scholarly research and 5 years of government service. I was Professor of Strategy at the Naval and National War Colleges and then the first scholar-in-residence at the Central Intelligence Agency. Since the 1970s I have published extensively on foreign and defense policy and developed conceptual and empirical critiques of coercive strategies of conflict management. Using case studies I have demonstrated how deterrence often provokes the kinds of challenges it is intended to prevent.[1] The brief opening of Soviet archives in the Gorbachev era allowed me and coauthor Janice Gross Stein to document in detail from both sides two critical Cold War crises: the Cuban missile crisis of 1963 and the October Middle East crisis of 1973.[2] More recently I developed a critique of hegemony with coauthor Simon Reich.[3] We demonstrate that the US has never been a hegemon, beyond its limited regional authority in Central and Latin America, and argue that hegemony is not in anybody's interest. We show how authority for security and economic wellbeing is becoming more diffused through international society and argue that it is a good thing. Janice Stein and I have explored other strategies of conflict management and resolution, most notably reassurance and diplomacy. In 2017, I wrote a book that nested this research in a holistic framework for conflict management and resolution.[4] In 2019, coauthor Feng Zhang and I applied this framework to Sino-American relations to show how further conflict might be prevented and current ones resolved or finessed.[5]

This book draws heavily on this earlier work. In some chapters I summarize findings of this research because they are so central to my critique of American foreign and defense policy. This part of the book rests on a firm scientific and empirical foundation—in sharp contrast to so many tomes on these subjects. The next part of the book—on the national interests, threats we need to take seriously, and intelligent ways of responding to them—rests on subjective judgments. The exception here is the threat posed by climate change, which also reflects good science. Science can inform our choices by telling us what is possible or likely, but those choices are inevitably based on our values, as they should be. I am very clear throughout when I am relying on or presenting scientific findings and when you, the reader, are being asked to make subjective judgments based on your values. In this connection I am very much hoping that we share common values and that you will see the logic of connecting them to the visions of foreign and defense policy that I offer.

London, UK   Richard Ned Lebow
Cambridge, UK
NH, USA

Notes

1. Richard Ned Lebow, *Between Peace and War: The Nature of International Crisis* (Baltimore: Johns Hopkins University Press, 1981); Robert Jervis, Richard Ned Lebow, and Janice Gross Stein, *Psychology and Deterrence* (Baltimore: Johns Hopkins University Press, 1984).
2. Richard Ned Lebow and Janice Gross Stein, *We All Lost the Cold War* (Princeton: Princeton University Press, 1994).
3. Simon Reich and Richard Ned Lebow, *Good-Bye Hegemony! Power and Influence in the Global System* (Princeton: Princeton University Press, 2014).
4. Richard Ned Lebow, *Avoiding War, Making Peace* (London: Palgrave Macmillan, 2017).
5. Feng Zhang and Richard Ned Lebow, *Taming Sino-American Rivalry*, forthcoming.

Contents

1

Introduction

The Iraq invasion of 2003 was intended to overthrow a gangster regime that had acquired weapons of mass destruction and replace it with a Western-oriented democracy. It was also meant to demonstrate American power, intimidate friend and foe alike, and lock in American hegemony. Saddam Hussein fled Baghdad and was later captured, tried, and clumsily executed on video, but no evidence of weapons of mass destruction or attempts to acquire them were ever found. The occupation provoked a violent and ongoing resistance to the Anglo-American military occupation that has been responsible for far more casualties than the invasion.[1] The invasion made Iran and North Korea more threatened and committed to developing nuclear weapons. It produced a power vacuum that invited the rise of ISIS and its short-lived but brutal and bloody occupation of swaths of the Middle East. It left the region more unstable than before, with intensified ethnic and religious rivalries, problems of drought and food shortages, and many more refugees. It significantly reduced American influence and strengthened the hold of the Taliban in Afghanistan.

Closer to home, successive American administrations have attempted to coerce or bribe Mexico to take action to interdict the flow of drugs into the US. Since the Nixon administration, Washington routinely negotiated

© The Author(s) 2020
R. N. Lebow, *A Democratic Foreign Policy*,
https://doi.org/10.1007/978-3-030-21519-4_1

agreements with Mexico and promptly violated them by carrying out unauthorized operations on its territory. These raids produced harsh and public reactions by Mexican officials who resented the US for infringing on their sovereignty. Mexican objections, reprisals, and refusal to cooperate in anti-drug efforts entrapped the US into progressively more restrictive agreements. The war against drugs in Mexico has not prevented the influx of cocaine and heroin into the US and has led to considerable spillover and cross-border violence. Most frightening of all, it has raised the prospect of a "failed state" along America's southern border.[2] President George Bush sought to break free of this cycle and put relations with Mexico on a more positive basis, but his efforts were torpedoed by a Republican Congress that refused to regularize the status of Mexican immigrants, and more importantly, of the many immigrants from failed states in Latin America who transit Mexico in search of safe havens in the US. In recent decades the drug and immigration problems have worsened considerably. Mexico has become increasingly unable to police its own territory, and the drug flow has increased. American policies made a bad problem worse.[3]

What do these stories have in common? In both situations the US pursued an illusory end with disastrous results. It defied political logic to think that in an era of nationalism a Muslim state deeply divided along ethnic and religious lines could successfully be governed by a foreign power or its puppet regime. In Iraq, as in Afghanistan, US forces, once they intervened, could not leave without turning these countries over to their enemies and could not stay without becoming their targets. Build-ups, surges, and cross-tribal and ethnic alliances were to no avail and often played into the hands of increasingly extreme adversaries. Mexican policy was equally ill-considered. The drug problem is not caused by imports from Mexico but by domestic demand, most of it from middle-class white Americans. Presidents and the Congress are unwilling to face this politically unpleasant truth. It is politically easier to blame foreigners. But it makes no sense to treat Mexico and Columbia as second-class countries whose sovereignty can be abridged at will. Terrorism has increased and the drug problem has not eased. US influence in the Middle East and Central America has declined.

These are only two of many possible examples of disastrous American foreign policies. Similar stories could be told about other security issues, foreign aid, trade, immigration, and even scientific and cultural exchanges.

Their root cause is a heavy-handed approach by American presidents, their advisors, and much of the national security establishment, who believe that power talks and other countries and peoples can be brought to heel at little or no cost. Many, moreover, mistakenly believe that it is America's right and mission to assert leadership in this manner and that others welcome its so-called leadership.

The country needs a more realistic and sophisticated approach to the world that begins with the understanding that, for all its might, America is just another country, and one deeply resented by others when it abuses its political, economic, or military power. Americans must reconnect with their national interests and the ways in which they should be anchored in the values they hold most dear. Foreign and national security policy in turn should seek to instantiate, protect, and advance these values. American leaders must further recognize that persuasion is more effective than coercion, multilateralism more efficacious than unilateralism, and that power, when exercised, needs to be masked, not publicized and paraded. Self-restraint is rarely perceived as weakness, contrary to the conventional wisdom in the national security establishment. Even more paradoxically, given how Americans think about the world, sitting back from time to time and letting others take the lead can build respect and influence in the longer term.

Americans must wean themselves from their fixation and overreliance on power. They must learn to distinguish between power and influence as they are not the same thing by any means. The crude exercise of power in the form of bribes, threats, and political coercion has seriously alienated other governments and peoples and reduced American influence to a marked degree. It has led to a remarkable conundrum that the most powerful political unit the world has ever witnessed is increasingly unable to persuade others to do what it wants. This book explores this seeming paradox and what can be done about it.

Foreign policy ought to protect and advance American interests abroad. Just what are those interests and how should they be advanced and protected? Here there is no agreement, nor has there been since the early days of the Republic, when political leaders and citizens were deeply divided over how to treat revolutionary France. Those committed to encouraging democracy, like Thomas Jefferson, favored supporting France. Those concerned with the country's material interests like Alexander Hamilton favored good relations with its British adversary.[4] American history indicates that the national interest reflects the subjective values and interests of citizens. There is no objective way to determine it because it is fundamentally a political issue. People offer and defend definitions of the national interest consistent with their values and goals.

I will offer my own take on the national interest in this book, and do so by deriving it from values I think central to most Americans. I do not expect my depiction of the national interest to be acceptable to everyone. I accordingly lay out a method for making connections between values and interest that should prove equally useful to those emphasizing different values or a different ordering of them. My goal is not to lead readers by the nose, but encourage them sniff around by themselves, to think about their core values and the interests to which they give rise, and also how those interests are best defended and advanced. For the same reason, I rarely advocate specific foreign policies, although I do in the China chapter. They depend on our values and interests, but also our understanding of what builds and maintains influence. I have a lot to say about the latter question.

My starting point is the tragic understanding of life and politics. As formulated by the Greek playwrights and Thucydides, and later in the dramas of Shakespeare and Goethe, tragedy teaches us that the world is complex enough to defeat our understandings of it, conflict is inevitable because of competing values and interests, rigid commitments to beliefs and principles put them at risk, and attempts to dominate others are costly and likely to be counterproductive. It further suggests ways of thinking that have the potential to reconcile us to the vagaries of life, make us grateful for what we have, and happier about ourselves and our relationships. Adopting a tragic perspective on life may also have the potential of reducing the harm that comes one's way, but it can never insure against it.

Tragedy speaks to the most fundamental questions of politics.[5] It offers a compelling critique of power, showing why and how it does not readily translate into influence, but also how it might help advance goals when suitably masked, used in support of shared goals, and with the willing cooperation of others. It provides insights into the role of a great power that are counterintuitive to the beliefs of Americans fed on a steady diet of American might, particularism, and the need to act as the world's policeman. Tragedy suggests that only rarely is there any agreement about national interest or how to advance it because people have differing beliefs, aspirations, and expectations. There is no way of adjudicating between clashing value systems. Rather, we must find ways of living with differences at home and abroad and the conflicts they generate while minimizing their negative consequences, and when possible, working around them to advance common goals.

Tragedy indicates that powerful people and states are their own worst enemies. Success goes to their heads. They seek further wealth and status, and in ways that threaten what they already have. This was true of Philip II's Spain, the France of Louis XIV and Napoleon, and the Germany of Kaiser Wilhelm and Hitler. The US gives evidence of the same pathology. True influence is based on shared identities that build common interests and make others willing to contribute to joint projects and possibly accept another state's leadership in carrying them out. Bribing and coercing others to do as you want—even more evident in the current administration—is costly and works only as long as others fear or need you. When they no longer do, or when your power ebbs, they will turn on you with a vengeance. Tragedy teaches us that settling for less often results in getting more.

The Trump administration was absolutely upfront about its intention of putting America first and riding roughshod over the interests of others. In his first years in office, the new president routinely engaged in bellicose rhetoric in the belief that nothing talks like military strength and money. The president also gave evidence of viewing foreign countries almost entirely through the lenses of his relations with their leaders, imagining friendships and respect when none existed.[6] The conventional wisdom among Trump's opponents and his supporters is that he represents something new and different. I maintain that the difference between the Trump and prior administrations is one of degree, not of kind. At least as far back as Reagan, most presidents and the national security establishment have sought hegemony. They have conceived of hegemony as recognition of America's dominant power and accordingly the only state capable of providing physical and economic security and therefore deserving special status, privileges, and the deciding voice in determining what is best for everyone. Trump played the same game, only more crudely and with even less to show for it.

The national security establishment has pursued hegemony for reinforcing reasons. Since 1945 America' role in the world has been significant, although never as dominant as Americans have been led to believe. American primacy has been widely hailed by politicians and the media as evidence of the country's superiority, if not its god-sponsored mission to bring democracy and capitalism to the rest of the world. American primacy, and the respect it brings with it, has become a key feature of national identity. Donald Trump's campaign slogan—"Make America Great Again"—spoke to an already committed audience. Hegemony is a claim for special privileges internationally, to be used to advance American business interests—especially his. It is ironic, but hardly surprising, that the country that loudly proclaims its mission to encourage democracy in other countries has consistently attempted to impose an authoritarian hierarchy on the world. Hegemony is a vehicle for creating and enforcing (or violating) norms that benefit some—by no means all—American corporations. I will examine and critique this quest in more detail later in the book.

The American commitment to hegemony is widely shared by members of the national security establishment, major politicians in both political parties, commentators in major newspapers, and realist and liberal scholars. It is matched by an unfounded belief in the efficacy of military power as a deterrent and means of fostering regime change. The US spends more on defense than the ten next largest military powers combined and, I will argue, derives relatively little advantage from it.

Deterrence was the foundation of national security throughout the Cold War and remains central in the post-Cold War era. It assumes that the principal threat to American security arises from the aggressive designs of foreign adversaries and that military strength and demonstrations of resolve are the best way of preventing them. Beginning in the 1960s American leaders and academics became consumed by the need to establish ever more impressive nuclear and conventional arsenals and to display resolve by gaining a reputation as trigger happy and possibly irrational.[7] Resolve was thought particularly critical because the use of nuclear weapons could be suicidal, which made nuclear threats by rational actors incredible.

In practice, deterrence more often provoked the behavior it was intended to prevent. The second Berlin (1960–61) and Cuban missile (1962) crises were the products of confrontational spirals provoked by mutual superpower attempts at deterrence. They took the form of arms build-ups, forward military deployments, and threatening rhetoric that convinced leaders on both sides of the other's aggressive designs, the need to stand firm in the face of threats, and, ironically, to practice deterrence even more forcefully. The October Middle East 1973 crisis took place in a different era; both superpowers were convinced of the other's fear of nuclear war and fundamental commitment to caution. This provided the opening for Henry Kissinger to pursue an aggressive policy that challenged the status quo by attempting to detach Syria and Egypt from the Soviet orbit.[8] Robust deterrence was the underlying cause of the last serious crisis of the Cold War.

When many Politburo and other Soviet documents became available at the end of the Cold War, they revealed that Soviet leaders never doubted American credibility. Khrushchev put missiles into Cuba not because he questioned Kennedy's resolve, but because he thought him a brash and risk-prone young man who would probably send his navy to stop or sink Russian ships transporting missiles openly to Cuba.[9] Kennedy and his advisors had decided that there was nothing they could do if Khrushchev deployed missiles publicly because it was so analogous to the American missile deployment in Turkey and thus neither NATO nor Latin American countries would back any confrontational move.[10] American policymakers, their advisors, and the military have not learned the lessons of these and more recent crises and continue to practice deterrence in an unnecessarily provocative manner.

Military power is used to serve a range of other political ends. These include compellence (i.e., forcing others to what you want), reassurance of allies, and regime change achieved through subversion or intervention. Reassurance of allies has often meant support for authoritarian regimes like Battista in Cuba and the Shah of Iran, making the US the automatic enemy of their successors. Compellence generally fails because leaders are loath to buckle under to threats and fear losing power if they do.

Enormous military power and an inflated belief in its efficacy have encouraged presidents to make more extreme demands on others than they would otherwise have. When their maximalist demands are rejected, presidents consider the use of force and possible goal of regime change. During the Cold War, the US attempted on 64 occasions to bring about regime change by covert means.[11] Interventions succeeded in removing governments in a number of countries but rarely in replacing them with either more democratic or more pro-American regimes. The cost in blood and treasure of these adventures has often been enormous—think of Vietnam, Afghanistan, and Iraq—and has generated enormous hostility toward the US around the world.

American military spending has risen throughout the post-Cold War era. The US gains little from having these forces and military spending has damaging economic consequences. Our country has consistently declined relative to others in education, health, longevity, infrastructure, and quality of life. Money wasted on defense could be redirected and also liberate considerable talent and labor for productive economic ends. One of the reasons the Soviet Union declined and ultimately collapsed was the siphoning of vast resources desperately needed elsewhere to sustain its bloated military establishment. The US is doing something similar. Although it is not in any way threatened with collapse, it is paying an increasingly heavy, political, economic, and social price.

Not content with its own military spending, successive administrations have pressured NATO allies and Japan to spend more on defense. The Europeans are reluctant to do so as they cannot imagine any military threats to their security. They worry about terrorism, illegal immigrants, domestic nationalism, and transnational phenomena that require different kinds of capabilities to address. The Japanese have gradually increased their defense spending and the Abe government appears ready to do so markedly. This will only intensify conflict with China, already mounting because of Japanese attempts to claim sovereignty over disputed islands. At least some of China's exaggerated territorial claims are in response to Japanese provocations.[12]

Early warning is another problem. Pearl Harbor, the first Soviet atom test, the launching of Sputnik, the terrorist attack on 9/11, and the so-called Arab Spring were all surprises. Intelligence failures are inevitable for many reasons, and more so because the CIA has traditionally used deterrence as a benchmark for assessment. It is inappropriate and misleading because attacks and other kinds of challenges are quite often independent of the military balance. They are more often the result of domestic and foreign pressures that put pressure on leaders to act and make self-serving and erroneous estimates of the capability and resolve of other actors. The motives of other leaders as well as the pressures acting on them are often opaque to outsiders, but good intelligence makes an effort to fathom them. When crises loom, the US typically buttresses deterrence without trying to assess if this might intensify the pressures on target leaders to do precisely what Washington seeks to prevent.

Many Republican and Democratic senators demonize China. Some academics and intelligence officials invoke something called power transition theory to justify their concern that a rising power like China is likely to challenge the US for world leadership, and possibly by military means. Power transition theory asserts that rising powers always challenge dominant powers for leadership, and by military means.[13] An alternative view argues that dominant powers attack rising power before they become strong enough to defeat them.[14] This theory in any of its variants totally lacks empirical support. History indicates that rising powers almost invariably seek entry into the club of great powers and are generally encouraged to do so by the leading powers of the day. There is no instance of a war of transition initiated by either a rising or a dominant power in the history of the modern state system. Transitions can be brought about by wars, but do not start them.[15] History aside, China's foreign and military policy give no indications of attempting to challenge the US militarily. I will present evidence in support of my contention that China's rise can be managed peacefully and to the advantage of American security and economic interests. Fearful of each other, the two countries are no acting in ways that intensify conflict. I will elaborate the strategy of reassurance, which, I believe, is more appropriate to managing relations with China.

Donald Trump has pursued hegemony more openly than any of his predecessors and in a cruder and counterproductive way. However, the goals he seeks are not so different from those of prior administrations. Focusing only on Trump and his ill-conceived, confrontational, and often aggressive, initiatives would be a distraction. It is the shared assumptions of the national security establishment that we must confront, not the egoistic views and policies of a single leader, no matter how offensive and disturbing. I will nevertheless describe and critique some Trump initiatives to show how they represent a more extreme version of the kinds of policies that preceded him and to which the national security establishment wants to return.

I have referred several times to the national security establishment and want to make clear to readers that I do not consider it as any kind of monolithic bloc, let alone a behind-the-scenes conspiracy. It is a term of convenience to describe a large group of influential people affiliated with both political parties—and some not affiliated with either—who have a professional interest in foreign and defense policy and share a common set of beliefs regarding them. They are the assumptions I critique in this book: America as hegemon, whose leadership is necessary for world order and widely recognized as such; the need for a supersized military so America can play world's policeman; the efficacy of nuclear and conventional deterrence and compellence; the belief—held by many realists—that ethics has no role in foreign policy, and that it is accordingly acceptable—even advisable—to violate international law and support the most retrograde regimes in pursuit of influence and possible leverage against adversaries. There are real differences within this elite about what policies to pursue in particular situations but rarely differences or debate about their shared assumptions. It is the latter I want to expose and critique.

Ethics and domestic politics do not stop at the water's edge, as realists so often allege. Rather, ethics must impose limits on goals and means. These ethics must reflect a domestic consensus about right and wrong, in goals sought and the means used to achieve them. They must also take into account what other states consider to be appropriate on goals and means. This key argument of my book explains the otherwise enigmatic cover design. It suggests that there is no water's edge, but an ebb and flow, and constant interaction between land and water. So should there be between domestic values and goals and foreign policy.

The existence of the national security elite is nicely documented by the reactions to Donald Trump's December 2018 order to withdraw American troops from Syria. It precipitated the resignations of Defense Secretary James Mattis and the special envoy to the coalition fighting the Islamic

State, Brett H. McGurk. With the exception of a few vocal isolationists like Kentucky Republican Senator Rand Paul, Trump's handling of the issue was condemned across the political spectrum."[16] Noam Chomsky on the left and Bill Kristol and Fox News morning host Brian Kilmeade on the right agreed that ISIS had not yet been defeated.[17] Other critics denounced the withdrawal as a surrender to Turkey, Russia, Syria, and Iran; a betrayal of the Kurds; and a victory for ISIS.[18] National Security Advisor John R. Bolton had only recently vowed that the US would not leave Syria as long as Iran or its proxies were active there.[19] Former deputy national security adviser to Mr. Obama, Benjamin J. Rhodes, suggested that American troops should stay put "until Iranian influence was gone was an unachievable goal and a recipe for potential escalation for a deployment."[20]

Striking too was the response to the resignation of Secretary of Defense James Mattis. He was for many years considered a hawk, irresponsible by many, and certainly on the right-wing fringe of the establishment. His departure elicited hand-wringing lamentations from the media and foreign policy talking heads who treated it as the equivalent of the Kaiser getting rid of Bismarck. Without supposed "adults" in the room, there would now be nobody to assure that the US would "stay the course" and maintain its open-ended military US commitment in the Middle East.[21] Others took his departure as a sign that the security consensus was at risk of shattering. They looked back with nostalgia to the era of Kissinger, Scowcroft, Schultz, and Albright "when certain values were broadly shared, like the imperative of America's global leadership and the nation's commitment to democracy, diplomacy and the North Atlantic alliance."[22]

Only a few voices were raised in favor of the withdrawal from Syria— although none of them approved the way Trump announced his policy without prior consultation with his secretary of defense and military chiefs. They thought—and I agree—that troop withdrawals in Syria would accelerate calls for withdrawals in Afghanistan and Iraq, and compel the US to rethink military commitments that have little public support and are no longer effective. Mark Landler suggested that "It could also force the Afghans and Syrians to confront their own deep-rooted problems, without the presence of foreign soldiers who often delay the day of reckoning."[23] Robert S. Ford, the last American ambassador to Syria, described the decision to withdraw as "sound and wise."[24]

There are alternative discourses about foreign and defense policy, but they are at least as problematic as the dominant one. There is a longstanding isolationist discourse which has been taken up by libertarians. It espouses non-involvement in an extreme form and depicts the country's security and economic wellbeing as largely independent of American alliances and military entanglements of almost any kind. On some issues its advocates align with the American right and on others with the left. It is most prominent, if inconsistent, spokesman is Rand Paul. Some of its scholarly advocates are thoughtful and offer powerful critiques of US foreign policy. They are pilloried by their counterparts in the national security establishment, and not infrequently parodied or misrepresented.[25]

There is a left-wing Marxist discourse that considers American defense and foreign policy the handmaiden of advanced capitalism. It describes every important foreign policy as somehow carried out at the behest or in support of American investments, trade, access to raw materials, or efforts to make these less available to competitors. This critique can open our eyes to the extent to which its foreign policy is influenced, and sometimes determined, by economic considerations. It is also on target in describing the Pentagon and Homeland Security budgets as largely giveaways to American businesses with political clout. It is nevertheless deeply flawed in its belief that all foreign and defense policy has economic roots and that large corporations and banks all but dictate it. The Marxist account of policy finds its most popular expression in the works of Noam Chomsky.[26] His treatments of the Vietnam and Iraq wars attribute them to economic goals. Oil was certainly a consideration in the latter conflict, but by no means the principal one. Bush and his advisors were more concerned, as noted earlier, with American standing and influence, and were willing to pay a considerable cost toward that end. They did, however, delude themselves into believing that their allies would cover the major costs of the war.[27]

The isolationist-libertarian and Marxist discourses have never been more than marginal in the postwar era. In recent years a third discourse has emerged and has found a powerful supporter in Donald Trump. It presents international relations as a contested arena in which the US should be dominant but is not because past presidents were bad negotiators, too anxious to please other countries, and too sensitive to issues of race and gender. They were "suckers" in short. Trump promised to "Make

America Great Again," that is, to restore its dominance. His parallel project was to restore the balance of power in domestic politics, where white, Protestant men were unfairly sidelined and lost status and income to less-deserving women, minorities, and immigrants.

I develop a discourse at odds with those of the national security establishment, libertarianism, Marxism, and the Alt Right. I challenge the deeply entrenched belief in the value and feasibility of hegemony and the extraordinary and counterproductive investment in military might that its pursuit entails. I argue that America's off-scale military power is more a curse than a blessing. It encourages leaders to make maximalist demands on others, downplay compromise, and promotes interventions which diminish rather than enhance American influence. It prompts military interventions with the goal of regime change. Even more common during the Cold War were efforts to bring about regime change through assassinations, US-sponsored *coups d'état*, meddling in Democratic elections, and secretly aiding foreign dissident groups. The US was ten times more likely to rely on covert rather than overt regime change during the Cold War.[28] In the 25-year period between 1951 and 1975, a US Senate committee found evidence for over 900 covert operations intended to influence or change foreign leadership.[29]

Of equal importance, I question the widely shared assumption that material capabilities translate into power and power into influence. Power has multiple sources and does not in and of itself confer influence. The most obvious example is nuclear weapons. They are undeniably a major source of power but are unusable for anything but retaliation to a nuclear attack, a very unlikely eventuality. Nuclear threats, explicit or implicit, have never been used successfully by the US, the Soviet Union, or any other nuclear power to persuade others to do what they want. Power can be translated into influence, but only certain kinds of power, and this outcome depends on diplomatic skills in support of policies that others can be convinced are in their interest.

This book is about both foreign policy and national security. In common parlance foreign policy refers to our relations with other states and regional and international actors, but also efforts to support American business and cultural activities abroad, and more generally to make foreign governments and peoples benignly disposed to the US. National security has a narrower focus and is limited to the range of activities intended to identify and respond to security threats. Some of these threats may be military, but others may be criminal, environmental, disease, or Internet related. There is an obvious overlap between foreign policy and national security, but they also differ in significant ways. So too is there an overlap in the institutions expected to address them. The State Department, the Treasury, and the Central Intelligence Agency figure prominently in both foreign and national security policy. The armed forces and Homeland Security are more focused on national security. The president and his central advisors are expected to provide guidance and coordination in both domains. Other institutions, and not only those at the national level, also contribute. Coordination is a big problem as these institutions have their own traditions and are fiercely jealous of one another. They also have vested interests in foregrounding certain kinds of threats and minimizing others.

I address both foreign policy and national security as they are so closely related. It is commonly assumed that security should have priority over other interests, a claim that has been used to justify off-scale military spending and creation of the ponderous and largely wasteful Department of Homeland Security. There can be little doubt that if someone is attacking you, other concerns must be set aside to deal with this immediate and existential threat. However, the US has not faced this situation since Pearl Harbor. The terrorist attacks of 9/11 were treated like another Pearl Harbor, when they were in reality pin pricks conducted by non-state actors and not followed up by any terror campaign against the homeland.

As Americans have been taught to believe that security trumps other goals, it is good politics by those in the military and other security-focused institutions—and all the businesses who supply them—to exaggerate as much as possible the threats faced by the country. The Soviet threat during the Cold War was greatly overblown and successfully exploited by the military and defense contractors to direct their way increasing percentages of an expanding federal budget. The 9/11 terrorist attacks were similarly exploited and led to a disproportionate response to the criminal activity of a small cell of terrorists. Misdirected resources benefit certain institutions, companies, and individuals at the expense of the country as a whole. Money spent on weapons and other gadgets, military personnel, and unnecessary and self-defeating wars in Afghanistan and Iraq is money not spent on infrastructure, schools, healthcare, and social programs.

Military spending has transformed America into something of a garrison state in which 54 percent of all discretionary spending goes to the military and its contractors, and more money still to security-related activities conducted by other governmental organizations. Spending of this kind, almost since the Cold War began more than 70 years ago, has greatly skewed the economy by creating entire sectors that are dependent on federal largesse. Capital, labor, engineering, and scientific know-how are directed away from productive research and economic activities to develop and produce unneeded weapons and sustain an unneeded level of military personnel and infrastructure. The economy suffers from this misdirected expenditure, but it is now so extreme that it would be extremely difficult to correct. So many firms in so many congressional districts are dependent on military and security-related spending that any efforts to cut back on it generate huge political protests.

This pressure to generate military contracts is so strong in the Congress that the military is regularly forced to accept weapons it does not want and do not work. A case in point is the Littoral Combat Ship (LCS). The ships' maiden voyages resulted in cracked hulls, engine failures, unexpected rusting, software snafus, weapons glitches, and persistent criticism of how vulnerable they were to attack. In 2017, Defense Secretary Ashton Carter ordered the overall number of new ships trimmed from 52 to 40, saving billions of dollars. But lawmakers on Capitol Hill, responding to a steady stream of contractor donations, appropriated the money anyway.[30]

Security is not a given. Like the national interest, it is subjective in nature and open to multiple interpretations. This is true in a double sense. We must decide what constitutes security and then what level of risk we are prepared to accept to protect ourselves against worst-case scenarios. It is not unlike insurance, where we decide what we need to insure ourselves against and how much we are willing to pay for it. It may make perfect sense to protect our home and possessions against fire, even if the premiums are high, but less advisable to buy earthquake insurance, even if the premiums are moderate, if we live in an area where they are very rare events.

In the course of the Cold War, the national security establishment dramatically extended the scope of national security. It was no longer just protection of the homeland, but preventing communists, or even left-wing governments, from coming to power anywhere in the world. With the help of academic theorists, they constructed a world in which the US had to defend itself by committing to the defense of regimes around the world and to many of their more questionable commitments. A good case in point was Taiwan and its control of offshore islands Kinmen (Quemoy) and Matsu close to the Chinese mainland. This commitment led to two war-threatening crises with China in the 1950s. Deterrence theory stipulated—and many American officials believed—that failure to uphold any commitment would lead to a loss of credibility and future challenges. By this logic, defending these worthless offshore islands became necessary to defend mainland US.[31] In home insurance, this would be akin to the agent arguing that you must also pay insurance for a rickety, fire-prone shack, some miles away for fear that if left uninsured it would invite arson, and if allowed to burn down would increase the likelihood of your home burning.

The military and their contractors and right-wing think tanks and intellectuals also insisted that we pay a fortune to insure ourselves against very remote threats. Almost no level of risk was acceptable. During and after the Cold War, it was official US doctrine that we must be prepared to fight two separate wars at the same time. There is now a move afoot, sponsored by the military, defense contractors, and the usual right-wing think tanks, to make us capable of fighting three wars simultaneously![32] With home or any other kind of insurance, we assess not only the value of what we are insuring and what we have to pay to insure it, but the opportunity cost. What else might we spend the money on? This was and is considered an unpatriotic way of thinking when it comes to military insurance.

By the 1950s national security had achieved an almost sacrosanct status. So much so that lobbyists wanting government money for unrelated expenditures often did their best to couch their demands in the language of national security. Arguably the most extreme example was the selling of the interstate highway system—pushed for by the trucking industry—as necessary for national security. Not that there was anything irrational or wasteful about building highways or economic justifications lacking for them.

The preceding examples should make it abundantly clear that new conceptions of foreign and national security policy that demand deep cuts in the military and more self-restraint abroad will provoke a firestorm of resistance. They will be opposed by powerful forces in the Congress and from the institutions and people charged with implementing foreign and national security policy. The Pentagon, defense contractors, right-wing think tanks, and much of the national security establishment will mobilize against them. They will dismiss those who advance or support these conceptions as naïve or worse. It is nevertheless a fight worth undertaking because the soul of the nation is at stake. Any transformation of American policy requires wide public support and effective national leadership. This book provides arguments in support of such change and hopes to build support for it.

Notes

1. The US suffered 5000 dead from the time of the invasion to March 2018. Philip Bump, "15 years after the Iraq War began, the death toll is still murky," *Washington Post*, 20 March 2018, https://www.washingtonpost.com/news/politics/wp/2018/03/20/15-years-after-it-began-the-death-toll-from-the-iraq-war-is-still-murky/?utm_term=.38439b834b69 (accessed 13 November 2018).

2. David Bohmer Lebow and Richard Ned Lebow, "Mexico and Iraq: Continuity and Change in the Bush Administration," in David B. MacDonald, *The Bush Leadership, the Power of Ideas and the War on Terror* (Farnham, Surrey: Ashgate, 2012), pp. 91–112; Ed Vulliamy, *Amexica: War Along the Borderline* (London: Bodley Head, 2010); Ioan Grillo, *El Narco: The Bloody Rise of Mexican Drug Cartels*, 2nd ed. (Bloomsbury Publishing, 2012); Anabel Hernández, *Narcoland: The Mexican Drug Lords And Their Godfathers* (London: Verso, 2013).

3. Ibid.

4. Albert H. Bowman, "Jefferson, Hamilton and American Foreign Policy," *Political Science Quarterly* 71, no. 1 (1956), pp. 18–41; Robert W. Tucker and David C. Hendrickson, "Thomas Jefferson and American Foreign Policy," *Foreign Affairs* (1990), https://www.foreignaffairs.com/articles/1990-03-01/thomas-jefferson-and-american-foreign-policy (accessed 13 November 2018).

5. Toni Erskine and Richard Ned Lebow, eds., *Tragedy and International Relations* (London: Palgrave Macmillan, 2012).

6. Bob Woodward, *Fear* (New York: Simon & Schuster, 2018), p. 232.

7. H. R. Haldeman, H. R., *The Ends of Power* (New York: Times Books, 1978), p. 122; Scott D. Sagan and Jeremi Suri, "The Madman Nuclear Alert: Secrecy, Signaling, and Safety in October 1969," *International Security* 27, no. 4 (2003), pp. 150–183.

8. Richard Ned Lebow and Janice Gross Stein, *We All Lost the Cold War* (Princeton: Princeton University Press, 1994), chs. 10 and 13.

9. Ibid., ch. 4.

10. Ibid., ch. 5.

11. Lindsey O'Rourke, *Covert Regime Change: America's Secret Cold War* (Ithaca: Cornell University Press, 2019).

12. Feng Zhang and Richard Ned Lebow, *Taming Chinese Rivalry*, forthcoming, chs. 3 and 7.

13. A. F. K. Organski and Jacek Kugler, *The War Ledger* (Chicago: University of Chicago Press, 1980); Charles F Doran and Wes Parsons, "War and the cycle of Relative Power," *American Political Science Review* 74, no. 4 (1980), pp. 947–965; Jacek Kugler and Douglas Lemke, *Parity and War: Evaluation and Extension of The War Ledger* (Ann Arbor: University of Michigan Press, 1996); Jacek Kugler and Douglas Lemke, "The Power Transition Research Program: Assessing Theoretical and Empirical Advances," in Manus I. Midlarsky, ed., *Handbook of War Studies II* (Ann Arbor; University of Michigan Press, 2000), pp. 171–94; Jonathan M. DiCicco and Jack S. Levy, "Power Shifts and Problem Shifts: The Evolution of the Power Transition Research Program," *Journal of Conflict Resolution* 43, no. 6 (1999), pp. 675–704; Woosang Kim and James D. Morrow, "When Do Power Shifts Lead to War?," *American Journal of Political Science*, 36, no. 4 (1992), pp. 896–922.

14. Robert Gilpin, *War and Change in International Relations* (Cambridge: Cambridge University Press, 1981).

15. Richard Ned Lebow and Benjamin Valentino, "Lost in Transition: A Critique of Power Transition Theories," *International Relations* 23, no. 3 (September 2009), pp. 389–410.

16. Mark Landler, "Trump Unites Left and Right Against Troop Plans, but Puts Off Debate on War Aims," *New York Times*, 27 December 2018, https://www.nytimes.com/2018/12/27/us/politics/trump-syria-afghani-stan-withdraw.html?action=click&module=Top%20Stories&pgtype=Homepage (accessed 27 December 2018).

17. Matt Gallagher, "The President's Field Trip to the Forever War," *New York Times*, 28 December 2018, https://www.nytimes.com/2018/12/28/opinion/sunday/trump-military-troops-iraq.html?action=click&module=Opinion&pgtype=Homepage (accessed 28 December 2018).

18. Patrick Cockburn, "Trump's Syria Withdrawal Is a Simple Case of Foreign Policy Realism," *Other News*, December 2018, http://www.other-news.info/2018/12/trumps-syria-withdrawal-is-a-simple-case-of-foreign-policy-realism/ (accessed 20 December 2018).

19. Ibid.

20. Ibid.

21. Gallagher, "The President's Field Trip to the Forever War."

22. Carlo Giacomo, "A Changing of the Guard," *New York Times*, 30 December 2018, https://www.nytimes.com/2018/12/30/opinion/foreign-policy-leaders-bush.html?action=click&module=Opinion&pgtype=Homepage (accessed 30 December 2018).

23. Landler, "Trump Unites Left and Right Against Troop Plans."

24. Ibid.

25. Ron Paul, "Opportunities for Peace and Nonintervention," *YouTube*, 5 January 2009, https://www.youtube.com/watch?v=DEJgFJBtlmY; Libertarian, "2018 Platform," July 2018, https://www.lp.org/platform/ (both accessed 20 November 2018).

26. Noam Chomsky, *Hegemony or Survival: America's Quest for Global Dominance* (New York: Metropolitan Books, 2003), *Hijacking Catastrophe: 9/11, Fear and The Selling of American Empire* (San Francisco: Kanopy Streaming, 2014), *Imperial Grand Strategy: The Conquest of Iraq and the Assault on Democracy* (Oakland: AK Press, 2006), *Perilous Power: The Middle East and U.S. Foreign Policy: Dialogues on Terror, Democracy, War, and Justice* (Boulder: Paradigm, 2007).

27. Richard Ned Lebow, *Cultural Theory of International Relations* (Cambridge: Cambridge University Press, 2008), ch. 9.

28. Lindsey A. O'Rourke, Covert Regime Change: America's Secret Cold War (Ithaca, N.Y.: Cornell University Press, 2018).

29. 94th Congress, 2nd Session, Report 755, *Final Report of the Select Committee to Study Governmental Operations with Respect to Intelligence Activities* [Church Report], 26 April 1976.

30. Jared Keller, "The US Navy basically admitted that the Littoral Combat Ship looks like a massive failure," *Business Insider*, 24 April 2018, http://uk.businessinsider.com/us-navy-littoral-combat-ship-problems-2018-4?r=US&IR=T (accessed 4 October 2018).

31. On the illogical nature of US beliefs about the seamless nature of deterrence and fear for American credibility, see Lebow and Stein, *We All Lost the Cold War*, ch. 2; Ted Hopf, *Deterrence Theory and American Foreign Policy in the Third World, 1965–1990* (Ann Arbor, Mich.: University of Michigan Press, 1994).

32. Paul D. Miller, "Why we need to move beyond the "Two War" doctrine," *Foreign Policy*, 6 January 2012, https://foreignpolicy.com/2012/01/06/why-we-need-to-move-beyond-the-two-war-doctrine/; John Gould, "The US may not be able to fight two big wars at once," *Defense News*, 3 October 2018; Jason Belcher, "Is The U.S. Prepared For A Two-Front War?," *Huffington Post*, 14 April 2017, https://www.huffingtonpost.com/entry/is-the-us-prepared-for-a-two-front-war_us_58f0f1fbe4b0156697224eb1 (all accessed 25 February 2019).

2

The Indispensable Nation?

Americans have been consistently smug about their political system, capitalist economy, social cohesion, and way of life. They have not for the most part questioned the stability of their political and economic institutions since the Great Depression of the 1930s. Their survival, in contrast to the collapse of so many European democracies, and subsequent robust performance in the postwar era, reaffirmed the view of many Americans that providence had blessed them. They were fulfilling their prophecy as "the city on the hill," a phrase from the Sermon on the Mount used by Puritan preacher Jonathan Edwards in 1630 to describe the Massachusetts Bay Colony on the eve of its founding.[1] President Kennedy would refer to Edward's sermon in his first post-election speech, as Ronald Reagan did on the eve of his presidency.[2]

This smugness also affects foreign policy. In the twentieth century it was most marked in Woodrow Wilson, president from 1913 to 1921, author of the Fourteen Points, and founder of the League of Nations. Son of a Presbyterian minister, he was a deep believer in Caucasian superiority and American superiority over other Caucasians. The country's God-given mission was to spread democracy, which he believed would eliminate the threat of war. Following World War II, the US sought to use the

© The Author(s) 2020
R. N. Lebow, *A Democratic Foreign Policy*,
https://doi.org/10.1007/978-3-030-21519-4_2

United Nations toward this end, but also as a vehicle to oppose the Soviet Union once the Cold War began.

The end of the Cold War and the collapse of the Soviet Union were greeted with triumphalist euphoria. Some commentators insisted that the world was now "unipolar" and that the US could and should impose its will on other countries. This belief lay behind the interventions in Afghanistan in 2001 and Iraq in 2003. Saner voices remained convinced that the world required US leadership, but in more muted form. America is "the indispensable nation," in the words of former Secretary of State Madeleine Albright.[3] President Obama said something similar in a presidential debate prior to his reelection.[4] Many Americans internalized these messages because it made them proud of their country and buttressed their self-esteem. The reality was, of course, different. American efforts to impose its will on the world were not very successful, especially in Afghanistan and Iraq, and many Americans were confused by these failures and accordingly receptive to Donald Trump's claim that Obama and other politicians had been taken advantage of by foreigners and the he would "Make America Great Again."

American power, the pursuit of hegemony, the belief in a special mission, and national self-esteem are closely connected. America's superiority and special mission had religious origins and did not become connected to and find expression until the presidency of Woodrow Wilson. It coincided with the Great War, now known as World War I, that ended with the US as the world's dominant power and transformed from a debtor into a creditor nation. World War II brought about an even more significant transformation. Most of the developed world lay in ruins, its infrastructure and economies devastated by war. The US economy, by contrast, escaped from the Depression by virtue of wartime production and in 1945 constituted more than one-third of the gross domestic product (GDP) of the entire world. America had 12 million men and women in uniform and occupying critical regions of Europe and Asia. It had become a global colossus. In the postwar era, even more than before, America's religious-based sense of mission and superiority was projected outward on to the world. It offered divine justification of the country's good fortune and inflated confidence in the success of spreading the gospel of America's way of life. It also encouraged Americans to frame the Cold War as a Manichean conflict between good and evil in which no compromise was possible.

In the post-Cold War era the collapse of the Soviet Union and its Eastern European satellite regimes, religious-inspired beliefs in America's world mission, and economic self-interest combined to make an even stronger claim on global leadership. It found expression in the assertion of hegemony and with it claims for special privileges. Let us unpack this concept and expose it for the unwarranted conceit it is.

Hegemony

Realist and liberal scholars offer differing definitions of hegemony, but they all stress the ability of a state whose power is grossly disproportionate to others to assert their preferences vis-à-vis other political actors.[5] The hegemon is expected to have the "power to shape the rules of international politics according to its own interests."[6] These scholars maintain that the US has been a hegemon since 1945, although only a partial hegemon during the long Cold War because of the opposition of the powerful Soviet Union and its allies. At the end of that conflict and the collapse of the Soviet Union, the conventional wisdom holds that the US became something closer to a global hegemon as bipolarity ended and, some claimed, gave way to unipolarity.

Realists and liberals differ somewhat in their understanding of the finer details of hegemony. Many realists contend that America's unrivaled military power enables it to impose its leadership on others, which they openly acknowledge as a form of domination.[7] Judging by the numbers, they are certainly correct about American military power.[8] The US accounts for well over 40 percent of the world's military spending and one-quarter of its economic activity. Its share of the world's gross domestic product (GDP) is larger than the EU and three times that of China, and some 65 percent of the world's currency reserve is held in US dollars.[9] This understanding of hegemony portrays it as the relatively unproblematic outcome of material capabilities.[10]

A more sophisticated conception of hegemony puts as much emphasis on legitimacy as power.[11] John Ikenberry and Charles Kupchan insist that "hegemony is most effectively exercised when the dominant state is able to establish a set of norms that others willingly embrace."[12]

Realists differ about whether consent derives from narrow self-interest—it is better to bandwagon with the dominant power or oppose it—or enlightened self-interest—from the hegemon's supposed protection of shared norms, values, and interests.[13] There can be little doubt that legitimacy matters because powerful states like Russia, who have not met their responsibilities in the eyes of other actors, are denied the standing and respect normally conferred on great power status.[14]

John Ikenberry suggests that for five decades the American-led liberal, rule-based hegemonic order "has been remarkably successful." The US has championed multilateralism, built global institutions, provided services and security and open markets as "the 'owner and operator' of the liberal capitalist political system."[15] Hegemony has "provided a stable foundation for decades of Western and global growth and advancement."[16] Through hegemony and a series of strategic partnerships, the US was able to orchestrate a relatively benign leadership, distinct from an "imperial hegemonic order." It helped to foster Western prosperity, democracy elsewhere, and a peaceful end to the Cold War. This is "a remarkable achievement."[17]

Realists and liberals share a state-centric view of the world and evaluate states in terms of their relative power. Despite America's enormous power, they worry that hegemony is fast disappearing in light of America's seeming economic decline. This fear surfaced in the 1970s with the rise of Japan and Germany. Some speculated that this shift in power might one day lead to war with Japan![18] In the 1980s, hegemons worried about the Soviet Union. Ignoring CIA estimates that the nuclear balance was robust, the American right insisted—entirely without reason—that the Kremlin had a strategic advantage and might exploit its "window of opportunity" to launch a "bolt-from-the blue" attack on the US.[19]

Today, the perceived threat is China, which pessimistic realists expect to challenge the US for world leadership within a decade or two.[20] Parallel arguments are made by "power transition theorists" who insist that all great wars arise when a rising power approaches a dominant one in military or economic power. Dominant powers go to war to preserve their position or rising powers attack them to remake the system in their interests.[21] Graham Allison at Harvard's Kennedy School offered a particularly crude formulation and historically ill-informed version of this thesis, which was rightly pilloried almost everywhere by reviewers. It nevertheless garnered considerable publicity and was seemingly taken seriously by many policymakers concerned with the rise of China.[22] The fear that the US as a declining power found an official voice in President Obama's 2010 *National Security Strategy*, the Cassandra-like warnings of right-wing voices like John Bolton, and Donald Trump's repeated campaign promises to increase the military budget to make American great again.[23]

Realists and liberals share a common normative agenda: preservation of American hegemony. Michael Mandelbaum, a prominent realist publicist, warns of the "chaos" that would result in the absence of US hegemony. He worries that US decline and Chinese ascendancy would result in a hegemonic war.[24] Ivo Daalder and James Lindsay, both of whom served in Democratic administrations, lament the decline in American leadership under Donald Trump. In a tellingly named book—*The Empty Throne*—they argue that allies have discovered that "Trump had no interest in leading the free world." America's foes have become "more emboldened" and nationalist and authoritarian regimes have become more popular. The international order is increasingly precarious because allies doubt American commitment and resolve.[25]

Liberals are just as committed to preserve what they believe to be America's preeminent position in the world and describe the US as "exceptional and indispensable" to global stability.[26] They disagree among themselves about the proper mix and relative importance of power projection, economic dominance, institutions, and cultural influence, but still find enough in common to collaborate on books and articles.[27] In a recent article, Brooks, Ikenberry, and Wohlforth, two liberals and a realist, assert that American hegemonic leadership is benign because it provides political and economic benefits for the US and its partners that outweigh its costs. These include the "reduction of transaction costs, establishment of credible commitments, facilitation of collective action, creation of focal points [and] monitoring." Hegemony thus produces many public goods, notably system stability, although the US, they concede, benefits disproportionately from its preeminence.[28]

Brooks, Ikenberry, and Wohlforth offer the binary choice of engagement and disengagement and make the case for the former. By focusing on the extreme alternative of near-total isolation, they find it correspondingly easier to argue for engagement in the form of hegemony, not acknowledging that it anchors the other. They offer a, parochial reading of the early Cold War in their assertion that US hegemony was "largely an empire by invitation."[29] Elsewhere, Ikenberry proclaims that "American global authority was built on a Hobbesian contract—that is, other countries, particularly in Western Europe and later in East Asia, handed the reins of power to Washington, just as Hobbes' individuals in the state of nature voluntarily construct and hand over power to the Leviathan."[30] This remarkable reading of Hobbes and more recent history ignores the US occupation troops in the defeated axis powers, the threats and coercion against communists in France and Italy, and efforts, in Europe and elsewhere, to impose US political and economic preferences—actions that lead critics to characterize America's efforts to assert authority as an "imperial project."[31] In Latin America and Asia, US efforts at hegemony were often achieved through support of right-wing dictatorships, coups against democratically elected governments, and outright military intervention. Brooks, Ikenberry, and Wohlforth's portrayal of benign American paternalism hardly tallies with historical facts or the ways in which America is perceived abroad, even among moderates in pro-Western countries.

Hegemony is as fiercely proclaimed and defended on the right. Neoconservative Robert Kagan, a major proponent of the Iraq War is a case in point. In a recent book, with a title that gives the argument away—*The Jungle Grows Back*—he insists that postwar peace, democracy, and prosperity was made possible by America's magnanimous decision to become the guarantor of a new world order.[32] The fall of the Berlin Wall and collapse of the Soviet Union made this order appear natural and inevitable to many Americans. Without American leadership and intervention, when necessary, "the jungle will grow back," and it is already beginning to do so because of the Trump administration relative isolationism and cozying up to rapacious dictators. According to Kagan, Trump is not so much letting the liberal world order die on the vine as he is actively trying to uproot it.

These voices insist that only American power can hold back the forces of evil, and they take the form of rising authoritarian power, illiberal regimes, and especially those with predatory ambitions. American leadership is equally essentially in the economic realm. It offers a currency of last resort and makes cooperation possible by example, coordination, and punishment of those who do not cooperate or defect. For all these reasons, thoughtful people around the world admire America, welcome its leadership, and lament the current administration's failure to exercise its essential role. They also worry about those voices who demand isolationism or deviation of any kind from the commitments American made throughout the postwar era.

The Emperor Has No Clothes

These authors and most of the security establishment believe that hegemony exists and is beneficial to almost everyone. They emphasize the abiding value of US military might in resolving security and non-security problems alike. I not only reject both claims but argue that the US constitutes as much a threat to global order and stability as it is a pillar of its preservation.[33] My jaundiced view of the US is shared by much of the world. Even among our closest allies—Canada, Britain, France, Germany, and Japan—public and much elite opinion considers us a threat to world peace, and this was before Trump assumed office.[34] The percentage has shot up since. Around the world, 70 percent of those surveyed by the Pew Research Center have no confidence in Trump. In Germany, only 10 percent have confidence in Trump, in France this figure is 9 percent. Fully 81 percent think the US does not consider the interests of countries like France when making foreign policy decisions.[35]

The national security establishment is blind to these realities and hostile to those who dare to point them out. In 2015, at the University of Cambridge, I debated the then-head of the Council on Foreign Relations, Richard Haas. He was close to Hilary Clinton and many expected him to be given a high post in the new administration if she had won the election. Haas gave the audience an intelligent Cook's Tour of the world's trouble spots and problems that any new administration would confront. I suggested that he had omitted one of the bigger problems that the world faced: American arrogance, sense of entitlement, confrontational policy toward China, and itchy trigger finger that prompted interventions like those in Afghanistan and Iraq. He looked uncomprehendingly at me and would not respond to my argument.

Instead he told the audience that he did not know what planet this fellow came from. The crowd being largely English smiled politely.

My criticism of the dominant hegemonic discourse is threefold: the claim of hegemony is empirically false, and the US has not behaved the way a hegemon should, and others do not recognize it as a hegemon. The regional American hegemony of the immediate postwar period eroded quickly. It was based on the extraordinary and short-lived economic and military power of the US in comparison to the rest of the non-communist world. In 1944, the US GDP peaked at 35 percent of the world total, a figure that had dropped to 25 by 1960 and 20 percent by 1980.[36] Western Europe and Japan not only rebuilt their economies but also regained much of their self-confidence; both developments reduced the need and appeal of American leadership. The Korean War stalemate in the early 1950s demonstrated the limits of this supposed hegemony, as did the failure of intervention in Indochina in the 1960s and 1970s and the delinking of the dollar from the gold standard in 1971. In the 1980s, the US systematically reneged on its own liberal trading rules by introducing a variety of tariffs and quotas instead of bearing the costs of economic adjustments.[37] More recently, imperial overstretch was evident in the interventions in Afghanistan and Iraq. In each instance, America's capacity was found wanting and its strategic objectives were frustrated. The supposed "unipolar moment" of US power in the early 1990s was accompanied by an unprecedented number of intra-state wars, with the US unable to impose solutions consistent with hegemony.[38]

The US fared no better when it intervened through third parties, as it is currently doing in Yemen. Saudi Arabia, the United Arab Emirates, and other Arab states, with US support, have been fighting since March 2015 against the impoverished Houthi rebels. They have been typecast as Iran's cat's-paw. Only a highly publicized, completely over-the-top slaughter recently forced the Pentagon to finally do a little mild finger wagging. On 7 August 2018, an airstrike hit a school bus with a laser-guided bomb made by Lockheed Martin killing 51 people, 40 of them schoolchildren. Conservative estimates by the United Nations and other organizations are that 6475 civilians have been killed and another 10,000 wounded since 2015. US weapons have been used to strike farms, homes, marketplaces, hospitals, schools, and mosques, as well as ancient historic sites in the capital of Sana'a. Saudi Arabia and its allies have imposed a blockade, which has led to a famine and cholera outbreak. President Trump stepped up American support for those fighting the Houthis and the Pentagon is now supplying them with additional weapons, including cluster bombs— banned by 120 countries in a 2008 treaty opposed by Washington. The US air force is refueling bombers in midair that are dropping these and other weapons.[39] In November 2018, the Trump administration stalled a United Nations resolution calling for a ceasefire and the resumption of humanitarian deliveries in Yemen after a lobbying campaign by Saudi Arabia and the United Arab Emirates.[40] The US role in Yemen is not so different from that of Russia in Syria—that has so shocked and horrified the world.[41]

Hegemony rests on legitimacy as well as power, and here too, the US position has seriously eroded. Public opinion in Europe was extremely sympathetic to the US after 9/11, but reversed itself after the invasions of Afghanistan and Iraq and came to regard it as a greater threat to world peace than North Korea.[42] In Britain, those with favorable opinions of the US dropped from 83 percent in 2000 to 56 percent in 2006. In other countries, the US suffered an even steeper decline.[43] This evaluation had not changed much by 2007, when an opinion poll carried out for the BBC World Service in 27 countries found that 51 percent of respondents regarded the US negatively—a figure surpassed only by their negative evaluations of Iran and Israel, 54 and 56 percent respectively. By comparison, North Korea was regarded negatively by only 48 percent of respondents.[44] Since the onset of the Iraq War, the US has undergone a shift in its profile from a status quo to a revisionist power.

While the election of Barrack Obama had a positive effect on these ratings, the US still trailed other advanced industrial states in popularity. Among Western countries, no country generated as many *negative* responses as the US (34 percent) in terms of global influence.[45] The "Obama bump did not last long, global opinion about his policies declining significantly by the spring of 2012."[46] With the Trump administration, these ratings plummeted further. In October 2018, 70 percent of public opinion among America's closest allies had a negative view of the president and 50 percent had a negative view of the US.[47] The American media and academic literature either ignores or minimizes the significance of these events or seeks to explain them away as somehow aberrant to a general trend that has allegedly sustained American power and its acceptance by others.

The US has abused its military and economic power. It has intervened around the world, often to help overthrow popular regimes or keep unpopular leaders in powers. Examples of the former include CIA-sponsored or supported coups in Iran in 1953, Guatemala in 1954, Chile in 1973, and, of the latter, support for right-wing dictatorships in South Vietnam, Central America, Greece. Military interventions in Cuba, Vietnam, Afghanistan, and Iraq all ended in disaster.

By the 1980s, the limits of US hegemony were just as evident in terms of the global economy when it systematically reneged on its own liberal trading rules, introducing a variety of tariffs and quotas against new cheaper Asian and Latin American producers, rather than bearing the costs of adjustment. Until the 1960s, when the dollar was the world's undisputed reserve currency, the US current account balance ran at zero or a small surplus. That position dramatically eroded in the 1980s, and the US current account deficit peaked at 6 percent in 2006, just before the financial crisis.[48] These imbalances were in part the result of deliberate American efforts to foster greater financial integration among advanced industrial economies in the 1980s. They were subsequently associated with efforts to integrate emerging markets, including China.

All of this took place at a time when there was a consistent decline in net US public and private savings.[49] The American public was no longer prudent. Successive administrations abandoned fiscal discipline in favor of consumption and defense expenditures. American policies accordingly had the effect of making the US government and consumers increasingly reliant on foreign capital to finance their expenditures. Runaway expenditure by Americans and their government, reflected in low personal savings rates coupled with increased government deficits, became important causes of global imbalances.[50]

The growth in American personal debt has been unmistakable. It reached a low of −0.5 percent in 2005, a negative rate not seen since the Great Depression.[51] As savings plummeted, debt increased. By 2005 total US household debt, including mortgage loans and consumer debt, stood at $11.4 trillion.[52] This growth in personal debt finds a parallel in the US federal budget deficit. By 2018, these figures had ballooned to

$15.6 trillion. Including intragovernmental holdings of $5.7 trillion, they make a total "National Debt" of $21.4 trillion. Debt held by the public was approximately 77 percent of the GDP in 2017, making the US the 43rd highest of 207 countries. The Congressional Budget Office forecast in April 2018 that the ratio will rise to nearly 100 percent by 2028, perhaps higher if current policies are extended beyond their scheduled expiration date.[53]

Figures for the US trade deficit, a third indicator, are just as illuminating. According to the US Census Bureau, the US has run a trade deficit in goods and services every year since 1969, with the exception of 1973 and 1975. Comparable to the budget deficit, these figures have worsened over time and have grown since the turn of the century, peaking in 2006 on the eve of the financial crisis. The growing trade imbalance has been exacerbated by US policy and a lack of regulatory mechanisms. Significant tax cuts introduced by the Bush administration, liberal policies designed to attract foreign funds, unregulated credit markets (that then made personal credit easier to obtain and led to a housing bubble) combined with low savings rates with dramatic effects. In several decades the US has gone from being the bulwark of the international economy to the principal source of its instability.

Liberals and realists contend that hegemony is legitimate in the eyes of other important actors who welcome American leadership and enforcement as beneficial to global stability and their national interests. The only foreign support for these claims comes from conservative politicians and authoritarian leaders, the latter for the most part direct beneficiaries of US military and economic backing. There has been a noticeable decline in pleas for US leadership since the end of the Cold War, and as previously noted, a corresponding increase in opposition to US military and economic initiatives. Since the Iraq War, the US has undergone a shift in its profile from a status quo to a revisionist power. Germany, Canada, and Japan now top the list of respected countries, followed by France, Britain, China, and India. Even pariah countries such as North Korea score better than the US on some surveys. More recent surveys reflect a sustained theme: the US is rarely perceived as acting in the interests of the international community, and that whatever legitimacy its leadership once had has significantly eroded.[54]

American policymakers are invested in hegemony because their policies remain largely state-centered and predicated on US leadership. Of equal importance, hegemony provides a justification for extraordinary defense spending. For most members of the American foreign policy elite, alternatives to US global leadership are, if not unthinkable, extremely distasteful. For the general public, fed on a steady diet of American exceptionalism and superiority, they are unacceptable. Almost every major policy speech on foreign policy invokes the superiority of American values, its messianic role in the world, and how responsible leaders everywhere welcome it.[55] The only alternative to leading, the American people are told, is following, and that is unpalatable. So US foreign policy remains focused on retaining something that no longer exists and is not welcomed by our closest allies.

Power Versus Influence

American "hegemony" eroded during the postwar decades as other nations regained their economic strength and political stability. Of equal importance, the postwar world witnessed movements and developments over which the US could exert little to no control, such as Third World nationalism, decolonization, and the rise of China. Efforts by Washington to maintain a puppet regime in South Vietnam and futile efforts to block Beijing from taking China's seat in the UN Security Council darkened America's image and publicized its impotence. The decline of the dollar did not help either. Yet American foreign policy still embraces hegemony and has not effectively adjusted to the long-since different reality. The glaring discrepancy between America's self-image and goals and others' perception of them, may explain one of the principal anomalies of contemporary international relations that I alluded to in the introduction: the extraordinary military and economic power of the US and its increasing inability to get other states to do what it wants. Examples of this phenomenon abound. In Iraq, the Bush administration claimed to have created "a coalition of the willing," but in practice the intervention was opposed by some of America's closest allies and the support of lesser states had to be purchased. In trade the US sought a critical

G-20 consensus on how to manage the 2008 Great Recession only to be rebuffed by Asians and Europeans alike.

To quote Alice, our story becomes "curiouser and curiouser." Although American hegemony has not existed for some time, prominent commentators and scholars paradoxically worry that it is about to disappear. In the aftermath of the Cold War, Charles Krauthammer famously proclaimed that the long-awaited "unipolar moment" had arrived and that American hegemony was secure for decades. Optimistic realists in the government, Congress, and the academy contend that America can finesse China's rise and remain dominant.[56] Pessimists worry about the challenge from a rising China. Some believe, as noted, that a power transition of this kind will almost certainly lead to war. Liberals share these fears, but their greatest concern, pace realists, is that a global system without a hegemon would become unstable and more war prone.[57]

Realists and liberals frame hegemony as a question of power. Realists in particular assume that material capabilities constitute power and that power confers influence. These categories are related but in more indirect and problematic ways. Material capabilities are only one component of power. Power also depends on the nature of a state's capabilities, how they are developed, and how they are used. Perhaps the most graphic illustration of this political truth is offered by the US and Soviet (now Russian) nuclear arsenals. These weapons and their delivery systems were expensive and all but unusable in any scenario other than retaliation to an attack by the other—something neither side ever wanted to do. Attack and counterattack would have constituted mutual, if not global, suicide. Intended to deter the other superpower, nuclear weapons increasingly became a cause of their conflict, and perhaps the principal one in the 1980s.[58] For the Soviet Union, its nuclear arsenal and conventional forces became its principal claim to superpower status. Extravagant expenditure on the military, despite a stagnating economy, is generally understood to have been a contributing cause of the Soviet collapse.[59]

The utility of conventional forces also became increasingly restricted. In an era of nationalism people are less willing to be coerced by foreign powers. Vietnam and Afghanistan became competitions in suffering, which foreign powers were bound to lose. The ability to inflict pain—the mechanism on which military power depends—can be offset by the ability of the militarily weaker side to absorb it. Disenchantment with the war in Vietnam on the home front convinced Lyndon Johnson not to seek reelection and Richard Nixon to withdraw American troops. The same phenomenon occurred in the Soviet Union and prompted Gorbachev's withdrawal from Afghanistan. The US-Mexican relationship offers another example. Repeated efforts by successive American administrations to violate its agreements with Mexico led to Mexican resistance and new agreements that Washington had to make more concessions to obtain.[60]

Attempts to translate power directly into influence rest on carrots and sticks. Such exercises, even when successful, consume resources and work only so long as the requisite bribes and threats are available and effective. More often than not they fail. Intervention in Vietnam and Iraq offer only the most dramatic examples. Raw power was ineffective when applied in a politically unsophisticated way and at odds with prevailing norms and practices. It eroded, not enhanced, American influence, involved the country in 15 years (and counting) of costly occupation of Afghanistan and Iraq, and enabled the rise of ISIS. Failures in Iraq and Afghanistan are anomalies for most realist and liberal understandings of power but not for an approach that disaggregates influence from power and directs our attention to its social as well as material basis. Such a shift grounds the study of influence in the shared discourses that make it possible. It builds on Hobbes' understanding that "the power of the mighty hath no foundation but in the opinion and belief of the people."[61]

The Vietnam case is worth some elaboration because it set a pattern from which American policymakers have not learned or deviated. I do this in the next chapter. Here let me just note that it offers a powerful illustration of the difficulties of equating material capabilities with power and power with influence. It further demonstrates an unfortunate and counterproductive disregard for ethics. Intervention and bombing on a large scale and the use of chemicals like Agent Orange to destroy crops were for American policymakers and generals just another instrument of war. Hans Morgenthau, a prominent international relations theorist and early opponent of intervention, insisted that both the ends and the means of foreign policy had to be consistent with the prevailing moral code—for ethical and practical reasons. America's brand of realism dispenses with all morality on the grounds that it had no place in a dangerous world populated by cutthroat adversaries and frightened allies. In making this move, American policymakers have lost sight of the limitations of power and the ways in which its exercise when at odds with conventional understandings of ethics can diminish a country's standing and influence.

The conceptual confusion of realism stems from its tendency to conflate power and influence, and to reduce both to material capabilities. This cramped and faulty understanding of power is not accidental. It reflects and panders to a particular American approach to the world that emphasizes power over persuasion and the material attributes of power over moral and psychological ones. This orientation attempts to reduce politics to a technical problem, in keeping with a longstanding American tradition.

For these reasons many liberals emphasize institutional arrangements and what Joseph Nye called "soft power." Soft power supposedly derives from the worldwide appeal of American culture and its way of life.[62] Consumption of Coca Cola, wearing of blue jeans, and interest in American TV and movies are expected—in unspecified ways—to make foreign publics more receptive and supportive of US foreign policy.[63] Nye is quick to concede that soft power, like material power, is diffuse, reliant on both local interpreters and a willing audience. Governments accordingly find it difficult to exploit soft power or anticipate its outcomes. Senior American policymakers nevertheless routinely invoke soft power as another mechanism for enhancing US influence.[64]

The concept of soft power is soft in conceptualization and weak in empirics. What is the leap of logic that leads from attraction to American culture or its material products to support for American foreign policy? The appeal of Japanese electronics, Chinese-made clothes, and Cuban cigars has not made Americans any more pro-Japanese, Chinese, or Cuban. Quite the reverse may be the case in response to the "invasion" of Chinese products in European and American markets.[65] There has been an equally negative reaction to some American exports, like McDonald's and fast food chains more generally. They have aroused anti-American feeling in Europe and have become the target of attacks and demonstrations. Most consumers seem capable of distinguishing between a country's products and its policies. Every anti-American demonstration in Europe and Asia features protesters clad in jeans. Many other popular

American exports—Apple products, for example—neither support nor oppose American foreign policy nor are seen as symbolic in this sense by those who purchase them. Those few American goods that are distinctly opposed to the American imperial project, like the widely acclaimed *South Park* and *The Daily Show*, are extremely popular abroad. They may build respect for American democracy and toleration of dissent, but certainly not for the country's foreign policies.

In practice, material capabilities and power are related in indirect, complex, and often problematic ways. Material capabilities are a principal source of power, but critical choices must be made about which capabilities to develop and how to use them.[66] During World War II, military power was the most important kind of power, and the US and USSR wisely invested in it. In the postwar period, its utility declined and its use undermined, rather than enhanced, the power of the two so-called superpowers. The overreliance of the USSR on its military power made it incapable of effectively building legitimacy for the communist regimes it imposed in Eastern Europe. We should note that the term bipolarity was developed and deployed in the US in the early 1950s and was part and parcel of the effort to justify the continuing expenditure on the military instrument. In today's world, military power is only maintained at the cost of other forms of power that are arguably at least as important.

Attempts to translate power directly into influence, even when successful, consume resources, and often at a prodigious rate. They succeed only so long as threats are available and effective. The same is true of bribes. Every year the US provides more than $1.5 billion of military aid to Egypt and $3 billion to Israel. It is not at all evident what, if anything, it gets in return. The Mubarak regime, the recipient of this aid until 2012, channeled much of it into the pockets of family members and regime supporters and spent the rest on a largely useless military. The same is true of aid to the current military junta.[67] Israel continually flouts administration wishes, most consistently on the question of settlements on the West Bank. In 2012, its leaders threatened to attack Iran's nuclear facilities in the face of US opposition.[68] Here too, bribery did not bring compliance.

The most effective form of influence is persuasion. It consists of efforts to convince others that it is their interest to do what you want. When successful, other actors are often willing to contribute resources of their own toward a common goal. American efforts to rebuild allied industrial economies after 1945, to encourage development and stabilize the world economy through the World Bank and International Monetary Fund, and strengthen European security by means of the North Atlantic Treaty Organization were successful institutional arrangements brought about largely by persuasion. More recent examples include the nuclear agreement with Tehran and the Paris environmental accords, both of which Trump has done his best to undermine.

Persuasion must build on shared values and advocate policies that involve accepted practices. If a state is asking other political units to acquiesce in its leadership it must make a serious effort to convince their leaders—and in some circumstances, their publics—that they will have meaningful input in formulating and implementing policies and that initiatives will not go beyond commonly agreed upon goals. Material capabilities can be critical, but so are the choice of goals others can support and the political skill necessary to build and maintain coalitions. Persuasion is greatly facilitated by prior instances of cooperation and leadership because they create a degree of trust and propensity to cooperate again. Of equal importance, cooperation helps to build shared, if not common, identities that make cooperation and persuasion more likely in the future. Coalition building and common implementation of foreign policy initiatives require what is best described as political and moral power, not only material capabilities. Depending on the nature of the initiative, it also benefits from institutional and technical expertise.

Persuasion ultimately rests on legitimacy. Legitimacy "refers to the normative belief by an actor that a rule or institution ought to be obeyed. It is a subjective quality, relational between actor and institution, and defined by the actor's perception of the institution. The actor's perception may come from the substance of the rule or from the procedure or source by which it was constituted."[69] Legitimacy facilitates authority. When other leaders or peoples believe that a rule is legitimate, their compliance is motivated by a sense of moral obligation at least as much as it is by calculations of self-interest or fear of retribution.[70] Legitimacy should be considered a long-run, low-cost, means of social control as compliance becomes habitual when values are internalized. Where states, leaders, and peoples accept a rule because it is perceived as legitimate, that rule assumes an authoritative quality. It then helps to shape behavior. Over time it contributes to the definition of national interests, even the identity, by those who obey.

Persuasion is far more effective than coercion, but it requires self-restraint and intelligent diplomacy. Both constitute a serious challenge for a country that has been notoriously lacking in the former and frequently unwilling to make the kinds of compromises around which consensus and common policies can be formed.

Notes

1. John Winthrop, "A Model of Christian Charity," Collection of Massachusetts Historical Society, http://history.hanover.edu/texts/winthmod.html (accessed 22 February 2017).
2. Address of President-Elect John F. Kennedy Delivered to a Joint Convention of the General Court of the Commonwealth of Massachusetts, 9 January 1961, https://en.wikipedia.org/wiki/City_upon_a_Hill; Ronald Reagan, "Election Eve Address: 'A Vision for America,'" 3 November 1980, The American Presidency Project, http://www.presidency.ucsb.edu/ws/?pid=85199 (both accessed 22 February 2017).
3. Michael Dobbs and John M. Goshko, "Albright's Personal Odyssey Shaped Foreign Policy Beliefs," *Washington Post*, 6 December 1996, p. A25.
4. Barrack Obama in the third presidential debate on foreign policy, "America remains the one indispensable nation. And the world needs a strong America." Transcript And Audio: Third Presidential Debate," 22 October 2012, http://www.npr.org/2012/10/22/163436694/transcript-3rd-obama-romney-presidential-debate.
5. Stuart J. Kaufman, Richard Little and William C. Wohlforth, *The Balance of Power in World History* (New York: Palgrave Macmillan, 2007), p. 7, describe hierarchy, which they all but equate with hegemony, as the political-military "domination" of a single unit "over most of the international system." Michael W. Doyle, *Empires* (Ithaca: Cornell University Press, 1986), p. 40, understands hegemony "to mean controlling leadership of the international system as a whole.
6. Michael Mastanduno, "Hegemonic Order, September 11, and the Consequences of the Bush Revolution," *International Relations of the Asia Pacific*, 5 (2005), pp. 177–96.

7. Stephen G. Brooks and William C. Wohlforth, *World Out of Balance: International Relations and the Challenge of American Primacy* (Princeton: Princeton University Press, 2008).

8. Robert Jervis, "The Remaking of a Unipolar World," *Washington Quarterly*, 29, no. 3 (2006), pp. 7–19.

9. Carla Norrlof, *America's Global Advantage: US Hegemony and International Cooperation* (Cambridge: Cambridge University Press, 2010), pp. 19–21.

10. Christopher M. Dent, "Regional Leadership in East Asia: Towards New Analytical Approaches," in Christopher M. Dent, ed., *China, Japan and Regional Leadership in East Asia* (Cheltenham: Edward Elgard, 2008); Brooks and Wohlforth, *World Out of Balance*, p. 28. For critiques, Lavina R. Lee, *Hegemony an International Legitimacy: Norms, Power and Followership in the Wars in Iraq* (London: Routledge, 2010); Ian Clark, *Hegemony in International Society* (Oxford: Oxford University Press, 2011).

11. Roger Simon, *Gramsci's Political Thought: An Introduction* (London: Lawrence and Wishart, 1982); Mark Haugard, "Power and Hegemony in Social Theory," in Mark Haugard and Howard H. Lentner, eds., *Hegemony and Power: Consensus and Coercion in Contemporary Politics* (Lanham, Md.: Lexington, 2006), p. 50; Richard Ned Lebow, *The Tragic Vision of Politics: Ethics, Interests and Orders* (Cambridge: Cambridge University Press, 2003), pp. 283–84; Clark, *Hegemony in International Society*, pp. 18–23.

12. John G. Ikenberry and Charles A. Kupchan, "Socialization and Hegemonic Power," *International Organization* 44, no. 3 (Summer 1990), pp. 283–315. Also Simon, *Gramsci's Political Thought*, p. 21.

13. Richard Ned Lebow, *Tragic Vision of Politics: Ethics, Interests, Orders*, (Cambridge: Cambridge University Press, 2003), pp. 283–84; Ian Hurd, "Making and Breaking Norms: American Revisionism and Crises of Legitimacy," *International Politics*, 44, nos. 2/3 (2007), pp. 194–213; Clark, *Hegemony in International Society*, pp. 23–28.

14. Lebow, *Tragic Vision of Politics*, pp. 283–84; Gerry Simpson, *Great Powers and Outlaw States: Unequal Sovereigns in the International Legal Order* (Cambridge: Cambridge University Press, 2004); Ian Hurd, "Making and Breaking Norms: American Revisionism and Crises of Legitimacy," *International Politics*, 44, nos. 2/3 (2007), pp. 194–213; Andrew Hurrell, *On Global Order: Power, Values, and the Constitution of International Society* (Oxford: Oxford University Press, 2007); Clark, *Hegemony in International Society*, pp. 23–28.

15. G. John Ikenberry, *After Victory: Institutions, Strategic Restraint, and the Rebuilding of Order after Major War* (Princeton: Princeton University Press, 2001).

16. G. John Ikenberry, *The Liberal Leviathan* (Princeton: Princeton University Press, 2011), p. 2.

17. Ibid., p. 3.

18. George Friedman, *The Coming War with Japan* (St-Martin Press, New York, 1991).

19. Richard Ned Lebow, "Windows of Opportunity: Do States Jump Through Them?," *International Security* 9, no. 1 (1984), pp. 147–86.

20. Christopher Layne, "The Waning of U.S. Hegemony—Myth or Reality? A Review Essay," *International Security* 34, No. 1 (2009), pp. 147–172, especially p. 148; Aaron L. Freidberg, "The Future of U.S.-China Relations: Is Conflict Inevitable?" *International Security*, 30, No. 2 (2005), pp. 7–45; John J. Mearsheimer, *The Tragedy of Great Power Politics*, p. 400; Michael H. Hunt, *The American Ascendancy: How the United States Gained and Wielded Global Dominance* (Chapel Hill, N.C.: University of North Carolina Press, 2007), p. 322; Michael Cox, "Is the United States in Decline—Again? An Essay," *International Affairs*, 83, no. 4 (2007), pp. 261–76; Fareed Zakaria, *The Post-American World* (London: Allen Lane, 2008); Hunt, *American Ascendancy*, p. 322; Cox, "Is the United States in Decline—Again?"; Fareed Zakaria, *The Post-American World* (New York: W. W. Norton & Company, 2008); Charles Glaser, "Will China's Rise Lead to War? Why Realism Does Not Mean Pessimism," *Foreign Affairs* (March/April 2011), http://www.foreignaffairs.com/articles/67479/charles-glaser/will-chinas-rise-lead-to-war; Steven W. Mosher, *Hegemon: China's Plan to Dominate Asia and the World* (San Francisco, CA: Encounter Books, 2000); Stefan Halper, *The Beijing Consensus: How China's Authoritarian Model Will Dominate the Twenty-First Century* (NY: Basic Books, 2010).

21. See Chap. 6 for a discussion.

22. Graham Allison, *Destined for War: Can America and China Escape Thucydides' Trap?* (New York: Houghton-Mifflin, 2017); Judith Shapiro, "America's collision Course with China," *New York Times*, 15 June 2017, https://www.nytimes.com/2017/06/15/books/review/everything-under-the-heavens-howard-french-destined-for-war-graham-allison.html; Richard Ned Lebow and Daniel Tompkins, "The Thucydides Claptrap," *Washington Monthly*, 28 June 2016, https://washingtonmonthly.com/thucydides-claptrap; Tom Christensen, (all accessed 9 October 2018).

23. United States National Security Council, *US National Security Strategy 2010*, p. 43, http://www.whitehouse.gov/nscnss/2010 (accessed 25 February 2013).

24. Michael Mandelbaum, *The Frugal Superpower: America's Global Leadership in a Cash-Strapped Era* (Philadelphia, Public Affairs, 2010), pp. 3–8; Roger C. Altman and Richard N. Haass, "American Profligacy and American Power," *Foreign Affairs* 89, no. 6 (2010), pp. 25–34.

25. Ivo Daalder and James Lindsay, *The Empty Throne: America's Abdication of Global Leadership* (New York: Global Affairs, 2018).

26. Michael Dobbs and John M. Goshko, "Albright's Personal Odyssey Shaped Foreign Policy Beliefs," *The Washington Post*, 6 December 1996, p. A25; Madeleine K. Albright, Interview on NBC-TV "The Today Show" with Matt Lauer, Columbus, Ohio, 19 February 1998; Daniel Deudney and G. John Ikenberry, *Democratic Internationalism: An American Grand Strategy for a Post-Exceptionalist Era* (New York: Council on Foreign Relations, 2012), p. 1.

27. G. John Ikenberry, Michael Mastanduno and William Wohlforth, eds., *Unipolarity and International Relations Theory* (New York: Cambridge University Press, 2011); G. John Ikenberry and Joseph Grieco, *State Power and World Markets: The International Political Economy* (New York: Norton, 2003); G. John Ikenberry and Michael Mastanduno, eds., *International Relations Theory and the Asia-Pacific* (New York: Columbia University Press, 2003); G. John Ikenberry, David A. Lake, and Michael Mastanduno, eds., *The State and American Foreign Economic Policy* (Ithaca: Cornell University Press, 1988); G. John Ikenberry and Charles A. Kupchan, "Socialization and Hegemonic Power," *International Organization* 44, no. 3 (Summer 1990), pp. 283–315; Stephen G. Brooks, G. John Ikenberry and William C. Wohlforth, "Don't Come Home, America: The Case against Retrenchment," *International Security* 37, no. 3 (Winter 2012/13), pp. 7–51.

28. Brooks, Ikenberry and Wohlforth, "Don't Come Home, America."

29. Geir Lundstadt, *The American "Empire"* (Oxford: Oxford University Press, 1990); Charles S. Maier, "Alliance and Autonomy: European Identity and U.S. Foreign Policy Objectives in the Truman years," in Michael Lacey, ed., *The Truman Presidency* (Cambridge: Cambridge University Press, 1991); John Lewis Gaddis, *We Now Know: Rethinking Cold War History* (New York: Oxford University Press, 1997); Thomas F. Madden, *Empires of Trust: How Rome Built—and America Is Building—A New World* (London: Plume, 2009).

30. Ikenberry, *Liberal Leviathan*, p. 10.

31. Walden Bellow, *Dilemmas of Domination: The Unmaking of the American Empire* (NY: Metropolitan Books, 2005); Chalmers Johnson, *Blowback: The Costs and Consequences of the American Empire* (London: Time Warner Paperbacks, 2002) and *Dismantling the Empire: America's Last Best Hope* (NY: Metropolitan Books, 2010). For American intervention in European domestic politics, Tony Judt, *Postwar: A History of Europe Since 1945* (NY: Penguin Press, 2005); Michael Cox and Caroline Kennedy-Pipes, "The Tragedy of American Diplomacy? Rethinking the Marshall Plan," *Journal of Cold War Studies* 7, no. 1 (2005), pp. 97–134; Michael J. Hogan, *The Marshall Plan: America, Britain and the Reconstruction of Western Europe, 1947–1952* (Cambridge: Cambridge University Press, 1987); Alan Milward, The Reconstruction of Western Europe, 1945–1951 (London: Methuen, 1984); William Appleman Williams, *The Tragedy of American Diplomacy* (New York: Norton, 1988).

32. Robert Kagan, *The Jungle Grows Back: America and Our Imperiled World* (New York: Knopf, 2018).

33. For a variant approach to global engagement, also rooted in a more pragmatic and less ideological and paradigmatic approach to foreign policy, see Steven Weber and Bruce W. Jentleson, *The End of Arrogance: America in the Global Competition of Ideas* (Cambridge: Harvard University Press, 2010).

34. See notes 42–43.

35. Richard Wike, Bruce Stokes, Jacob Poushter, Laura Silver, Janell Fetterolf and Kat Devlin, "Trump's International Ratings Remain Low, Especially Among Key Allies," *Pew Research Center*, 1 October 2018, http://www.pewglobal.org/2018/10/01/trumps-international-ratings-remain-low-especially-among-key-allies/ (accessed 17 November 2018).

36. Angus Maddison, *Monitoring the World Economy, 1820–1992* (Paris: Organization for Economic Cooperation and Development, 1995). Even Robert Gilpin, renowned proponent of hegemonic stability theory, acknowledges the fact that the US's global dominance was fleeting. See his *War and Change in World Politics* (New York: Cambridge University Press, 1987), pp. 173–175.

37. Charles P. Kindleberger, "Dominance and Leadership in the International Economy: Exploitation, Public Goods, and Free Rides," *International Studies Quarterly*, 25, no. 2 (1981) pp. 242, 248; Simon Reich, *Restraining Trade to Invoke Investment: MITI and the Japanese Auto*

Producers: Case Studies in International Negotiation (Washington, D.C.: Institute for the Study of Diplomacy, 2002).

38. Andrew Mack, "The Changing Face of Global Violence (Part 1)," in *The Human Security Report 2005* (Oxford: Oxford University Press, 2005), http://www.humansecurityreport.info/HSR2005_PDF/Part1.pdf (accessed 5 February 2013).

39. Rajan Menon, "Yemen's descent into hell," *Le Monde* Diplomatique, 18 September 2018, https://mondediplo.com/openpage/yemen-hell (accessed 9 October 2018).

40. Julian Borger, "Yemen ceasefire resolution blocked at UN after Saudi and UAE 'blackmail'," *Guardian*, 29 November 2018, https://www.theguardian.com/world/2018/nov/29/un-yemen-ceasefire-resolution-blocked-saudi-uae-blackmail (accessed 29 November 2018).

41. Gardiner Harris, Eric Schmitt, Helene Cooper and Nicholas Fandos, "Senators, Furious Over Khashoggi Killing, Spurn President on War in Yemen," *New York Times*, 28 November 2018, https://www.nytimes.com/2018/11/28/us/politics/trump-saudi-arabia-yemen.html?emc=edit_mbe_20181129&nl=morning-briefing-europe&nlid=69950465201811129&te=1 (accessed 28 November 2018).

42. Steve Schifferes, "U.S. names coalition of the willing," *BBC News*, 18 March 2003. http://news.bbc.co.uk/2/hi/americas/2862343.stm, (accessed 5 February 2013); *Time Europe* 2 June 2003, http://www.time.com/time/europe/gdml/peace2003.html (broken link).

43. The Pew Global Attitudes Project, "America's Image Slips, but Allies Share U.S. Concerns over Iran, Hamas," released 13 June 2006, http://www.pewglobal.org/2006/06/13/americas-image-slips-but-allies-share-us-concerns-over-iran-hamas/ (accessed 25 February 2013).

44. BBC World Service Poll, "Israel and Iran Share Most Negative Ratings in Global Poll," 6 March 2007, http://news.bbc.co.uk/2/shared/bsp/hi/pdfs/06_03_07_perceptions.pdf (accessed 5 February 2013); Wike, Stokes, Poushter, Silver, Fetterolf and Devlin, "Trump's International Ratings Remain Low, Especially Among Key Allies."

45. WorldPublicOpion.org, Program on International Policy Attitudes (PIPA), *Global Views of United States Improve While Other Countries Decline*, http://www.worldpublicopinion.org/pipa/articles/views_on_countriesregions_bt/660.php, 10 April 2010 (accessed December 22, 2010).

46. Pew Global Attitudes Project, "Global Opinion of Obama Slips, International Policies Faulted," 13 June 2012, http://www.pewglobal.org/2012/06/13/global-opinion-of-obama-slips-international-policies-faulted/ (accessed 17 August 2012).

47. Pew Research Center, Global Attitudes and Trends, "Trump's International Ratings Remain Low, Especially Among Kew Allies," 1 October 2018, http://www.pewglobal.org/ (accessed 9 October 2018).

48. Joshua Aizenman, "On the causes of global imbalances and their persistence: Myths, facts and conjectures," in Stijn Claessens, Simon Evenett and Bernard Hoekman, eds., *Rebalancing the Global Economy: A Primer for Policymaking* (Centre for Economic Policy Research: London, 2010), pp. 23–30.

49. Ibid., p. 24.

50. The personal savings rate is calculated by taking the difference between disposable personal income and personal consumption expenditures and then dividing this quantity by disposable personal income.

51. Massimo Guidolin and Elizabeth A. La Jeunesse, "The Decline in the U.S. Personal Saving Rate: Is It Real and Is It a Puzzle?" *Federal Reserve Bank of St. Louis Review* 89, no. 6 (2007), pp. 491–514. See Figure 1, pp. 492.

52. Board of Governors of the Federal Reserve System, Federal Reserve Statistical Release, "Z.1-Flow of Funds Accounts of the United States," 9 March 2006, http://www.federalreserve.gov/releases/Z1/20060309/data.htm, p. 8, 102 (accessed 29 January 2011).

53. Wikipedia, "National Debt of the United States," citing US Treasury sources, January 2018, https://en.wikipedia.org/wiki/National_debt_of_the_United_States#cite_note-treasurydirect.gov-5 (accessed 9 October 2018).

54. Pew Survey, "Obama More Popular Abroad Than At Home, Global Image of U.S. Continues to Benefit," 17 June 2011, http://www.pewglobal.org/2010/06/17/obama-more-popular-abroad-than-at-home/ (accessed 26 September 2011); Wike, Stokes, Poushter, Silver, Fetterolf and Devlin, "Trump's International Ratings Remain Low, Especially Among Key Allies."

55. For one prominent example, The White House, Office of the Press Secretary, "Remarks by the President in State of Union Address," United States Capitol, Washington, D.C., 25 January 2011, http://www.whitehouse.gov/the-press-office/2011/01/25/remarks-president-state-union-address (accessed January 29, 2011).

56. James Traub, in "Wallowing in Decline," *Foreign Policy*, September 24, 2010. http://www.foreignpolicy.com/articles/2010/09/24/wallowing_in_decline?page=0,1 (accessed December 27, 2010) http://walt.foreignpolicy.com/posts/2010/09/22/the_virtues_of_competence (accessed December 27, 2010); Aaron L. Freidberg, "The Future of U.S.-China Relations: Is Conflict Inevitable?" *International Security*, 30, no. 2 (2005), pp. 7–45; Michael Mandelbaum, *The Frugal Superpower: America's Global Leadership in a Cash-Strapped Era* (Philadelphia, Public Affairs, 2010), especially pp. 3–5. For critics, Stephen G. Brooks and William C. Wohlforth, *World Out of Balance: International Relations and the Challenge of U.S. Primacy* (Princeton: Princeton University Press, 2008); William C. Wohlforth, "The Stability of a Unipolar World," *International Security* 24, No. 1 (1999), pp. 5–41; William C. Wohlforth, "U.S. Strategy in a Unipolar World," in G. John Ikenberry, ed., *America Unrivaled: The Future of the Balance of Power* (Ithaca, N.Y.: Cornell University Press, 2002), pp. 98–120. For a summary of realist views, see Christopher Layne, "The Waning of U.S. Hegemony—Myth or Reality?" *International Security* 34, no. 1 (2009), pp. 147–172.
57. Robert O. Keohane, *After Hegemony: Cooperation and Discord in the Modern World* (Princeton: Princeton University Press, 1984); G. John Ikenberry, *Liberal Leviathan: The Origins, Crisis, and Transformation of the American World Order* (Princeton: Princeton University Press, 2011); Joseph S. Nye, Jr., "The Future of American Power," *Foreign Affairs* 89, no. 6 (2010), pp. 2–12; Bruce Russett and John Oneal, *Triangulating Peace: Democracy, Interdependence and International Organizations* (NY: Norton, 2001).
58. Richard Ned Lebow and Janice Gross Stein, *We All Lost the Cold War* (Princeton: Princeton University Press, 1994), ch. 14, for elaboration.
59. Central Intelligence Agency, "Intelligence Report: The Economic Impact of Soviet Defense Spending," April 1975, https://www.cia.gov/library/readingroom/docs/DOC_0000380724.pdf; William Easterly and Stanley Fischer, "The Soviet Economic Decline," *World Bank Economic Review* 9, no. 3 (1995), pp. 341–371.
60. David Bohmer Lebow and Richard Ned Lebow, "Mexico and Iraq: Continuity and Change in the Bush Administration," in David B. MacDonald, *The Bush Leadership, the Power of Ideas and the War on Terror* (Farnham, Surrey: Ashgate, 2012), pp. 91–112.
61. Thomas Hobbes, *Behemoth* (Chicago: University of Chicago Press, 1990), p. 16; Steven Weber and Bruce W. Jentleson, *The End of Arrogance:*

America in the Global Competition of Ideas (Cambridge: Harvard University Press, 2010), for a related approach.

62. Joseph Nye, Jr., *Soft Power: The Means to Success in Worlds Politics* (New York: Public Affairs, 2004) pp. 5–11.

63. Joseph S. Nye, Jr., "The Future of American Power," *Foreign Affairs* 89, no. 6 (2010), pp. 2–14; G. John Ikenberry, *Liberal Order and Imperial Ambition* (Cambridge: Polity, 2006), widely discussed in the introduction, pp. 1–18 and *America Unrivaled: The Future of the Balance of Power* (Ithaca: Cornell University Press, 2002); John M. Owen IV, "Transnational Liberalism and American Primacy: or, Benignity Is in the Eye of the Beholder," pp. 239–259 and Thomas Risse, "U.S. Power in a Liberal Security, pp. 260–283, both in Ikenberry, *America Unrivaled*.

64. Hillary Rodham Clinton, "Leading Through Civilian Power: Redefining American Diplomacy and Development," *Foreign Affairs* 89, no. 6 (2010), pp. 13–24.

65. Globescan/PIPA poll, "Global views of United States improves while others decline," BBC Views, April 18, 2010, p. 7.

66. The Cold War demonstrated the irrelevance of certain raw forms of power. The USSR and US developed impressive nuclear arsenals and diverse delivery systems for them. These weapons were all but unusable. The principal purpose for which they were designed—all-out superpower war—would have constituted mutual, if not global, suicide. Intended to deter the other side, nuclear weapons and forward deployments of their delivery systems became a principal cause of superpower conflict and greatly extended the Cold War. See Lebow and Stein, *We All Lost the Cold War*, ch. 13.

67. Joel Greenberg, "Israel: Egypt's President Mohamed Morsi pledges new peace efforts," *The Washington Post*, 31 July 2012, http://articles.washingtonpost.com/2012-07-31/world/35489115_1_netanyahu-and-peres-president-morsi-peace-efforts (accessed 25 February 2013).

68. Cf., Calev Ben-David, "Israel Plans Iran Strike; Citizens Say Government Serious," *Bloomberg.com*, 15 August 2012, http://www.bloomberg.com/news/2012-08-14/israel-plans-for-iran-strike-as-citizens-say-government-serious.html (accessed 25 February 2013).

69. Ian Hurd, "Legitimacy and Authority in International Politics," *International Organization* 53, no. 2 (1999), pp. 379–408.

70. Ibid.

3

Starve the Beast

In the post-Cold War era, the US continues to devote a disproportionate percentage of its wealth to developing and maintaining extraordinary military capabilities. Most countries cut back on their armed forces in the aftermath of the Cold War, but US spending went up. Between 2001 and 2010 the US defense budget increased by 128 percent.[1] In 2003, the US spent $417 billion on defense, 47 percent of the world total.[2] In 2008, it spent 41 percent of its national budget on the military and its two ongoing wars.[3] In absolute terms this was *twice* the total of Japan, Russia, the UK, Germany, and China *combined*. On 16 March 2017, President Trump submitted his request to Congress for $639 billion in military spending, which represented a 10 percent increase over Fiscal Year (FY) 2017. With a total federal budget of $3.9 trillion for FY2018, the increase in military spending is predicated on deep cuts to many other federal agencies and domestic programs, as well as the State Department.[4] For FY2019 Trump's would boost military spending by $94 billion.

The Pentagon has used its funding to establish a global military reach; it is the only state with this capability.[5] In 2018 the US military had troops stationed in 177 countries, deployed 140,000 soldiers in Afghanistan, and dropped over 20,000 pounds of ordnance.[6] Democratic and Republican

© The Author(s) 2020
R. N. Lebow, *A Democratic Foreign Policy*,
https://doi.org/10.1007/978-3-030-21519-4_3

administrations alike argue that off-scale levels of military expenditure will sustain, if not increase, the standing and influence that traditionally comes with military dominance. Is there any truth to this claim? In the previous chapter I argued there is not. Military dominance encourages interventions and all the major ones have ended in disaster. They have eroded rather than enhanced American influence. This is true of Vietnam, Cambodia, Afghanistan, Iraq, and the current proxy war in Yemen.

These wars have been fought without authorization from appropriate regional or international organizations, most resulted in large numbers of civilian dead—"collateral damage" in the obfuscating jargon of the American military—and most became increasingly unpopular at home. In all these interventions American presidents and their advisors exaggerated—or invented—threats to mobilize public and congressional support at the outset. Or, as in the case of Yemen, waged war furtively and out of the public eye as far as they could. They won military victories in Vietnam, Afghanistan, and Iraq but could not translate them into political successes on the ground because they intervened in support of unpopular regimes or sought to install puppets with little in the way of local support.

Carl von Clausewitz, the famous Prussian theorist of war, rightly observed that war is an extension of politics by other means. States use military force to bend or break the will of adversaries to gain from them what they cannot achieve by diplomacy. Military might permit America to defeat the armed forces of their adversaries, but this is not victory in the Clausewitzian sense. Victory can only be claimed when the state going to war can translate success on the ground—or in the air or on the seas—into political success; that is, use force to achieve the goals for which it went to war. American political leaders and generals seem never to have learned this most fundamental lesson. Military might encourage false confidence and start wars they cannot win—even if they win every battle, as they did in Vietnam, Iraq, and Afghanistan.

President George Bush famously proclaimed victory on the deck of an aircraft carrier not long after US forces had "liberated" Baghdad.[7] Fifteen years later American soldiers continue to die in that country, the insurgency remains very much alive, and Islamic fundamentalists and Iran have become more powerful. America is also increasingly hated. In 2013, the Watson Center at Brown University estimated that the war had killed at least 134,000 Iraqi civilians and may have contributed to the deaths of as many as four times that number.[8] In Afghanistan, a UN report said that 3804 civilians were killed in 2017 and another 7189 wounded: the highest toll since they began compiling statistics in 2009. The deaths are attributable to suicide bombings and US airstrikes.[9] Up to 2013, three successive administrations had spent a conservative total of $2 trillion in Iraq alone.[10] By 2016, the estimated cost had risen to $5 trillion and there is no end in sight. Critics have pointed to extraordinary waste in this expenditure, with money, goods, and weapons being siphoned off by crooked contractors or simply stolen or discarded.[11] The bigger picture suggests that the entire enterprise has been a waste because it serves no useful end—quite the reverse.

Our analysis is not complete without considering the opportunity costs. What if the US had not intervened in Indochina, Afghanistan, and Iraq? How else might this vast sum of money have been spent? How might it have benefitted the economy in a productive way and perhaps have improved internal security by encouraging employment and reducing drug dependency, crime, and other social problems? Consider the grander counterfactual that throughout the post-Cold War era the US had followed its European allies in cutting back on military spending rather than increasing it? Suppose it had used this money to fund education, scientific research, the creation and maintenance of infrastructure, and the beefing up and enforcement of rules governing banking, investment, and income tax? This kind of outlay would almost certainly have promoted a more robust and innovative economy, avoided the banking crisis, and with it the most recent recession. It would also reduce the federal deficit and avoided costly loans from China. A stronger and more independent American economy would have made the US a more powerful arbiter of international economic issues and made others more willing to accept its leadership. So too would have restraint in dealing with Afghanistan and Iraq.

Military expenditure is also wasteful. We have all read stories of $900 toilet seats and other inexplicable costs run up by the Pentagon for all kinds of goods and services. For decades, Department of Defense (DoD) leaders and accountants have been perpetrating a gigantic and illegal accounting fraud. They have cooked their books to mislead the Congress and drive their budgets ever higher, regardless of military necessity. The DoD has literally been making up numbers in its annual financial reports to Congress—representing trillions of dollars' worth of seemingly non-existent transactions—knowing that Congress would rely on those misleading reports when deciding how much money to give the DoD the following year.[12] Congress ordered an independent audit of the DoD, and in November 2018 Ernst & Young and other firms announced that they could not complete the job because the financial records were riddled with so many bookkeeping deficiencies, irregularities, and errors that a reliable audit was simply impossible.[13]

A Longer View

America has fought five wars since 1945: in Korea, Indochina, the Persian Gulf, Afghanistan, and Iraq. The Persian Gulf War was successful, Korea was a stalemate, and Indochina, Afghanistan, and Iraq were unmitigated failures. This is not a very good record. Moreover, all these wars were expensive, and with the exception of the least expensive and most successful, the Persian Gulf War, resulted in loss of influence for the US.

Korea: The Korean intervention was a response to the invasion of South Korea by North Korea in June 1950. President Truman and his advisors put little value in South Korea but believed they had to make a stand against communism lest the Soviet Union become more aggressive in Europe. American forces were rushed across the Strait from Japan and held a narrow perimeter at the bottom of the Korean Peninsula. In September, General MacArthur landed troops at Inchon, not far from South Korea's capital of Seoul and the border with North Korea. They almost trapped the North Korean army further south and left the North all but defenseless. Political pressure grew on the president to invade the North even though his UN mandate and the initial US war aim was the liberation of the South. Truman reluctantly agreed to cross the 38th Parallel and pursue the retreating North Korean army. MacArthur deliberately misled the Joint Chiefs of Staff and the president about the disposition of his forces and military intelligence indicating large-scale Chinese troop movements into North Korea. In October, the Chinese army attacked and severely defeated MacArthur's poorly positioned and largely isolated army and marine units. The Americans retreated and ultimately reestablished a front in South Korea. Two years of costly positional warfare followed until China and the US agreed to an armistice in July of 1953.[14]

The Korean War preserved South Korean independence and would have done so without the ill-fated attempt to liberate North Korea. An American presence along the Yalu River, the border with Manchuria, China's principal industrial zone, was unacceptable to Beijing. Ironically, the striking American success at Inchon created a power vacuum in the North that generated the pressures on Truman to invade the North. Even then, an invasion that overran the North Korean capital and stopped at the narrow neck of the peninsula might have succeeded. The US pursued instead a strategy that made both intervention seem necessary to Beijing and its forces vulnerable to attack. MacArthur's arrogance and ego, and military planning unconnected to—and really at odds with—political goals turned a stunning success into a catastrophe from which routed American forces had to claw their way back at great cost to the 38th Parallel. Not surprisingly, public euphoria with MacArthur's success at Inchon gave way to deep pessimism following Chinese intervention. Korea was an extremely unpopular war, resulting in a sharp drop in President Truman's public support and a Republican presidential victory in 1952.[15]

The Korean experience did not deter Lyndon Johnson from intervening in Vietnam, or the Nixon administration from expanding that war into Cambodia despite mounting opposition to the war at home.[16] Security was once again the motive, but security even more poorly conceived than in Korea. On both occasions American leaders were prisoners of erroneous lessons they had learned from World War II. They were convinced that if the democracies had stood firm, Hitler would have backed down and World War II could have been prevented. There was no evidence for this belief at the time or since; the best historical evidence indicated that Hitler wanted war and was furious at France and Britain for backing down at Munich.[17] Faith in the efficacy of deterrence nevertheless becomes something of an American mantra and makes deterrence—the subject of the next chapter—the foundation of postwar national security policy. Deterrence focused attention on credibility: the need to make adversaries believe that America would defend its territorial and other commitments even if it meant war. American leaders from Truman on worried about American credibility and believed, again without evidence, that the Soviets doubted it. Evidence that became available from Soviet archives after the Cold War indicated just how misplaced this American fear was. Soviet leaders from Khrushchev on never doubted US resolve but rather worried that their American counterparts—especially Kennedy, Nixon, and Reagan—were aggressive, trigger happy, and difficult to deter.[18]

Vietnam: President Johnson and his advisors inherited the Vietnam problem from their predecessors. At the end of World War II, the Truman administration, convinced that communism needed to be opposed everywhere, provided the airlift, and later, many of the weapons, for French forces to reimpose colonial rule in Indochina. They were resisted by local communist-nationalists who initially bore no ill-will toward the US. Ho Chi Minh, political leader of the Vietnamese forces opposing the French, had hoped for US support, which he sought as a means of offsetting Chinese power and preventing encroachments against his country from the North. Washington was blind to this dynamic because it erroneously conceived of communism as monolithic with its headquarters in Moscow and branch offices in Beijing and Hanoi. The Eisenhower administration accordingly supported the French, and when they were defeated used its political clout at the 1954 Geneva Conference to have Vietnam temporarily divided into two parts. The communist Vietminh would control the North, and France's former puppet, the Emperor Bao Dai, would rule in the south.[19]

Free elections were to be held and Vietnam reunified. Eisenhower and his Secretary of State John Foster Dulles refused to honor this part of the agreement because they recognized that Ho Chi Minh and the communists would win any fair election. Their push for permanent independence for the south triggered a civil war that pitted the North Vietnamese-backed southern-based Viet Cong against the increasingly unpopular regime of Catholic landlords that Washington supported in Saigon led by Ngo Dinh Diem. The Kennedy administration backed a military coup against Diem but the military junta that came to power grew shakier and the Viet Cong grew stronger. Lyndon Johnson's civilian and military advisors pushed him into intervention on the grounds that it was necessary to demonstrate American resolve and prevent falling dominos. If the US "lost" South Vietnam, the argument went that the rest of Southeast Asia might also fall to the communists. President Johnson had a bad feeling about intervention but did not have the self-confidence when it came to foreign policy to oppose the nearly unanimous push for intervention from his civilian and military advisors. As MacArthur misled Truman, so too did Defense Secretary Robert McNamara and National Security Advisor McGeorge Bundy mislead the president about the extent of local support for the South Vietnamese government.[20]

American intervention was gradual. It began with military training missions, advisors who went into combat, naval and air support, escalated to insertion of "light" marine, and then "heavy" army divisions, and bombing initially intended as a signal of resolve to all-out efforts to punish North Vietnam, interfere with its supply lines to the south in Vietnam and then Cambodia, destruction of suspected Viet Cong strongholds in the South by B-52 "carpet bombing," and the defoliation of vast swatches of territory with "Agent Orange" to deprive the Viet Cong of food and cover.[21] By April 1968, there were 543,482 US military personnel in Vietnam, but the insurgency did not weaken. In the end the US was forced to withdraw its forces when American public opinion went against the war.

There were two reasons for this outcome. Vietnam was a political struggle as much as it was a military one, and US support for a repressive, unpopular regime and its replacement by puppet rulers from the military did nothing to win the hearts and minds of the Vietnamese people. Neither did military escalation and indiscriminate bombing with its growing civilian casualties. According to North Vietnamese strategic analyst Colonel Quach Hai Luong: "The more you bombed, the more the people wanted to fight you."[22] Department of Defense studies confirmed that bombing "strengthened, rather than weakened, the will of the Hanoi government and its people."[23] The Viet Cong and its North Vietnamese backers, by contrast, were indigenous forces, represented nationalism, introduced land reform, and successfully presented themselves a mass, popular, and even Democratic movement.

The second reason is really an extension of the first. Clausewitz astutely observed that war is a competition in sacrifice. What counts is not only the ability to deliver pain but the willingness to absorb it. The US with its modern arsenal possessed the ability to inflict more pain on the Viet Cong and North Vietnamese than they could on the US, but the reverse was true when it came to absorbing it. The ability to accept punishment and persevere derives even less from material capabilities and may even be inversely related to them. Vietnam was less vulnerable to bombing than Pentagon planners supposed because its economy was underdeveloped. There were fewer high-value targets to destroy or hold hostage. With little in the way of factories, highways, and railroads, the economy was more difficult to disrupt, and the population was less dependent on existing distribution networks for its sustenance and material support. It is apparent in retrospect that the gap between the protagonists in material and military capabilities counted for less than their differential ability to absorb punishment, and that in turn was a function of the North Vietnamese and Viet Cong to convince ordinary people that their victory mattered and was worth fighting for. The US won every battle but lost the war because its citizens would not pay the moral, economic, and human cost of victory. Washington withdrew from Indochina after losing 58,000 American lives, a fraction of Viet Cong and North Vietnamese deaths even at conservative estimates.

The war became increasingly unpopular because many Americans could see no point to it. This was especially true of the many young men who could be called up for military service, sent to Vietnam, and possibly die there. The anti-war movement grew in strength the more bogged down American forces became. President Nixon, who followed Johnson in office, sought to end the war through negotiations and stepped-up bombing toward this end. Nixon and Kissinger negotiated an agreement with the North Vietnamese behind the back of South Vietnam and its leader. It enabled the withdrawal of American ground forces, placating domestic opinion in part, but the war continued as did American bombing. At a propitious moment, North Vietnam invaded the south, took over the country, and the world was treated to film of the humiliating spectacle of the remaining American diplomats and officers being evacuated by helicopter from the roof of the American embassy.

Once again arrogance was the root cause of failure. Americans learned nothing from France's defeat at the hands of the Viet Minh; they blamed it on French incompetence and political weakness. Washington framed the Vietnam problem in narrow military terms, not recognizing that any number of military successes might not solve the political problem but make it worse. In the absence of a regime with legitimacy and popular support, no amount of bombing and search-and-destroy missions could stabilize the country. Escalation of all kinds only alienated the Vietnamese population and public opinion at home. Nixon's "Vietnamization" of the war eased the domestic pressure on him, but he was regarded as a sell-out by his remaining supporters in the South, thereby creating the conditions for a North Vietnamese takeover. Efforts to demonstrate American resolve came close to undermining it. The war prompted legislation limiting the president's ability to send armed forces into action without prior congressional support.[24]

Gulf War: Less than a generation later, President George H. W. Bush put together an international coalition to expel Iraqi forces from Kuwait after they invaded and overran the oil rich country in August 1990. Bush and his advisors sought and gained international support for a limited, Korea-like mandate for the liberation of Kuwait. Support from the public and Congress was forthcoming in light of the obvious nature of Iraq's aggression, the United Nations' authorization of a war of liberation, and the formation of an international coalition that received financial support from countries that did not participate in the fighting. The Persian Gulf War of 1990–91 was welcomed by a large segment of the American people as a vehicle for overcoming the trauma associated with the American defeat in Indochina. It provoked a display of yellow ribbons on cars, houses, and trees, many of them with a "Support Our Troops" logo. Following the earlier lead of Ronald Reagan, right-wing revisionists encouraged the myth that America would have won in Vietnam if public opinion had only supported their forces overseas.[25]

The Gulf War produced a military victory and a qualified political success. The Iraqi army was decisively defeated and expelled from Kuwait. However, Republican Guard, the main tank army, was allowed to retreat and Saddam Hussein, Iraq's ruler, used them to carry out punitive wars against separatist groups in the North and South of Iraq. President Bush decided for strategic and domestic political reasons not to invade Iraq and remove Saddam from power. He exercised the restraint that President

Truman did not because he feared that an invasion would encourage centrifugal ethnic and religious forces, break up Iraq, and strengthen the power of Iran in the region.[26]

Iraq: The Anglo-American invasion of Iraq was arguably the dominant military event of the first decade of the twenty-first century. Intended as a lightning strike to remove Saddam Hussein from power and to "shock and awe" friend and foe alike, it turned into an open-ended, increasingly costly, and unsuccessful occupation whose consequences for the Middle East will be felt for years to come. It transformed the US from a country for which there was enormous sympathy in the aftermath of the terrorist attack of 9/11 into an overextended, intensely disliked, quasi-pariah, whose military power was still enormous but unusable for anything but the most obvious defensive missions.[27]

When George Walker Bush assumed office in January 2000, Secretary of State Colin Powell cheerfully admitted to reporters that his predecessor's Iraq policy was successful: "We have kept Saddam contained, kept him in a box."[28] The president and his closest advisors were not satisfied with mere containment or with the international constraints under which they operated. Vice President Cheney, Secretary of Defense Donald Rumsfeld, Deputy Secretary of Defense Paul Wolfowitz, and Undersecretary of Defense Douglas Feith wanted to remove Saddam from power. Their neoconservative allies in the media and think tanks had long been pushing for war against Iraq, and stepped up their campaign after the terrorist attacks on 11 September.[29]

The events of 11 September provided the much-desired pretext for the American invasion, first of Afghanistan and then of Iraq. In the week following the attacks, Rumsfeld, CIA Director George Tenet, and Vice President Cheney's chief of staff Scooter Libby made the case for the invasion of Afghanistan and Iraq.[30] George Bush would ultimately be persuaded by their appeals, and not by the advice to proceed cautiously as proffered by Secretary of State Colin Powell, James Baker, and Lawrence Eagleburger—his father's two secretaries of state—Republican Majority Leader Dick Armey, former National Security Advisor Brent Scowcroft and retired Marine Corps General Anthony Zinni.[31] "Fuck Saddam," Bush told National Security Advisor Condoleezza Rice, "We're taking him out."[32]

The administration began a media blitz with the goal of connecting Saddam to Al-Qaeda, the group responsible for the attacks on 9/11.[33] In his State of the Union Address on 28 January 2003, he described the kinds of WMDs Saddam possessed, spoke of his efforts to buy uranium in Africa, and accused him of harboring of Al-Qaeda terrorists.[34] All of these claims would later be discredited.[35] Secretary of State Powell tried unsuccessfully to win UN support for military action against Saddam. On 20 March 2003, Anglo-American forces opened their campaign against Iraq with massive air strikes directed against military and political targets throughout the country. The following day, ground forces went on the offensive, and three weeks later US forces entered Baghdad. On 1 May, aboard the aircraft carrier *Abraham Lincoln*, President Bush proudly proclaimed victory.[36] Little did he suspect that the real war was about to begin. It is hardly surprising that Bush was blindsided this way. One of the most striking aspects of the run-up to war in Iraq was the extraordinary willingness of the Bush administration to embrace risk. Critiques of the administration's Iraq policy universally emphasize its failure to gather and use available intelligence for any kind of serious risk assessment, to employ a level of forces that would have reduced military risks or devised in advance an occupation policy designed to achieve its political goals.[37]

To make sense of the Iraq fiasco, we need to understand why the Bush administration was so committed to overthrowing Saddam that it was prepared to act unilaterally, "cherry pick" and manipulate intelligence to support its claims that he possessed WMDs, and ride roughshod over the advice and objections of high-ranking military officers concerning its on-the-cheap invasion plans. It made no preparations for an occupation beyond protection of the oil ministry and well heads, was dilatory in responding to the post-occupation insurgency, did so with tactics that only made the situation worse, installed a corrupt, "puppet" émigré leader with no local support, and was subsequently slow and ineffective in building a coalition representative of Iraqi opinion. A large body of literature has developed to address intelligence, military planning, and execution, the occupation and efforts to quell the insurgency, and attributes these failures largely to hubris.[38] The most fundamental question remains unanswered: the administration's reasons for invading Iraq rather than continuing its predecessor's policy of political, economic, and military containment.

Despite frequently voiced claims by Noam Chomsky and others that the invasion was driven by the desire to control Middle Eastern oil, the US had traditionally allowed oil companies, interested primarily in the flow of reasonably priced oil, to make deals with all kinds of authoritarian regimes in the Middle East.[39] If the administration wanted access to Iraqi oil, all it had to do was end sanctions against Iraq, as many people were urging on humanitarian grounds. Saddam would have been happy to sell oil to all comers as he was desperate for income, and the price of oil would have dropped as Iraq's production reentered the international market. The Republican radical right would not consider ending sanctions and buying Iraqi oil. Invasion and occupation were their preferred strategy.[40]

Security is an equally dubious motive. Saddam had been defeated in the Gulf War, although he was able to reassert his authority within Iraq. Iraq's air force and air defense network were in a shambles and "no-fly" zones had been imposed over the Shi'a and Kurdish regions of Iraq and enforced by NATO with frequent sorties. The UN maintained economic sanctions and interdicted any strategic materials that could assist in the development of WMDs. Saddam repeatedly limited inspections and expelled United Nations weapons inspectors, but there was never credible evidence indicating that he had recommenced his pre-war efforts to acquire a nuclear arsenal. A band of uncertainty nevertheless remained, and it was reasonable, even prudent, to compel Saddam to readmit UN inspection teams and give them unrestricted access. In the absence of WMDs and a useable air force, and with a poorly equipped and trained army, Saddam was more a nuisance than a threat to his immediate neighbors.

In the first weeks of the Bush administration, high-ranking officials indicated to foreign officials and the media that they were deeply offended by the survival of Saddam's regime and were clearly on the lookout for any pretext to invade Iraq.[41] They confided to friendly listeners that Saddam's removal would allow Washington to remake the map of the Middle East and dramatically increase its influence worldwide. They assumed Iraqis would welcome their American "liberators" with open arms and accept émigré puppet Ahmed Chalabi as their new ruler. A pro-American regime in the heart of the Middle East was expected to provide significant leverage over Saudi Arabia, Iran, and the Palestinians. Administration officials also reasoned that a high-tech military campaign of "shock and awe" that paralyzed

Iraqi forces at the outset with precision bombing and missile attack and overthrew Saddam with few American casualties would intimidate North Korea and Iran. "Iraq is not just about Iraq," a senior official confided, "but about Iran, Libya and North Korea."[42] Victory was expected to encourage widespread "bandwagoning," making countries around the world more intent on currying favor with the US, while allowing Washington to put more pressure on countries like France that opposed its vision of world order.[43] The US was king of the hill and the Bush administration was basking in its "unipolar" glory.[44]

Anger also played a role. The attacks of 9/11 wounded the US physically and psychologically, as Al-Qaeda killed a sizeable number of people, although many less than initial estimates. They destroyed a major landmark—the World Trade Center—an icon of American economic power—and damaged an even more hallowed landmark—the Pentagon—the nerve center of American military might. The attacks were not conducted by another state, but by a rag-tag cabal of terrorists, which made the offensive more intolerable still. That such an unworthy adversary could so successfully attack the US aroused strong desires for revenge. It also soon became apparent that terrorist attacks had succeeded because of refusal at the highest levels of government to take seriously the threat of terrorism and the remarkable incompetence on the part of the Federal Bureau of Investigation (FBI).[45] The administration successfully exploited American anger, deflecting it away from itself and toward Saddam.

The history of American intervention suggests that to succeed, presidents must sell it to the public on compelling grounds of national security and win quick victories with low casualties. The First Gulf War met these conditions and established the precedent that the subsequent Bush administration tried and failed to emulate. It was unable to secure UN authorization for intervention and could not put together an impressive multilateral coalition. Britain aside, other major powers opposed intervention, among them France and Germany, two of America's closest allies.[46] After invading Iraq and overthrowing Saddam's regime, the occupying forces failed to find any weapons of mass destruction, which had provided the public justification for American intervention. They were also were unable to withdraw, as originally planned, because of a growing insurgency. Although Obama won the presidential election in 2008, in part because of his promise to end the war in Iraq, he made it clear upon taking office that American troops would have to remain in that country for some time and ordered a build-up of forces in Afghanistan. These moves antagonized the left wing of the Democratic Party but did not generate any kind of widespread opposition.

Sonderweg?

German historians and the media have long debated the extent to which Germany had a unique path (*Sonderweg*) of development that distinguished it from other Western countries, encouraged authoritarianism, and was ultimately responsible for Hitler. We might ask a similar question about the US: has it gone down a pathway different from other Western democracies? Have its foreign wars and the effects of globalization led to Donald Trump? And is he a passing phenomenon or the beginning of a sustained assault on the constitution, the media, tolerance of diverse opinions, respect for political opponents, and the willingness to make the kinds of compromises that sustain democracy?

When we examine the record of war initiation since 1945, the US is among the countries that have most often used their military instruments. Of 31 wars fought in the postwar era, Israel was involved in six, the US and China in five, Vietnam in four and India and Pakistan in three. Israel and the US are tied in war initiation. Israel initiated four wars and fought in two others (1948 and 1973) in which it was attacked by Arab coalitions. The US initiated four of the six wars in which it participated.[47]

The US is unique in other ways. Prodigious wealth allows the US to spend an extraordinary percentage of its GDP on its armed forces in comparison to other countries. Democratic and Republican administrations alike have bet that extraordinary levels of military expenditure will sustain, if not increase, the standing and influence that traditionally comes with military dominance. US defense expenditure also reflects the political power of the military-industrial complex. Defense spending encouraged dependence on the government by numerous companies and helped bring others into being. In 1991, at the end of the Cold War,

12 million people, roughly 10 percent of the US workforce, were directly or indirectly dependent upon defense dollars. The number has not changed significantly since. Having such a large impact on the economy gives defense contractors enormous political clout.[48] Those who land major weapons projects are also careful to sub-contract production across the country, not infrequently offering something to companies in every state. This too gives them enormous political leverage in Congress, often enough to force reluctant administrations to buy weapons that the military does not want.[49]

Congress and presidents are witting participants to a vicious cycle. Propaganda, sponsored by think tanks and so-called patriotic organizations, many with funding from defense contractors, creates foreign enemies for the public and greatly exaggerates the threats they pose. This process began with the Cold War and identification of the Soviet Union as an enemy, but also China. In the post-Cold War era, North Korea, Iran, and Islamic fundamentalism are the enemies, with China perhaps on its way to becoming one again. Arms build-ups, forward deployments, bellicose rhetoric, and military and diplomatic support for countries more directly in the firing line exacerbate tensions with these enemies, helping to make depictions of their hostility self-fulfilling. In the Cold War, behavior of this kind by both superpowers helped to provoke a series of war-threatening crises, culminating in the Cuban missile crisis.[50] In the post-Cold War period, the invasions of Afghanistan and Iraq have escalated tensions with the Islamic world, seemingly emboldened Iran and North Korea, and have probably made the US an even more likely target of territorial attacks. It has certainly put American soldiers and civilians in harm's way throughout the Middle East. These conflicts not only make American fears self-fulfilling but provide justification for the kinds of arms build-ups and forward deployments that helped to bring this situation about. It is a well-known adage that people with hammers look for nails. With such a large and capable military, there is a continuing temptation to try to influence outcomes around the world and to rely heavily on the nation's military capabilities to do this.

In comparison to its peer group of democracies, the US is the only country in which elements of a historical honor culture remain important.

In Prussia and Wilhelminian Germany, the Junkers (East Elbian, land-owning aristocrats) constituted a distinct class whose hold on power was justified by the military service and legendary bravery. Their class values and representatives helped to shape Prussian and German foreign and military policy and contributed significantly to the outbreak of World War I.[51] The Junkers bled to death in World War I although enough survived to provide proficient and compliant leadership of the *Wehrmacht* in Hitler's wars of aggression. Two world wars purged Germany and other European countries of such elites and, more importantly, thoroughly discredited their values. The Civil War did not do the same for the US.[52] The South's honor culture continued to produce officers and enlisted personnel who gradually came to dominate the American military and who are still over-represented within it. Since the draft was abolished in 1973, the percentage of military enlistments from the south and west has risen. Between 1985 and 2001, recruits from the South increased from 34 to 42 percent. In 2016, 44 percent of recruits for all the armed forces came from the South.[53] The regional distribution of newly commissioned officers is roughly similar; the South accounted for 44 percent of new Army ROTC commissioned officers in 2006 and 38 percent of West Point graduates in 2007.[54] Southern influence in the military is growing, making it an institution like the Prussian officer corps, in the sense that it is cut off from the rest of society by virtue of its very different values. In the case of the American military this is true not only of officers but of enlisted men and women.

Fortunately, American officers differ from their Prussian counterparts in that they have only indirect input into the policymaking process. As Leslie Gelb and Richard Betts convincingly demonstrated, it is civilian officials, not the military, who generally push for the use of force, although the military prefers to use it on a more massive scale once a decision for war is made. This was the case in Iraq, where the military was appalled by the small size of the force Secretary of Defense Donald Rumsfeld was willing to commit to the operation.[55] However, like its Junker counterpart, the US military is on the whole a compliant tool of political authorities in its willingness to sacrifice itself, even become spokesmen for, the most questionable military adventures. Only one general resigned his commission when the military was pushed into invading Iraq; the others bit the bullet and prepared to attack with forces they believed inadequate for the task.[56]

Equally striking is the willingness of the military and their families to back wars like Afghanistan and Iraq despite the personal price they pay in fighting them. Public opinion polls consistently reveal that there is more support for ongoing wars and interventionist foreign policies within the military than among civilians, and more among Southerners than people from other parts of the country.[57] Southerners and the military are much more likely to identify with the Republican Party, which is more likely than the Democrats to support interventions and has a higher tolerance for casualties. Pro-war attitudes also reflect the honor culture from which many professional soldiers come or to which they are socialized.[58] This orientation makes it easier to sell wars to the public because the people who have to fight and die in them are the least likely to oppose them. It also makes it more difficult to oppose war because under the guise of "Support Our Troops" dissenters who have never served in the military must bear the onus of appearing unpatriotic.

The US further differs from Europeans and Japanese in the strength of its religious faith. Gallup polls from 1947 to 1994 show that about 95 percent of Americans believe "in god or a universal spirit," in contrast to about 50 percent for Europeans and Japanese.[59] Gallup polls further reveal that between 81 and 93 percent of Americans believe in heaven, although, strikingly, only 54–85 percent give credence to hell.[60] Belief in a deity and in heaven is far more prevalent within the military than outside, and more in the south than the rest of the country.[61] Both beliefs soften the consequences of death and make it more acceptable, especially if a military causality is understood as god's will and family members hope, even expect, to be reunited in heaven with departed loved ones. The commitment to honor has the same effect by imparting important meaning to loss of life in combat and conferring status on their families within the community that shares these values.[62]

These unusual features of American political, economic, and social culture come together to produce what might be called the perfect national security storm. Wealth provides the material capability for the US to attempt to play a hegemonic role in the international system while its parvenu status and military-industrial complex provides the means and public support for such a policy. Southern honor sub-culture and the pervasiveness of religious beliefs ensure willing agents to execute wars and interventions and quietly accept the human costs they entail. It is not without reason that a significant percentage of the population in other democracies considers the US the greatest threat to peace.

Starving the Beast

Republicans want to starve the beast, by which they mean the civilian branches of the federal government. They are motivated by reinforcing economic and ideological reasons. Government costs money and it is raised from taxes. Many Republicans are well off, or at least in the higher tax brackets, and want to keep as much of their income as possible. They particularly resent that part of the budget that goes to social and related services, which they condemn as income redistribution. They want to get or stay rich at the expense of the poor. They are happy, by contrast, to spend more and more on the military.

The country needs to pursue just the opposite policy. The beast that needs starving is the defense establishment and equally bloated Homeland Security. They waste money prodigiously in ways that spending on social services and spending on infrastructure do not. Of equal importance, I have argued, an expensive military needs justification and finds it in unsuccessful interventions, support for proxy interventions—as in Yemen—and threatening forward deployments. These actions occur because with such military might US presidents and their advisors fell less need to compromise with foreign actors and are more inclined to make maximum demands that they are likely to reject. With the rare exception, these actions have been seriously damaging to American security and prestige. They have undermined, not strengthened, American influence in the world. Then there is the hidden cost of wasting so much money, brainpower, and labor on the military when it could otherwise be directed to economically productive and socially useful activities. Less is more when it comes to military spending.

Any efforts to trim the military will provoke powerful opposition and charges from the military, the right wing, and powerful lobby groups that cuts border on treason. This veritable and inevitable storm of opposition must be confronted head-on with reasoned arguments and incremental cuts that reduce the military budget by 50–70 percent over the course of an administration. This will mean laying off people and mothballing or sending to the scrapheap planes, ships, and other weapons. These cuts should be premised and justified by a strategic planning document that makes reasonable estimates of security threats and identifies appropriate ways of protecting against them.

The threat of budget cuts to the Pentagon and Homeland Security will inspire the same kind of doomsday rhetoric that efforts to ban chloro-fluorocarbons did in the run-up to the Montreal Protocol and subsequent agreements to reverse the hole in the ozone layer. The companies that complained discovered that the alternatives they had to produce gave them more market share and profit. The hoopla the right wing currently makes about the costs of confronting climate change are also more ideology than fact. European countries that have taken climate change seriously have discovered that the costs are much less than imagined and that it has inspired technical innovation and profit making. The same would be true of drastic cutbacks in military spending. Richard Nixon punished the state of Rhode Island for voting Democratic in the 1968 election by relocating the fleet from Newport to Norfolk, Virginia. Newport feared a serious economic downturn. The reverse proved true as the fleet's disappearance created the conditions for redevelopment and a tourist boom that made the economy stronger than before.

The national security establishment will also raise the threat of Russia and China, whom they will assert will see us as weak and act more aggressively. At the same time, they will insist, our allies will lose faith in us and bandwagon with our adversaries. These charges are readily deflected. If the US cut its military spending by half, it would still be spending five times more than the next ten military powers combined. Surely, this is enough to guarantee our security! It is also premised on the belief that Russia and China harbor aggressive designs against Western Europe or our Pacific allies, and there is no evidence for this whatsoever. They are not nice regimes, to be sure, and I will treat China in detail in a later chapter.

Change will require a committed, skillful, and courageous president with strong support in the Congress and backed by an effective public relations campaign. Even then the going will be tough. But then weaning people off drugs to which they are addicted is never easy. Once they are free of their addiction, most feel empowered and happier and cannot imagine going back to it.

Notes

1. Stockholm International Peace Research Institute, *SIPRI Yearbook 2011* (Oxford: Oxford University Press, 2011), p. 158.
2. SIPRI, "The Major Spenders in 2003," http://www.sipri.se.
3. *SIPRI Yearbook 2011*, p. 9.
4. Zachary Cohen, "Trump proposes $54 billion defense spending hike," *CNN*, 26 March 2017, https://edition.cnn.com/2017/03/16/politics/donald-trump-defense-budget-blueprint/index.html; Andrew Taylor, "Trump budget would slash domestic programs to boost military," *Boston Globe*, 16 March 2017, https://www.bostonglobe.com/news/politics/2017/03/16/trump-unveils-trillion-budget/5Wa4rRxxdgrrBBqrSueUjO/story.html (both accessed 12 October 2018).
5. Global Issues, "World Military Spending," 25 February 2007, http://www.globalissues.org/Geopolitics/ArmsTrade/Spending.asp#USMilitarySpending; Christopher Hellman, "Highlights of the Fiscal Year 2008 Pentagon Spending Request," 5 February 2007, available at www.armscontrolcenter.org.
6. Katrina Manson, "The Future of War," *Financial Times Magazine*, 17–18 November 2018, pp. 12–10.
7. Karen DeYoung, "Bush Proclaims Victory," *Washington Post*, 2 May 2003, p. A1.
8. Watson Institute for International Studies, Brown University, "Costs of War Project: The $5.6 Trillion Price Tag of the Post-9/11 Wars." https://watson.brown.edu/news/2017/costs-war-project-56-trillion-price-tag-post-911-wars (accessed 12 October 2018); Philip Bump, "15 years after the Iraq War began, the death toll is still murky," *Washington Post*, 20 March 2018, https://www.washingtonpost.com/news/politics/wp/2018/03/20/15-years-after-it-began-the-death-toll-from-the-iraq-war-is-still-murky/?utm_term=.38439b834b69 (accessed 17 November 2018).
9. Associated Press, "Civilian deaths in Afghan war rise to highest level in ten years," *Guardian*, 25 February 2019, p. 21.
10. Daniel Trotta, "Iraq war costs US more than $2 trillion: study," *Reuters*, 14 March 2013, https://www.reuters.com/article/us-iraq-war-anniversary-idUSBRE92D0PG20130314 (accessed 9 October 2018).
11. David Wood, "Iraq Reconstruction Cost US $60 Billion, Left Behind Corruption And Waste," *Huffington Post*, 3 June 2013, https://www.huff-

ingtonpost.co.uk/entry/iraq-reconstruction_n_2819899; Keith Perry, "Afghanistan has cost more to rebuild than Europe after Second World War," *Telegraph*, 31 July 2014, https://www.telegraph.co.uk/news/world-news/asia/afghanistan/11004928/Afghanistan-has-cost-more-to-rebuild-than-Europe-after-Second-World-War.html; CBS News, "Much of $60B from US to rebuild Iraq wasted, special auditor's final report to Congress shows," 6 March 2013, https://www.cbsnews.com/news/much-of-60b-from-us-to-rebuild-iraq-wasted-special-auditors-final-report-to-congress-shows/; James Risen, "Investigation Into Missing Iraqi Cash Ended in Lebanon Bunker," *New York Times*, 12 October 2014, https://www.nytimes.com/2014/10/12/world/investigation-into-missing-iraqi-cash-ended-in-lebanon-bunker.html (all accessed 10 October 2018).

12. *Economist*, Daily Dispatch, 19 October 2018, https://mail.google.com/mail/u/0/#inbox/FMfcgxvzLFCCHPGvnBkWDkdgzZDhsXnL (accessed 20 October 2018).

13. Dave Lindorff, "Exclusive: The Pentagon's Massive Accounting Fraud Exposed," *Nation*, 16 November 2018, https://www.thenation.com/article/pentagon-audit-budget-fraud/ (accessed 16 November 2018).

14. Rosemary Foot, *The Wrong War: American Policy and the Dimensions of the Korean Conflict, 1950–1953* (Ithaca: Cornell University Press, 1985).

15. Casey, *Selling the Korean War, Propaganda, Politics, and Public Opinion in the United States, 1950–1953* (New York: Oxford University Press, 2008), p. 326–36.

16. Leslie Gelb and Richard K. Betts, *The Irony of Vietnam: The System Worked* (Washington, D. C.: Brookings, 1978); Fredrik Logevall, *Embers of War: The Fall of An Empire and The Making of America's Vietnam* (New York: Random House, 2012); David Kaiser, *American Tragedy: Kennedy, Johnson, and the Origins of the Vietnam War* (Cambridge: Harvard University Press, 2002).

17. Gerhard L. Weinberg, *The Foreign Policy of Hitler's Germany*, 2 vols. (Chicago: University of Chicago Press, 1970–80), I, pp. 462–63.

18. Ted Hopf, *Peripheral Visions: Deterrence Theory and American Foreign Policy in the Third World, 1965–1990* (Ann Arbor: University of Michigan Press, 1994); Richard Ned Lebow and Janice Gross Stein, *We All Lost the Cold War* (Princeton: Princeton University Press, 1994), ch. 13.

19. Logevall, *Embers of War*; Kaiser, *American Tragedy*.

20. Logevall, *Embers of War*; Kaiser, *American Tragedy*; Personal conversation with McGeorge Bundy, (New York City, 20 April 1990).

21. Stanley Karnow, *Vietnam: A History*, 2nd ed. (New York: Penguin, 1997); Max Hastings, *Vietnam: An Epic Tragedy, 1945–1975* (New York: Harper, 2018).

22. Robert S. McNamara, James G. Blight, and Robert K. Brigham, *Argument Without End: In Search of Answers to the Vietnam Tragedy* (New York: Public Affairs, 1999), p. 194.

23. Ibid., pp. 191, 341–45.

24. Louis Fisher, *Presidential War Power*, 3rd ed. rev. (Lawrence, Kans.: University of Kansas Press, 2013).

25. *Neo-Neocon*, "Mind is a Difficult Thing to Change: Vietnam Interlude—after the Fall," 28 April 2005, http://neo-neocon.blogspot.com/2005/04/mind-is-difficult-thing-to-change.html, "Breaking the Big Stick: Removing the Threat of War to Achieve Peace," 31 May 2007, http://neoneocon.com/category/war/vietnam/; Robert Buzzanaco, "How I Learned to Stop Worrying and Love Vietnam and Iraq," *Counterpunch*, 16–17 April 2005, http://www.counterpunch.org/buzzanco04162005.html. For serious analyses, Lembcke, *The Spitting Image*; Hixon, *Historical Memory and Representations of the Vietnam War* (New York: New York University Press, 2000).

26. Steve A. Yetiv, *Explaining Foreign Policy: US Decision-Making in the Gulf Wars* (Baltimore: Johns Hopkins University Press, 2011); William Thomas Allison, *The Gulf War, 1990–91* (New York: Palgrave Macmillan, 2012); W. Lance Bennett and David L. Paletz, eds., *Taken by Storm: The Media, Public Opinion, and US Foreign Policy in the Gulf War* (Chicago: University of Chicago Press, 1994).

27. "What the World Thinks in 2002," http://people-press.prg/reports/display.php3?ReportID=165. There was overwhelming support in Europe for the war against the Taliban: 73 percent in the UK, 64 percent in France, and 61 percent in Germany.

28. Colin Powell, "Press Briefing en Route to Cairo Egypt," 23 February 2001, www.state.gov/secretary/former/powell/remarks/2001/931.htm.

29. William Kristol and Zalmay Khalilzad, "We Must Lead the War in Deposing Saddam," *Washington Post*, 9 November 1997; PNAC Statement of Principles available at the Project for a New American Century website, http://www.newamericancentury.org/statementofprinciples.htm; Bob Woodward, *Bush at War* (New York: Simon & Schuster, 2002), p. 349–50; Michael Gordon and Bernard Trainor, *Cobra II* (New York: Pantheon Books, 2006), p. 15, quoting from an interview with Lt.-Gen.

Gregory S. Newbold in which he quotes Douglas Feith. Ivo H. Daalder and James M. Lindsay, *America Unbound: The Bush Revolution in Foreign Policy*, rev. ed. (Hoboken, N.J.: Wiley, 2005) pp. 163–4; James Fallows, "Blind into Baghdad," *Atlantic Monthly* (January/February 2004). Halper and Clarke, Stefan Halper and Jonathan Clarke, *America Alone: The Neo-Conservatives and the Global Order* (New York: Cambridge University Press, 2004), pp. 201–31; Michael Isikoff and David Corn, *Hubris: The Inside Story of Spin, Scandal, and the Selling of the Iraq War* (New York: Crown, 2006), pp. 33–191 on the public relations campaign by neoconservatives and administration officials to win public support for war against Iraq. Ricks, Thomas E., *Fiasco: The American Military Adventure in Iraq* (New York: Penguin, 2006), pp. 13–28 on containment.

30. Patrick Tyler and Elaine Sciolino, "Bush Advisors Split on Scope of Retaliation," *New York Times*, 20 September 2001, p. A5; Bob Woodward and Dan Balz, "At Camp David, Advise and Dissent," *Washington Post*, 31 January 2002, p. A1; Richard Cheney on *Meet the Press*, 16 September 2001, https://www.youtube.com/watch?v=KQBsCIaxMuM (accessed 26 February 2019); Fallows, "Blind into Baghdad"; Purdham, *A Time of Our Choosing*, p. 10; Woodward, *Bush at War*, pp. 48–50, 83; James Mann, *Rise of the Vulcans: The History of Bush's War Cabinet* (New York: Penguin, 2004), p. 302, citing an 18 June 2003 interview with Paul Wolfowitz; Gordon, and Trainor, *Cobra II*, pp. 14–15, and interview with Francis Brooke, p. 19, on Rumsfeld.

31. National Commission on Terrorist Attacks, *The 9/11 Commission Report: Final Report of the National Commission on Terrorist Attacks upon the United States* (New York: Norton, 2004), pp. 334–35; Woodward, *State of Denial*, pp. 332–34 on the Powell-Bush meeting of 5 August 2002; Transcript of interview with Brent Scowcroft, *Face the Nation*, 4 August 2002; Brent Scowcroft, "Don't Attack Saddam," *Wall Street Journal*, 15 August 2002, p. A12; Todd Purdum and Patrick E. Tyler, "Top Republicans Break with Bush on Iraq Strategy," *New York Times*, 16 August 2002, p. A1; James A. Baker II, "The Right Way to Change a Regime," *New York Times*, 25 August 2002, section 4, p. 9; Transcript of Lawrence Eagleburger, *Crossfire*, 19 August 2002; Interview with Lawrence Eagleburger, Fox *News* Sunday, Washington, D. C., 18 August 2002; Walter Gibbs, "Scowcroft Urges Wide Role for the U.N. in Postwar Iraq," *New York Times*, 9 April 2003; Eric Schmitt, "Iraq is Defiant as G.O.P. Leaders Opposes Attack," *New York Times*, 9 August 2002, p. A6; Ricks, *Fiasco*, pp. 30–32, 50–52: Isikoff and Corn, *Hubris*, pp. 27–28.

32. Quoted in Michael Elliot and James Carney, "First Stop Iraq," *Time*, 31 March 2003, p. 173; Gordon, and Trainor, *Cobra II*, p. 17, quoting from an interview with Hugh Shelton. Bush is reported to have said, "We will get this guy but at a time and place of our choosing." Lott, *Herding Cats*, pp. 235–36, also reports that Bush indicated his intention to go to war in private conversations with him.

33. George Bush, "President Bush Outlines Iraqi Threat," October 7, 2002, (http://www.whitehouse.gov/news/releases/2002/10/20021007-8.html); State of the Union Address, 28 January 2003, http://www.whitehouse.gov/news/releases/2003/01/20030128-19.html (both accessed 25 February 2019).

34. George Bush, State of the Union Address, 28 January 2003, http://www.whitehouse.gov/news/releases/2003/01/20030128-19.html (accessed 12 October 2018).

35. *National Commission on Terrorist Attacks Upon the United States*, pp. 61, 161, 334–35; *Iraq Survey Group Final Report*, Global Scan, http://www.globalsecurity.org/wmd/library/report/2004/isg-final-report/isg-final-report_vol3_cw_key-findings.htm (accessed 4 March 2018).

36. Karen DeYoung, "Bush Proclaims Victory," *Washington Post*, 2 May 2003, p. A1.

37. Rick's, *Fiasco*, pp. 42–43, 66–84, on military dissatisfaction.

38. Daalder and Lindsay, *America Unbound*, pp. 143–83; Fallows, "Blind into Baghdad"; David L. Phillips, *Losing Iraq: Inside the Postwar Reconstruction Fiasco* (Boulder, Co: Westview, 2005); Isikoff and Corn, *Hubris*, pp. 191–210; Ricks, *Fiasco*, pp. 149–202; Gordon, and Trainor, *Cobra II*; Galbraith, *End of Iraq*, pp. 114–224; Bob Woodward, *Plan of Attack* (New York: Simon & Schuster, 2004); Seymour M. Hersh, *Chain of Command: The Road from 9/11 to Abu Ghraib* (New York: Harper, 2004).

39. Noam Chomsky and David Barsamian, *Imperial Ambitions: Conversations in the Post-9/11 World* (New York: Metropolitan Books, 2005); "Imperial Ambition," Interview with Noam Chomsky by David Barsamian, *Monthly Review*, May 2003, http://www.monthlyreview.org/0503chomsky.htm; "Iraq: Yesterday, Today, and Tomorrow," Michael Albert interviews Noam Chomsky, 27 December 2006, http://www.chomsky.info/articles/20050704.htm; Callinicos, *New Mandarins of American Power*, pp. 93–98; Phillips, *American Dynasty*, pp. 248–59, 313–14; Harvey, *The New Imperialism*, pp. 1–25; Edward Ingram, "Pairing off Empires: The United States as Great Britain in the Middle East," in Tore T. Petersen,

Controlling the Uncontrollable? The Great Powers in the Middle East (Trondheim: Tapir Books, 2006), pp. 1–32.

40. *Debate*, 5 March 2007, "Is Oil or Big Business an Undisclosed Motive for the War on Iraq?," http://www.thedebate.org/thedebate/iraq.asp; MSNBC, 11 November 2002, "Oil: The Other Iraq War," http://www.msnbc.msn.com/id/3071526/, for a more moderate version of the argument.

41. Hersh, *Chain of Command*, pp. 163–71; Mann, *Rise of the Vulcans*, pp. 294–310; Halper and Clarke, *America Alone*, pp. 28–35; Isikoff and Corn, *Hubris*, p. 16.

42. David E. Sanger, "Viewing the War as a Lesson to the World," *New York Times*, 6 April 2003.

43. Frum and Perle, *An End to Evil*, p. 33, 212–13, 247–66.

44. Charles Krauthammer, "The Unipolar Moment," *Foreign Affairs* 70 (1990/1991), pp. 23–33; Stephen Brooks and William Wohlforth, "American Primacy in Perspective," *Foreign Affairs* 81 (2002), pp. 20–33; William Wohlforth, "The Stability of a Unipolar World," *International Security* 24 (1999), pp. 5–41; Chris Reus-Smit, *American Power and World Order* (Cambridge: Polity Press, 2004), ch. 4 on the "idealism of preponderance."

45. Dan Eggen, "Pre 9/11 Missteps by FBI Detailed," *Washington Post*, 10 June 2005, p. AO1.

46. Isikoff and Corn, *Hubris*; Gordon and Trainor, *Cobra II*; Lebow, *Cultural Theory of International Relations*, ch. 9; Rich, *Greatest Story Ever Sold*.

47. Prepared by Benjamin Valentino and the author.

48. John J. Accordino, *Captives of the Cold War Economy: The Struggle for Defense Conversion in American Communities* (Westport, Conn: Praeger, 2000), p. 1.

49. For a nice case in point, consider the F-22, which Obama finally killed in the Senate with the threat of a veto. Leslie Wayne, "Air Force Jet Wins Battle in Congress," *New York Times*, 28 September 2006; Editorial, "We Don't Need the F-22," *New York Times*, 19 June 2009; "White House Threatens Veto over F-22 Jet Fighters," Associated Press, 24 June 2009; Bryan Bender, "A Dog Fight Obama Seems Bound to Lose," *Boston Globe*, 12 July 2009, pp. A1, 10; Christopher Drew, "Bowing to Veto Threat, Senate Blocks Money for Warplanes," *New York Times*, 22 July 2009, p. A1.

50. Lebow and Stein, *We All Lost the Cold War*, ch. 2.

51. Holger Afflerbach, *Falkenhayn: Politisches Denken und Handeln in Kaiserreich* (Munich: Oldenbourg, 1994), p. 61; Annika Mombauer, *Helmuth von Moltke and the Origins of the First World War* (Cambridge: Cambridge University Press, 2001); Lebow, *Cultural Theory of International Relations*, ch. 7.

52. Bertram Wyatt-Brown, *Southern Honor: Ethics and Behavior in the Old South* (New York: Oxford University Press, 1986) and *The Shaping of Southern Culture: Honor, Grace and War, 1760s–1890s* (Chapel Hill: University of North Carolina Press, 2001).

53. Michael Lind, "Bush's Martyrs," *New Statesman*, 1 March 2004, p. 20; Shanea Watkins and James Sherk, *Who Serves in the US Military? The Demographics of Enlisted Troops and Officers* (Washington, D.C.: Heritage Foundation Center for Data Analysis Report: 2008), p. 13.

54. US Department of Defense, *Population Representation in the Military Services, Fiscal Year 2016* (Washington, D. C.: Department of Defense, 2016); George M. Reynolds and Amanda Shendruk, "Demographics of the US Military," Council on Foreign Relations, 24 April 2018, https://www.cfr.org/article/demographics-us-military (accessed 12 October 2018).

55. Mombauer, *Helmuth von Moltke and the Origins of the First World*; Ricks, *Fiasco*, pp. 40–43, 66–84.

56. Ricks, *Fiasco*, p. 67, Lt. Gen. Gregory Newbold is the only known pre-invasion departure from senior military ranks for opposition to the war.

57. Valentino and Valentino, "An Army of the People?"

58. Ole R Holsti, "Of Chasms and Convergences: Attitudes and Beliefs of Civilians and Military Elites at the Start of a New Millennium," in Peter D. Feaver and Richard H. Kohn, eds., *Soldiers and Civilians: The Civil-Military Gap and American National Security* (Cambridge: MIT Press, 2001), pp. 15–99; Christopher Gelpi, Peter Feaver and Jason Reifler, *Paying the Human Costs of War* (Princeton: Princeton University Press, 2009); Peter D. Feaver, and Christopher Gelpi, *Choosing Your Battles: American Civil-Military Relations and the Use of Force* (Princeton: Princeton University Press 2004) or contrary findings about close association with the military and willingness to support war.

59. Gallup Polls, reported at Religious Tolerance.org, http://www.religioustolerance.org/godpoll.htm The Pew Forum on Religion and Public Life, "US Religious Landscape Survey," 1 July 2009, http://religions.pewforum.org/reports (nevertheless shows an across the board decline in

formal affiliation); Association of Religious Data Archives, http://www.thearda.com/internationalData/compare.asp (all accessed 10 October 2018). Steven Pfaff, "The Religious divide: Why Religion Seems to Be Thriving in the United States and Waning in Europe," in Jeffrey Kopstein and Sven Steinmo, eds., *Growing Apart? America and Europe in the Twenty-First Century* (New York: Cambridge, 2007), pp. 24–52.

60. Gallup Organization poll in 1994-DEC. Quoted in George Bishop, "What Americans Really Believe," *Free Inquiry*, Summer 1999, pp. 38–42. Gallup Poll, described by *Charisma*, 7 June 2000, http://www.mcjonline.com/news/00/20000225e.htm (accessed 10 February 2019).

61. Holsti, "Of Chasms and Convergences."

62. Lebow, *Cultural Theory of International Relations*, chs. 3 and 4 for the characteristics of honor societies and how they regard death.

4

Deterrence and Compellence

Deterrence and compellence were foundational strategies during the Cold War. They have made a comeback in the light of widespread fears of an aggressive Russia, more assertive China, and always troublesome North Korea. There are notable differences between the present and the past. Terrorism is the most immediate security threat to the West, foreign adversaries are increasingly non-state groups and movements, and chaos in North Africa and the Middle East has brought a flood of refugees to Europe. Globalization has significantly increased the mobility of pathogens, and with it the possibility that a newly evolved virus in East Asia or Africa could devastate populations worldwide. Most threatening of all in the longer term is global warming and the economic dislocation, water shortages, and domestic and international conflicts it is likely to provoke. Threat-based strategies are not relevant to these problems. But they are pertinent to more traditional kinds of conflicts—or thought to be—by those who make or seek to influence policy—and to combatting terrorism as well. Arguments in favor of them frequently invoke the so-called lessons of the Cold War or other past conflicts. It is worth revisiting these lessons, and all the more so because I think they are wrong. Toward this end I offer a critique of deterrence and compellence, based on the same cases but better historical evidence.

© The Author(s) 2020
R. N. Lebow, *A Democratic Foreign Policy*,
https://doi.org/10.1007/978-3-030-21519-4_4

Threat-based strategies have always been central to international relations. Deterrence and compellence represent efforts to conceptualize these strategies to make them more understandable in theory and more effective in practice. Deterrence can be defined as an attempt to influence other actors' assessment of their interests. It seeks to prevent an undesired behavior by convincing the party who may be contemplating such an action that its cost would exceed any possible gain.[1] Deterrence presupposes decisions made in response to a rational cost-benefit assessment, and further assumes that this assessment can be successfully manipulated from the outside by increasing the cost of noncompliance. Compellence, a related strategy, employs the same tactics to attempt to convince another party to carry out some action it otherwise would not. Deterrence has always been practiced, but the advent of nuclear weapons made it imperative for policymakers to find ways of preventing catastrophically destructive wars while exploiting any strategic nuclear advantage for political gain.

Scholars and policymakers became interested in deterrence following the development of the atom bomb. The early literature began with the assumption of fully rational actors and was deductive in nature. It stipulated four conditions of successful deterrence: defining commitments, communicating them to adversaries, developing the capability to defend them, and imparting credibility to these commitments. It explored various tactics that leaders could exploit toward this end, concentrating on the problem of credibility. This was recognized as the core problem when deterrence was practiced against another nuclear adversary—and the implementation of the threats in question could entail national suicide.[2,3] One prominent theorist argued that it was rational for a leader to develop a reputation for being irrational so his threats might be believed.[4] Richard Nixon took this advice to heart in his dealings with both the Soviet Union and North Vietnam.[5]

Contemporary Deterrence and Compellence

The contemporary debate is more international than it was during the Cold War. There are additional nuclear powers, and there are also more targets for deterrence for existing one. Deterrence has been extended to non-state actors and to the new domain of cyber warfare.[6] Russia has been modernizing its nuclear forces and even before he took the oath of office President Trump insisted that the US should expand its nuclear capability.[7] For me the big question is not whether deterrence helped to prevent World War III, but why so many officials and academics believe it did. Reputable scholars also routinely claim that nuclear weapons keep the peace between India and Pakistan and promote more peace generally.[8] As in the Cold War, what theorists and analysts say about deterrence often reveals more about their ideological assumptions and national strategic culture than it does about the efficacy of threat-based strategies.

During the Cold War, the theory and practice of deterrence and compellence focused on making credible threats on the assumption that they were necessary to moderate adversaries. Self-deterrence—the reluctance of actors to assume the risks of war independently of efforts by others to deter them—received little attention or credence when it did. Post-Cold War research suggests that self-deterrence was a more important source of restraint than deterrence practiced by adversaries.[9] Successive leaders of the superpowers were terrified of a conventional war, let alone, a nuclear one.

Self-deterrence is equally evident in the post-Cold War era. In Somalia, the US withdrew its forces after losing 18 US Army Rangers.[10] In Rwanda, genocidal Hutus deterred Western intervention by killing ten Belgian soldiers.[11] In Bosnia, compellence clearly failed against Milosevic, who continued his policy of ethnic cleansing of Bosniaks in Bosnia despite Western threats. Pushed by Western public opinion, NATO finally screwed up its courage to intervene, but then failed to go after known war criminals because of the vulnerability of its lightly armed forces, whose primary mission was the distribution of aid.[12] Self-deterrence also kept the Western powers from intervening in Syria or taking a harder line against Russia in the Ukraine crisis.

In the aftermath of the Cold War, the focus of American deterrence turned away from restraining large state actors with nuclear weapons to smaller, so-called rogue states or non-state actors. Washington and its European allies sought to deter Iraq, Iran, and North Korea from developing or testing nuclear weapons.[13] Deterrence did not achieve its goal. Iraq was invaded, Iran was persuaded to put its program on hold in return for concessions, and North Korea continues to build its nuclear arsenal. In all three countries, there are grounds for arguing that deterrent threats might make these weapons more attractive. There is persuasive research that suggests countries are most likely to give up their nuclear programs when new governments come to power that seem to them as inimical to their interests or values.[14] Neither deterrence nor compellence is very relevant to these calculations, but the promise of recognition and acceptance is.

Since 11 September 2001, there has been an ongoing debate about the applicability of deterrence to the problem of terrorism. Libya, North Korea, and Iran have been the major target of US pressure because of their support of terrorism in addition to their pursuit or funding of nuclear weapons programs. Regional actors have attempted to deter non-state actors, notably Palestinians, Kurds, and Islamic fundamentalists.[15] One of the emerging conclusions is that it is impossible to deter groups who are willing to give up their lives, but there it may be possible to reduce overall terrorism by deterrence that promises other kinds of punishment and is coupled with non-coercive efforts to reduce some of the incentives for this kind of violence.[16]

Nuclear strategy has made a comeback in the academic and policy world in response to a more aggressive Russia and China.[17] Its advocates claim it is a demonstrable successful strategy, and some claim that nuclear weapons would be usable if the US had an effective counter-damage strategy.[18] The Obama administration, criticized by Trump, spent more on nuclear weapons upgrades than the Reagan administration did during its extraordinary build-up in the early 1980s.[19] The Obama build-up spawned numerous critiques that challenge the concept of first use, the feasibility of limited nuclear war, and more fundamentally, the assumption that nuclear threats, explicit or implicit, have value.[20] It triggered a renewed debate in the strategic community about the possible first use of nuclear weapons against Russia, China, North Korea, or other adversaries.[21] Those advocating first use seem not to grasp the possibly dangerous consequences of encouraging others to believe that the US might act this way.

Three observations are in order with regard to the present and the past. The first grows out of the record of deterrence and compellence during the Cold War and its aftermath. These conflicts suggest that powerful states focus on the punishment term of the Clausewitzian equation and less powerful ones on the absorbing cost side. This has the potential to promote misleading conclusions about relative advantage. To date, the more serious miscalculations have been on the part of the powerful. They tend to assume an equal vulnerability to punishment and accordingly consider their side greatly advantaged by its ability to inflict greater costs to their adversaries. This helps to explain why highly developed industrial powers are willing to consider military intervention against weaker, less developed, more traditional countries, and also why they so often fail; they, in fact, have a much lower tolerance for loss of life than countries in which honor remains strong or nationalism is a more powerful motive and source of solidarity. How many Westerners are willing to suffer 50-percent casualty rates in battle or volunteer for suicide missions?

The second concerns the general efficacy of deterrence as a strategy. Its political and psychological drawbacks do not mean that it should be discarded. Rather, scholars and statesmen must recognize its limitations and make greater use of other strategies of conflict prevention and management. I contend that the downside of deterrence can sometimes be minimized when it is combined with reassurance and other diplomatic efforts to reduce fear and resolve or finesse substantive differences.

Finally, there is a failure of strategists to take history seriously. Much of the current debate about conventional and nuclear strategy shows little cognizance of past debates or repeats many of the discredited Cold War claims about the political and military utility of nuclear weapons. A case in point is Paul Bracken's *The Second Nuclear Age*, a book that has attracted considerable attention. He contends that "nuclear weapons were very useful weapons during the cold war," and the nuclear threats were frequently successful in preventing or stopping "Soviet expansion, coercion, and tyranny."[22] He repeats the old canard that preparations for war undertaken by the Truman administration in 1948–49 prevented the Soviet Union from invading Berlin or interfering with the airlifting of food and supplies to the beleaguered city.[23] He cites two studies of the crisis conducted during the Cold War that assume Stalin's motives—incorrectly as it turns out—and infer deterrence success on the basis of his restraint.[24] This kind of circular reasoning was endemic during the Cold War and applied to the Taiwan Straits and Cuban missile crises, among others.[25]

A Critique

During and after the Cold War, Janice Stein and I developed a critique of deterrence and compellence that has three interlocking components: political, psychological, and practical. Each exposes a different set of problems of deterrence in theory and practice.

The political component examines the motivations behind foreign policy challenges. Deterrence is unabashedly a theory of "opportunity." It asserts that adversaries seek opportunities to make gains, and that when they find these opportunities they pounce. It accordingly prescribes a credible capacity to inflict unacceptable costs as the best means to prevent challenges. Empirical investigations point to an alternative explanation for a resort to force, which I call a theory of "need." The evidence indicates that strategic vulnerabilities and domestic political constraints often constitute incentives to use force. When leaders become desperate, they may resort to force even when the military balance is unfavorable and there are no grounds to doubt their adversarial resolve. Deterrence may be an inappropriate and even dangerous strategy in these circumstances. If leaders are driven less by the prospect of gain than they are by the fear of loss, deterrent policies can provoke the very behavior they are designed to forestall by intensifying the pressures on an adversary to act.

The psychological component is directly related to the motivations for deterrence challenges. To the extent that leaders believe in the necessity of challenging the commitments of their adversaries, they become predisposed to see their objectives as attainable. This encourages motivated errors in information processes. Leaders can distort their assessments of threat and be insensitive to warnings that the policies to which they are committed are likely to end in disaster. They can convince themselves, despite evidence to the contrary, that they can challenge an important adversarial commitment without provoking war. Because they know the extent to which they are powerless to back down, they expect their adversaries to recognize this and be accommodating. Leaders may also seek comfort in the illusion that their country will emerge victorious at little cost if the crisis gets out of hand and leads to war. Deterrence can and has been defeated by wishful thinking.

The practical component describes some of the most important obstacles to the successful implementation of deterrence. They derive from the distorting effects of cognitive biases and heuristics, political and cultural barriers to empathy, and differing cognitive frames of reference that deterrer and would-be challengers use to frame and interpret signals. Problems of this kind are not unique to deterrence and compellence; they are embedded in the very structure of international relations. They nevertheless constitute particularly severe impediments to these strategies because of deterrer needs to understand the world as it appears to the leaders of a would-be challenger in order to manipulate effectively their cost-benefit calculus. Failure to do so correctly can result in deterrent policies that make the proscribed behavior more attractive to challengers or the required restraint less attractive in the case of compellence.

Our critique explains why deterrence is a risky and unreliable strategy. The problems associated with each component can independently confound deterrence. In practice, they are often reinforcing; political and practical factors interact with psychological processes to multiply the obstacles to success. In this section I unpack this critique to offer some observations about the conditions in which deterrence is most applicable and the foundations for more sophisticated understandings of conflict management.

Political Failings: A good strategy of conflict management should build on a good theory of the nature and causes of aggression. Such a theory should describe the causes of the malady it seeks to control or prevent. Theories of deterrence make no attempt to do this. They finesse the fundamental question of the causes of aggression by assuming both the existence of marked hostility between adversaries and a desire on the part of leaders of one of them to commit acts of aggression against the other. Deterrence further assumes that these leaders are under no political or strategic compunction to act aggressively but will do so if they see an opportunity in the form of a vulnerable commitment of their adversary. It accordingly prescribes defensible, credible commitments as the most important means of discouraging aggression.

Case studies of international conflict contradict this depiction of aggression in important ways. They indicate that the existence of a vulnerable commitment is neither a necessary nor a sufficient condition for a challenge.

At different times in history "vulnerable" commitments have not been challenged and commitments that most observers would consider credible have. The evidence suggests, then, that deterrence theory at best identifies only one cause of aggression: outright hostility. It reflects a Cold War mentality. Deterrence theorist assumed that Stalin, Khrushchev, and Mao Zedong were cut from the same mold as Hitler and intend on conquering the world. This homology was a matter of belief, not the product of careful analysis. They generalized from these cases to conflict in general, another unwarranted leap. The theory and practice of deterrence are accordingly rooted in and inseparable from a view of the Cold War subsequently refuted by evidence.

Deterrence takes for granted that when leaders undertake a cost assessment and conclude that they confront a credible commitment by a stronger adversary to defend its commitment, they will not initiate a challenge, at least not an irreversible one. However, there are many conflicts where the weaker side challenged the stronger one. Leaders convinced themselves that they could design around their adversary's advantage, as the Southern Confederacy did in 1861, the Japanese in 1941, or Egypt in 1973.[26]

Deterrence mistakes the symptoms of aggression for its causes. It ignores the political and strategic vulnerabilities that can interact with cognitive and motivational processes to prompt leaders to choose force or challenge and adversarial commitment. This can be attributable to hubris but is more often the result of their perceived need to carry out a challenge in response to pressing foreign and domestic threats. In contrast to the expectations of the theory and strategy of deterrence, there is considerable evidence that the leaders considering challenges or the use of force often fail to carry out any kind of serious risk assessment. This was true of the French failure in 1897–98 in the Fashoda crisis between Britain and France, the Austrian, German, and Russians in 1914 in the run-up to World War I, India's failure in 1962 border war with China, and the Soviet Union's in the 1962 Cuban missile deployment, and the Anglo-American invasion of Iraq in 2003.[27] Other well-documented cases are Israel in 1973 and Argentina and Britain in 1981.[28]

When challengers are vulnerable or feel themselves vulnerable, a deterrer's effort to make important commitments more defensible and credible will have uncertain and unpredictable effects. At best, they will not dissuade. They can also be malign by intensifying those pressures that are pushing leaders toward a choice of force. Great power interactions in the decade prior to World War I, and the US oil and scrap metals embargo against Japan in 1940–41 illustrate this dynamic.[29] Both helped to provoke the confrontations they sought to avoid.

Once committed to a challenge, leaders become predisposed to see their objective as attainable. Motivated error can result in flawed assessments and unrealistic expectations; leaders may believe an adversary will back down when challenged or, alternatively, that it will fight precisely the kind of war the challenger expects. Leaders are also likely to become insensitive to warnings that their chosen course of action is likely to provoke a serious crisis or war. In these circumstances, deterrence, no matter how well practiced, can be defeated by a challenger's wishful thinking. Motivated bias blocks receptivity to signals, reducing the impact of efforts by defenders to make their commitments credible. Even the most elaborate efforts to demonstrate prowess and resolve may prove insufficient for discouraging a challenger who is convinced that a challenge or use of force is necessary to preserve vital strategic and political interests.

Deterrence is beset by a host of practical problems. It is demonstrably difficult to communicate capability and resolve to would-be challengers. Theories of deterrence assume that everyone understands, so to speak, the meaning of barking guard dogs, barbed wire, and "No Trespassing" signs. This assumption is unwarranted. Signals only acquire meaning in the context in which they are interpreted. When sender and recipient use quite different contexts to frame, communicate, or interpret signals, misjudgments multiply. Receivers may dismiss signals as noise or misinterpret them when they recognize that they are signals. This problem is endemic to international relations and by no means limited to deterrence because of the different historical experiences and cultural backgrounds of policymaking elites. It is, however, more likely in tense relationships, where both sides use worst-case analysis, and are emotionally aroused.

If credible threats of punishment always increased the cost side of the ledger—something deterrence theory takes for granted—it would be unnecessary for would-be deterrers to replicate the value hierarchy and preferences of target leaders. This convenient assumption is belied by practice. As we have seen, leaders may be driven primarily by "vulnerability," not by "opportunity." When they are, raising the costs of military action may have no effect on their unwillingness to tolerate what are perceived as the higher costs of inaction. Even when motivated by opportunity, leaders may reframe their cost calculus in the opposite direction than intended in the face of threats. They may conclude that giving in to them is costlier than resistance, especially if they believe that compliance will be interpreted by their adversary as a sign of weakness and give rise to new demands.

Deterrence in the Long Term: Case evidence of deterrence failures and successes indicates that deterrence is a risky and uncertain strategy. Deterrence only works in a narrow range of conflicts: those in which adversarial leaders are motivated largely by the prospect of gain rather than by the fear of loss, have the freedom to exercise restraint, are not misled by grossly distorted assessments of the political-military situation, and are vulnerable to the kinds of threats that a would-be deterrer is capable of making credibly. Deterrence must also be practiced early on, before an adversary commits itself to a challenge and becomes correspondingly insensitive to warnings that its action is likely to meet with retaliation. Unless these conditions are met, deterrence will at best be ineffective and at worst counterproductive.

These conditions apply only to deterrence in the short term, that is, to immediate deterrence. My analysis of deterrence would be incomplete if I failed to examine its implications for the management of adversarial relationships in the longer term. Does deterrence facilitate or retard the resolution of international conflict?

Deterrence proponents maintain that it can play a positive role by convincing a challenger that its fundamental objectives cannot be met through a use of force. It may give the parties to a dispute time to work out an accommodation and, in so doing, reduce tensions and the potential for overt conflict.[30] But deterrence can also retard conflict resolution by exacerbating the causes of the conflict or by creating new incentives to use force. Three different processes can contribute to this kind of negative outcome.

As noted, deterrence can intensify the pressures on adversarial leaders to resort to challenges or the use of force. American deterrence did this for

Khrushchev in the Cuban missile crisis and in the second Taiwan Straits crisis. In the wake of the 1954–55 crisis, the US reinforced deterrence in the Straits. President Eisenhower committed the US to the defense of Taiwan and the offshore islands and, in 1957, authorized the deployment of nuclear-tipped surface-to-surface Matador missiles on Taiwan. To the president's annoyance, Chiang Kai-shek began a major military build-up on the islands and by 1958 had stationed 100,000 troops there, one-third of his total ground forces. To leaders in Beijing, the increased military preparedness and troop deployments indicated that Washington was preparing to "unleash" Chiang. A series of provocative speeches by Secretary of State John Foster Dulles, suggesting that Chinese Nationalist forces might invade the mainland if significant domestic unrest provided the opportunity, intensified the Chinese perception of threat. This led the Chinese leadership to demonstrate resolve through a renewed artillery assault on Quemoy and Matsu Islands.[31]

Deterrence can also aggravate conflict by encouraging defenders to develop an exaggerated concern for their bargaining reputation. Deterrence does not attach great significance to the impact of the interests at stake in influencing an adversary's judgments of a commitment's credibility. It assumes—incorrectly that the most important component of credibility is the defender's record in honoring past commitments.[32] Thomas Schelling, author of one of the most influential studies of deterrence, emphasized the interdependent nature of commitments; failure to defend one, he argued, will make willingness to defend any commitment questionable in the eyes of an adversary. "We tell the Soviets," a prominent deterrence theorist wrote in 1966, "that we have to react here because, if we did not, they would not believe us when we said that we will react there."[33]

Schelling and other deterrence advocates do not consider the possibility of escalation inherent in the connections among commitments. More importantly, they ignored the likelihood that deterrence pursued this way would make the state practicing deterrence look more aggressive than defensive. This phenomenon was particularly striking in the run-up to the Cuban missile crisis, where Soviet and American efforts at deterrence convinced the other of its aggressive intentions and prompted them to take a series of reciprocal actions that culminated in the Cuban missile deployment.[34] Fears for credibility are in any case misplaced. Ted Hopf examined Soviet reactions to 38 cases of American intervention over a 25-year period of the Cold War and could not discover a single Soviet document that drew negative inferences about American resolve in Europe or Northeast Asia. Janice Stein and I demonstrated that neither Khrushchev and his advisors nor Brezhnev and his ever doubted American credibility but rather considered the Americans rash, unpredictable, and aggressive.[35]

Concern for credibility gives rise to symbolic commitments like that of John Foster Dulles to defend the Taiwanese occupied offshore islands of Kinmen (Quemoy) and Matsu. Such commitments can easily become entangling because they tend to become at least as important to leaders as commitments made in defense of substantive interests. Their exaggerated importance is probably due in large part to the pernicious effect of post-decisional rationalization. Once a commitment is made, leaders, understandably uncomfortable about risking war for abstract, symbolic reasons, seek to justify the commitment to themselves and to others. This need motivates them to "discover" important substantive reasons for these commitments—reasons absent in and irrelevant to their original calculations.

In the case of the Taiwan Straits, top-level administration officials, who previously had questioned the importance of the offshore islands, subsequently came to see them as the linchpin of security throughout Asia. Most senior policymakers subscribed in all solemnity to an astonishing version of the "domino" theory. In a classified policy statement meant only for internal use, Eisenhower and Dulles both argued that loss of the islands would likely not only endanger the survival of the Nationalist regime on Taiwan, but also that of pro-American governments in Japan, Korea, the Philippines, Thailand, and Vietnam, and would bring Cambodia, Laos, Burma, Malaya, and Indonesia under the control of communist forces.[36] The most far-reaching expression of this "logic" was Vietnam. American leaders had no substantive interests in the country but committed forces to its defense in large part because they were persuaded that failure to defend their commitment in Southeast Asia would encourage Moscow to doubt US resolve elsewhere in the world.[37]

Finally, deterrence can intensify conflict by encouraging leaders to interpret even ambiguous actions as challenges that require a response. This exaggerated sensitivity to challenge is very much a function of the heavy emphasis that deterrence places on a state's bargaining reputation. Invitations to play chicken in the international arena, however, are rarely direct and unambiguous. Challenges must be inferred from the context of events, and given the inherent complexity of international affairs, policymakers have considerable leeway in determining their meaning. Leaders are much more likely to perceive a challenge—and often falsely so— when they believe damage to their state's interests and reputation is the principal goal of another's actions, not just its by-product.

These three processes are important contributing causes of tension, misunderstanding, and fear between adversaries. They point to the greatest long-term danger of deterrence: its propensity to make the worst expectations about an adversary self-fulfilling. Threats and military preparations— the currency of deterrence—inevitably arouse the fear and suspicion of those they are directed against. As noted, they tend to provoke the very behavior that they are designed to prevent. Over time, military preparations, initially a consequence of tensions between or among states, can become an important cause. This kind of dynamic has operated between the US and the Soviet Union, Israel and the Arab states, China and the Soviet Union, and some fear is now operating between China and the US. In all these cases, the misunderstanding and tension caused by deterrence, overlain on substantive issues that divide protagonists, made these conflicts more acute, more difficult to manage, and less amenable to resolution.

The outlines of the policy dilemma are clear. Protagonists may need deterrence to prevent their adversaries from resorting to force, but the use of deterrence can simultaneously make the conflict more acute and more likely to erupt into war. Because deterrence can be ineffective, uncertain, and risky, it must be supplemented by other strategies of conflict management.

Thinking Holistically

Any sophisticated strategy of conflict management must combine deterrence—in muted form—with other strategies of conflict management, most notably reassurance and diplomacy. The relative importance of each will vary from case to case and so too will the ways they are combined or staged.

Diplomacy has long been recognized as the essential mechanism of conflict management and resolution. There are many classical works extolling its virtues and achievements in eighteenth- and nineteenth-century Europe, and globally in the twentieth century.[38] Diplomacy has diverse goals with regards to conflict management. Diplomats seek to clarify national interests and commitments to prevent misunderstandings. In a broader sense they attempt to enlighten other countries and their leaders about the perspectives of national leaders, their international and national goals, the constraints under which they operate—although those may sometimes be downplayed. This kind of information and education is intended to make it easier for foreign leaders to understand or predict the likely responses to their initiatives. Diplomats and intelligence agencies serve the same function for their own countries; they educate leaders about the interests, commitments, perspectives, goals, and reactions to the policies of the home country.

Mutual exchanges and education have the potential to lay the ground work for finding ways of reducing, finessing, or resolving clashes of interest or other points of contention between countries. Here too diplomats are expected to play an important role. Not surprisingly, diplomacy was central to every instance of successful conflict management or resolution in the postwar era. A partial list includes the territorial dispute between Italy and Yugoslavia over Trieste, the ceasefire that ended the Korean War, the Geneva Conference and resulting peace treaty that allowed France to withdraw from Indochina, resolution of the Cuban missile and October 1973 crises between the US and the Soviet Union, the Israel-Egyptian peace brokered by the US, ping-pong diplomacy that broke the ice in Sino-American relations, the Good Friday agreement that brought peace to Northern Ireland, the end of the Cold War, agreement with Iran to end its nuclear weapons program, and various ceasefires and regime changes in Africa.

In most of these cases diplomats acted as agents of their respective governments. They often had considerable leeway in how they present proposals, to whom, when, and under what circumstances. Not infrequently they exercise creativity in performing their assigned tasks, and benefit, as does their country, from personal relationships they have established with their opposites and foreign leaders. Skilled diplomats who establish a reputation for honesty and probity, who represent their country accurately and effectively, who provide important heads-up to their foreign counterparts and own governments, and who exercise creativity and restraint in appropriate circumstances are an asset of inestimable value.

The US has all but reduced the State Department and corps of skilled diplomats to the role of pencil pushers who have little say in the implementation and formulation of policy. Presidents surround themselves with people with whom they feel comfortable—people, that is, who think like themselves or agree—or pretend to agree—with everything they think, say, and feel. By doing so they often deprive themselves of people knowledgeable about the problems they face and willing to put forward another point of view. One purpose of government is to widen the circle of expertise on which leaders can draw. The marginalization of the State Department by the National Security Council and its diminution in authority in turn by a small circle of "friends" around the president is not in the national interest.

In its heyday State still had to put up with many ambassadors given their position on the basis of their financial contributions to the victorious president's campaign chest. Political appointments dropped from a high of 44 percent under Franklin Roosevelt to a low of 29 percent under Obama. This pattern was reversed with Trump, climbing back to the Roosevelt level. Not surprisingly, of the 119 ambassadors he has appointed, 94 percent are white men.[39] More than any previous president, Trump has also left important federal offices unfilled. In January 2018 he had no appointees for high-ranking 245 position, including ambassador to South Korea, Austria, and the European Union. Other positions include deputy secretary at Treasury and Commerce, director of the Census, director of Alcohol Tobacco and Firearms, director of the Office on Violence Against Women at Justice and commissioner of the Social Security Administration.[40]

Trump's first Secretary of State Rex Tillerson was, in the opinion of many of those who follow foreign affairs, the worst holder of that office in the history of the Republic. Formerly CEO of Exxon Mobil, he failed to wield any influence in administration debates over key issues like North Korea and Russia and actively alienated the president. He happily went along with cuts in the Department's budget, sought to slash the so-called inefficiencies, surrounded himself with outsiders, and sidelined long-time staff familiar with the Department's workings and the problems it addressed and even refused to spend money allocated to the Department. He reassigned Department Staff from substantive postings to search for "dirt" on former Secretary Hilary Clinton. On his watch, 60 percent of State's top-ranking career diplomats resigned and new applications to join the foreign service fell by half. George Washington University's Elizabeth Saunders alleges that this "hollowing-out" of the foreign service has weakened the State Department for a "generation."[41]

Professional diplomacy gets short shrift because, Stephen Walt laments, "Americans have long viewed it with a certain suspicion and disdain. Instead of thinking of foreign policy as primarily the art of pursuing arrangements of mutual benefit and adjustment—where we get most of what we want while others get some of what they want as well—Americans prefer the moral clarity of unconditional surrender." That approach is usually short-sighted, however, because it encourages others to fight harder and longer and because losers who are not reconciled to their defeat (such as Saddam Hussein after the first Gulf War or the Confederate states after the Civil War and Reconstruction) will try to renege on whatever the United States forced them to accept."[42]

Downgrading State has no doubt played well with Trump's base. After freezing hiring, the president proclaimed—and may even believe—that most positions at the State Department are "unnecessary." He repeatedly told reporters "I'm the only one that matters."[43] We are left with a president who makes policy and even meets with foreign leaders—as he did with North Korean President Kim Jong-un—without the benefit of professional advice and input.

Diplomats and diplomacy must be resuscitated and diplomacy combined effectively with deterrence and reassurance to manage international conflicts in a sophisticated and successful manner. A political leader must listen with an open mind—they do not have to agree—to those who have spent their career studying and practicing foreign policy in the service of their country.

Reassurance is the third component of conflict management. It seeks to ease or alleviate causes of competition and conflict and induce accommodation and cooperation by reducing fear, mistrust, misunderstanding, and miscalculation between adversaries. It does so by attempting to convince adversarial leaders that you are not hostile to them and would prefer to reach an accommodation. This is often difficult to do in any conflict with a history. Leaders, and often peoples, on both sides have come to view the other side as hostile, aggressive, and willing to exploit any opportunity to weaken or humiliate them. Well-meaning words and gestures are often discounted and viewed warily as efforts to entrap one into easing off or making concessions.

Leaders, their advisors, and public opinion, have a tendency to rely on worst-case analyses to adversarial relationships. They convince themselves that the adversary is unremittingly hostile, constrained only by superior force, and intent on achieving a decisive military advantage.[44] As noted, deterrence operates on this assumption, and may help to confirm it. Fear can readily become the central dynamic governing adversarial relations, as it did for much of the Cold War. Reassurance aims to reduce fear so that leaders can focus more on interests, and by finding common ones, reduce conflict between them.

Successful reassurance generally relies on more than words. It seeks incremental changes in policy through reciprocity, thus minimizing the costs of possible defection to both sides. It may break through mistrust by means of an irrevocable commitment, as Egyptian President Anwar Sadat did when he expressed willingness to come to Israel and address its parliament. He made a conciliatory speech that in effect burned his bridges with Arab hardliners. Soviet President Mikhail Gorbachev did more or less the same thing when he withdrew Soviet forces from Afghanistan and told Eastern Europeans they could choose their own governments. Reassurance also benefits from self-restraint and efforts to develop through diplomacy norms of competition.

In the most ambitious applications of reassurance, leaders attempt to shift the trajectory of the conflict and induce cooperation through reciprocal acts of de-escalation and bargaining over substantive issues. They may begin with unilateral and irrevocable concessions. If they are pessimistic about the likely success of this approach, or politically constrained from attempting it, they can pursue more modest variants of reassurance. They can exercise self-restraint in the hope of not exacerbating the foreign or domestic pressures and constraints pushing an adversary to act aggressively. They can try to develop informal "norms of competition" to regulate their conflict and reduce the likelihood of miscalculated escalation.

Leaders can attempt through diplomacy informal or formal regimes designed to build confidence, reduce uncertainty, and diminish the probability of miscalculated war. Known as "confidence building measures," they were extensively used during the Cold War to reduce strategic anxiety, especially in situations where misunderstandings might have provoked a military incident.[45] Examples include advance notification of troop movements, information exchanges on arms programs, inviting officers from the other side to attend maneuvers, independent technical means of verification, creation of neutral territorial zones, with third-party observers always present to report any violations to both sides. This last measure was key to the tension reduction and then a peace treaty between Egypt and Israel.[46] These several approaches to reassurance are neither mutually exclusive nor logically exhaustive.

Strategies of reassurance, like those of deterrence and compellence, are difficult to implement successfully. They too must overcome strategic, political, and psychological obstacles. Cognitive barriers to signaling, for example, can just as readily obstruct reassurance as they can deterrence.[47] Other obstacles are specific to reassurance, and derive from the political and psychological constraints that leaders face when they seek to reassure an adversary. Nevertheless, reassurance can be used effectively and was a significant component of all longstanding rivalries that were resolved. Reassurance played a major role in facilitating accommodations between Britain and France, France and Germany, Egypt and Israel, America and China, and the Soviet Union and the West.

Conflicts have multiple causes, some of the follow-on effects of conflict. Superpower nuclear build-ups are a case in point. They were a response to their territorial conflict in the heart of Europe but soon became causes in their own right. They continued to poison superpower relations for almost two decades after the Helsinki Accords of 1975 resolved their territorial dispute in Central Europe. There is no general rule about which cause to address first. Opportunity must dictate strategy. Leaders should be guided by their judgment of which cause of conflict is easiest to address. These judgments are never scientific but reflect, or should, politically informed

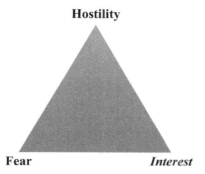

Fig. 4.1   Conflict triangle

understandings about the causes of conflict, their openness to resolution, and all the conditions, noted earlier, for setting a process of accommodation in motion. Analysis is useful, but leadership is critical.

Different strategies are more appropriate to different causes of conflict. We might represent these choices with the graphic of a conflict triangle with each vertex representing a generic source of conflict (Fig. 4.1). Hostility can be a source of conflict, as it was for Hitler's Germany vis-à-vis its neighbors, if not the world. More often, hostility is a follow-on effect of conflict. Leaders, and perhaps public opinion as well, become convinced that their adversary is unremittingly hostile and committed to their demise. We observed this phenomenon in the Cold War. Americans believed the Soviet Union and China sought to destroy their political system, a belief reciprocated by Soviet and Chinese leaders.

Deterrence is the appropriate strategy to use against a hostile adversary whom it is believed only superior force can restrain from attacking. But it is only likely to work when this perception is accurate, which, as we have seen, is often not the case. Deterrence is only likely to succeed when adversarial leaders are motivated largely by the prospect of gain rather than by the fear of loss, free to exercise restraint, are not misled by rosy assessments of the political-military balance and are vulnerable to the kinds of threats a deterrer is capable of credibly making. If challengers do not share these motivational, cognitive, and political attributes, the strategy of deterrence is more likely to intensify conflict. The timing of deterrence is also important. Its effectiveness is enhanced if it is used early, that is, before an adversary becomes committed to a challenge or the use of force and becomes correspondingly insensitive to warnings and threats.

Fear and hostility are closely related. To the extent that leaders believe an adversary is hostile, they become fearful. Reassurance seeks to reduce fear by changing this perception. It can be used duplicitously, as Hitler did to encourage French and British appeasement. More frequently, it is intended to reduce tensions by demonstrating benign or cooperative intentions. As noted, attempts at reassurance must overcome disbelief on the part of target leaders. They may believe, rightly or wrongly, that their adversary is unremittingly hostile, and interpret communications and behavior to the contrary as nefarious and designed to lull them or public opinion into letting down their guard. Key members of the Reagan administration felt this way about Gorbachev and tried to prevent and then to sabotage arms control negotiations.[48]

The best historical example may be the coupling of reassurance with compellence in the Cuban missile crisis. Compellence in the form of the American naval quarantine of Cuba and the threat of an invasion of Cuba and air strike against the Soviet missile bases on that island raised the risk of war, and reassurance, as practiced by President Kennedy, reduced the cost of concession to Khrushchev. The Soviet premier came to believe that Kennedy was not a tool of the American military and Wall Street bankers, but someone with a fair degree of independence and committed, as he was, to avoiding war. By withdrawing the missiles in Cuba, he would not invite new demands but rather resolve the crisis and reduce the likelihood of a future one. Khrushchev and Kennedy became partners as much as adversaries in the end game and aftermath of the crisis, paving the way for a subsequent détente.[49]

Reassurance and diplomacy are the strategies relevant to the fear and interest vertices of the triangle. Different readings of context and the history of the conflict in question lead to different assessments and perhaps different strategic preferences. Most importantly, they lead to different assessments about whether conflict can be reduced or resolved. People can be deeply committed to their perspectives for motivated and cognitive reasons. The former primes them to see the world in a manner consonant with the political and psychological needs. The more their worldview, career, status, or wealth derives from or is associated with a particular view of a conflict and its causes, the less open they are to information that suggests another perspective. The latter leads people to see what they expect to see, and the more developed their schema, the more resistant they are to discrepant information.

Scholars are just as likely as policymakers, their advisors, and the media to succumb to motivated and cognitive biases. This may help explain why hardly anybody in the US or the Soviet Union thought the end of the Cold War possible, or that Gorbachev and Reagan could do away with theater nuclear weapons, that Gorbachev would allow Eastern European states to reject the communist government and agree to the reunification of Germany. It is exceedingly difficult to separate our analysis of politics from our political beliefs and expectations. To break through motivational and cognitive barriers to meaningful change and accommodation may take leaders who are not strongly committed to particular views of the conflict or strongly motivated for other reasons to seek accommodation.

Notes

1. Richard Ned Lebow, *Between Peace and War: The Nature of International Crisis* (Baltimore: Johns Hopkins University Press, 1981, p. 83.
2. William W. Kaufmann, *The Requirements of Deterrence* (Princeton: Center of International Studies, 1954); Henry Kissinger, *Nuclear Weapons and Foreign Policy*. New York: Harper, 1957); Bernard B. Brodie, "The Anatomy of Deterrence," *World Politics* (1959) 11 no. 1, pp. 173–92; Morton A. Kaplan, "The Calculus of Deterrence," *World Politics* 11, no. 1 (1958) pp. 20–43.
3. Thomas Schelling, *The Strategy of Conflict* (Cambridge: Harvard University Press, 1960) and *Arms and Influence* (New Haven: Yale University Press, 1966).
4. Schelling, *Arms and Influence*.
5. Jeffrey Kimball, *Nixon's Vietnam War* (Lawrence: University Press of Kansas, 1998), pp. 76–86.
6. Emanuel Adler, "Complex Deterrence in the Asymmetric-Warfare Era," in T. V. Paul, Patrick M. Morgan and James Wirtz, eds., *Complex Deterrence:*

Strategy in the Global Age (Chicago: University of Chicago Press, 2009), pp. 85–109; Alex Wilner, "Deterring the Undeterrable," *Journal of Strategic Studies*, 3, no. 5 (2010), pp. 597–619: Ivan Arreguin Toft, "Unconventional Deterrence: How the Weak Deter Strong," in Wirtz, *Complex Deterrence*, pp. 222–259, and "Targeted Killings in Afghanistan: Measuring Coercion and Deterrence in Counterterrorism Counterinsurgency," *Studies in Conflict and Terrorism* 33 (2010), pp. 53–94; Patrick B. Johnston, "Does Decapitation Work? Assessing the Effectiveness of Leadership Targeting in Counterinsurgency Campaigns," International Security 36, no. 4 (2002), pp. 47–79.

7. Michael D. Shear and James Glanz, "Trump Says US Should Expand its Nuclear capability," *New York Times*, 22 December 2016, http://www.nytimes.com/2016/12/22/us/politics/trump-says-us-should-expand-its-nuclear-capability.html?_r=0; Michael D. Shear David E. Sanger, "Trump Says U.S. Would 'Outmatch' Rivals in a New Nuclear Arms Race," *New York Times*, 23 December 2016, http://www.nytimes.com/2016/12/23/us/politics/trump-nuclear-arms-race-russia-united-states.html?hp&action=click&pgtype=Homepage&clickSource=story-heading&module=first-column-region&region=top-news&WT.nav=top-news&_r=0 (both accessed 12 October 2018).

8. For this debate, Scott Sagan and Kenneth Waltz, *The Spread of Nuclear Weapons: A Debate* (New York: Norton, 1995).

9. Richard Ned Lebow and Janice Stein *We All Lost the Cold War* (Princeton: University Press, 1994); T. V. Paul, *The Tradition of Non-Use of Nuclear Weapons.* (Stanford: Stanford University Press, 2009).

10. Walter Clarke and Jeffrey Herbst, eds., *Learning from Somalia: The Lessons of Armed Humanitarian Intervention* (Boulder: Westview, 1997).

11. Mahmood Mamdani, *When Victims Become Killers: Colonialism, Nativism, and the Genocide in Rwanda (Princeton: Princeton University Press, 2002)*; Roméo Dallaire, *Shake Hands with the Devil: The Failure of Humanity in Rwanda* (London: Arrow Books, 2002); Gerard Prunier, *The Rwanda Crisis: A History of a Genocide*, 2nd ed. (London: Hurst, 1998).

12. Daniel L. Byman and Mathew C. Waxman, "Kosovo and the Great Air Power Debate," *International Security* 24, no. 4 (2000), pp. 5–38; Lawrence A. Freedman, *Deterrence* (Cambridge: Polity, 2004), pp. 124–30.

13. Frank Harvey and Patrick James, "Deterrence and Compellence in Iraq, 1991–2003: Lessons for a Complex Paradigm," in Paul, Morgan and Wirtz, *Complex Deterrence*, pp. 222–58; Jacquelyn K. Davis and Robert

L. Pfaltzgraff, Jr., *Anticipating a Nuclear Iran: Challenges for U. S. Security* (New York: Columbia University Press, 2013); Er-Win Tan, *The US Versus the North Korean Nuclear Threat: Mitigating the Nuclear Security Dilemma* (New York: Routledge, 2013).

14. On renouncing the weapons programs, Jacques E. Hymans, *The Psychology of Nuclear Proliferation: Identity, Emotions, and Foreign Policy* (Cambridge: Cambridge University Press, 2006); Etel Solingen, *Nuclear Logics: Contrasting Paths in East Asia and the Middle East* (Cambridge University Press, 2007).

15. Shmuel Barr, "Deterrence of Palestinian Terrorism: The Israeli Experience," in Andreas Wenger and Alex Wilner, eds., *Deterring Terrorism: Theory and Practice.* (Stanford: Stanford University Press, 2012), pp. 205–27; Michael D. Cohen, "Mission Impossible? Influencing Iranian and Libyan Sponsorship of Terrorism," in Wenger and Wilner, *Deterring Terrorism*, pp. 251–72; Fred Wehling, "A Toxic Cloud of Mystery: Lessons from Iraq for Deterring CBRN Terrorism," in Wenger and Wilner, *Deterring Terrorism*, pp. 273–300; David Romano, "Turkish and Iranian Efforts to Deter Turkish Attacks," in Wenger, Andreas and Alex Wilner, *Deterring Terrorism*, pp. 228–50.

16. Janice Gross Stein, "Deterring Terrorism, Not Terrorists," in Wenger and Wilner, *Deterring Terrorism*, pp. 46–66.

17. Stephen van Evera, *Causes of War: Power and the Roots of Conflict* (Ithaca: Cornell University Press, 1999), ch. 8; Daniel Deudney, *Bounding Power: Republican Security Theory from the Polis to the Global Village* (Princeton: Princeton University Press, 2007) and "Unipolarity and Nuclear Weapons," in G. John Ikenberry, Michael Mastanduno, and William Wohlforth, eds., *International Relations Theory and the Consequences of Unipolarity* (Cambridge: Cambridge University Press, 2011), ch. 10; Avery Goldstein, *Deterrence and Security in the twenty-first Century: China, Britain, France and the Enduring Legacy of the Nuclear Revolution* (Palo Alto: Stanford University Press, 2000); Randall Schweller, *Unanswered Threats: Political Constraints on the Balance of Power* (Princeton: Princeton University Press, 2006), pp. 2–3; Susan B. Martin, "The Continuing Value of Nuclear Weapons: A Structural Realist Analysis," *Contemporary Security Policy* 34, no. 1 (2013), pp. 174–94; Casper Sylvest and Rens van Munster, *Nuclear Realism: Global Political Thought During the Thermonuclear Revolution* (London: Routledge, 2016); Charles Glaser and Steve Fetter, "Should the United States Reject MAD? Damage

Limitation and U.S. Nuclear Strategy Towards China," *International Security* 41 no. 1, pp. 49–98; Nuno Monteiro, *Theory of Unipolar Politics* (Cambridge: Cambridge University Press, 2014).

18. Keir Lieber and Daryl Press, "The End of MAD? The Nuclear Dimension of US Primacy," *International Security* vol. 30, no. 4 (2006), pp. 7–44; Lieber and Press, "The New Era of Nuclear Weapons, Deterrence and Conflict," *Strategic Studies Quarterly* 7, no. 1 (2013) pp. 3–12; Larsen and Kartchner, *On Limited Nuclear War*; Matthew Kroenig, "Nuclear Superiority and the Balance of Resolve: Explaining Nuclear Crisis Outcomes," *International Organization* 67, no. 1 (2013), pp. 141–171 and "Facing Reality: Getting NATO Ready for a New Cold War," *Survival: Global Politics and Strategy* 57 no. 1, (2015), pp. 49–70; Brad Roberts, *The Case for U.S. Nuclear Weapons in the Twenty-First Century* (Palo Alto: Stanford University Press, 2015), ch. 6; Austin Long and Brendan Rittenhouse-Green, "Stalking the Secure Second Strike: Intelligence, Counterforce, and Nuclear Strategy," *Journal of Strategic Studies* 38, nos. 1–2 (2015), pp. 38–73; Francis Gavin, "Strategies of Inhibition: U.S. Grand Strategy, the Nuclear Revolution, and Nonproliferation," *International Security* 40, no. 1 (2015), pp. 16–17.; ISFF "Policy Roundtable 9–4 on U.S. Nuclear Policy," with an introduction by Francis J. Gavin and essays by James M. Acton, Keir A. Lieber, Austin Long, Joshua Rovner, and Nina Tannenwald, *H-Diplo*, 22 December 2016, https://networks.h-net.org/node/28443/discussions/157862/issf-policy-roundtable-9-4-us-nuclear-policy (accessed 22 December 2016).

19. Jon Wolfsthal, Jeffrey Lewis, and Marc Quint, "The Trillion Dollar Nuclear Triad,"

20. James Cartwright, Richard Burt, Chuck Hagel, Thomas Pickering, Jack Sheehan, and Bruce Blair, "Global Zero U.S. Nuclear Policy Commission Report: Modernizing U.S. Nuclear Strategy, Force Structure and Posture," www.globalzero.org (accessed 12 October 2016); James Cartwright and Bruce Blair, "End the First-Use Policy for Nuclear Weapons," *New York Times*, August 15, 2016, p. A39; Thomas Nichols, *No Use: Nuclear Weapons and U.S. National Security* (Philadelphia: University of Pennsylvania Press, 2014).

21. James Martin Center for Nonproliferation Studies, Monterey, 2014. Scott Sagan, "The Case for No First Use," *Survival* vol. 51 no. 3 (2009) pp. 163–182; Morton Halperin, Bruno Tertrais, Keith B. Payne, K. Subrahmanyam, and Scott Sagan, "The Case for No First Use: An Exchange," *Survival* 51, no. 5 (2009) pp. 17–46.

22. Bracken, *Second Nuclear Age Strategy, Danger, and the New Power Politics* (New York: Times Books, 2012), pp. 33–35.

23. Ibid., pp. 50–57.

24. Ibid., pp. 289–90 for his references. Mihail M. Narinskii, "The Soviet Union and the Berlin Crisis, 1948–9," in Francesca Gori and Silvio Pons, *The Soviet Union in the Cold War, 1943–53* (New York: St. Martin's, 1996), pp. 57–75; Victor Gorbarev, "Soviet Military Plans and Actions During the First Berlin Crisis," *Slavic Military Studies* 10, no. 3 (1997), pp. 1–23. Vladislav Zubok and Constantine Pleshakov, *Inside the Kremlin's Cold War* (Cambridge: Harvard University Press, 1997), pp. 134–37, 194–97.

25. Lebow and Stein, *We All Lost the Cold War*, chs. 2–4 for discussion and exposure of these kinds of argument with reference to the Cuban missile crisis.

26. Michael A. Barnhart, *Japan Prepares for Total War: The Search for Economic Security, 1919–1941* (Ithaca, N.Y.: Cornell University Press, 1987); Gerhard L. Weinberg, *A World at Arms: A Global History of World War II* (Cambridge: Cambridge University Press 1994), pp. 260, 323, 329–330; Janice Gross Stein, "Calculation, Miscalculation and Deterrence: The View from Cairo," in Robert Jervis, Richard Ned Lebow, and Janice Gross Stein, *Psychology and Deterrence* (Baltimore: Johns Hopkins University Press, 1984), pp. 34–59.

27. Lebow, *Between Peace and War*, chs. 4–5.

28. Jervis, Lebow, and Stein, *Psychology and Deterrence*, ch. 4–5, 7; Richard Ned Lebow, *A Cultural Theory of International Relations* (Cambridge: Cambridge University Press, 2008), chs. 7–9.

29. Barnhart, *Japan Prepares for Total War: The Search for Economic Security, 1919–1941* (Ithaca, N.Y.: Cornell University Press, 1988); *Weinberg, A World at Arms*, pp. 260, 323, and 329–330.

30. Alexander L. George, and Richard Smoke, *Deterrence in American Foreign Policy: Theory and Practice* (New York: Columbia University Press, 1974), p. 5.

31. Melvin Gurtov and Byung-Moo Hwang, *China under Threat: The Politics of Strategy and Diplomacy* (Baltimore: Johns Hopkins University Press, 1980), pp. 63–98; Jian Chen, *Mao's China and the Cold War: Beijing and the Taiwan Strait Crisis of 1958* (Chapel Hill, N.C.: University of North Carolina Press, 2001), ch. 7.

32. Glenn H. Snyder and Paul Diesing, *Conflict Among Nations: Bargaining, Decision Making, and System Structure in International Crisis* (Princeton: Princeton University Press, 1977), pp. 183–184; George and Smoke, *Deterrence in American Foreign Policy*, pp. 550–561.

33. Thomas Schelling, *Arms and Influence* (New Haven: Yale University Press, 1966), p. 55.
34. Lebow and Stein, *We All Lost the Cold War*, ch. 2.
35. Ted Hopf, *Deterrence Theory and American Foreign Policy in the Third World, 1965–1990* (Ann Arbor: University of Michigan Press, 1994). Also, Daryl G. Press, *Calculating Credibility: How Leaders Assess Military Threats* (Ithaca: Cornell University Press, 2007); Lebow and Stein, *We All Lost the Cold War*, chs. 2, 10–11.
36. Morton H. Halperin and Tang Tsou, "The 1958 Quemoy Crisis," in Morton H. Halperin, ed., *Sino-Soviet Relations and Arms Control* (Cambridge: M.I.T. Press, 1967), pp. 265–304; George and Smoke, *Deterrence in American Foreign Policy*, pp. 386, 578, for quote.
37. Fredrik Logevall, *The Origins of the Vietnam War* (London: Routledge, 2001), ch. 4; Brian VanDeMark, *Into the Quagmire: Lyndon Johnson and the Escalation of the Vietnam War*, (New York: Oxford University Press, 1995).
38. Henry Kissinger, *Diplomacy* (New York: Simon & Schuster, 1994); G. R. Berridge, *Diplomacy: Theory and Practice*, 5th ed. (London: Palgrave Macmillan, 2015); Jean-Robert Leguey-Feilleux, *The Dynamics of Diplomacy* (Boulder, CO: Lynne Rienner, 2009); Andrew F. Cooper, Jorge Heine, and Ramesh Thakur, eds., *The Oxford Handbook of Modern Diplomacy* (Oxford: Oxford University Press, 2003).
39. "Tag Archives: career vs. political appointees," *Diplopundit*, 13 October 2018, https://diplopundit.net/2016/09/29/obamas-career-ambassadorship-appointments-highest-on-record-at-70-8-thanksobama/; Robbie Gramer, Jefcoate O'Donnell, "White and Male: Trump's Ambassadors Don't Look Like the Rest of America," *Foreign Policy* 17 September 2018, https://foreignpolicy.com/2018/09/17/white-male-trump-ambassadors-dont-look-like-america-us-state-department/ (both accessed 13 October 2018).
40. James Hohman, "The Daily 202: Trump has no nominees for 245 important jobs, including an ambassador to South Korea," *Washington Post*, 12 January 2018, https://www.washingtonpost.com/news/power-post/paloma/daily-202/2018/01/12/daily-202-trump-has-no-nomi-nees-for-245-important-jobs-including-an-ambassador-to-south-korea/5a57cce830fb0469e8840085/?noredirect=on&utm_term=.b8d6babe-aed1; Tara Palmiri, "Trump administration has yet to fill many US ambassador posts in Europe," *ABC News*, 9 December 2017, https://abcnews.go.com/International/trump-administration-fill-us-ambassa-dor-posts-europe/story?id=51691373 (both accessed 13 October 2018).

41. Zach Beauchamp, "Rex Tillerson has been fired. Experts say he did damage that could last 'a generation,'" *Vox*, 13 March 2018, https://www.vox.com/world/2018/3/13/16029526/rex-tillerson-fired-state-department (accessed 13 October 2018); Ronan Farrow, "Inside Rex Tillerson's Ouster," *New Yorker*, 18 April 2008, https://www.newyorker.com/books/page-turner/inside-rex-tillersons-ouster; Stephen M. Walt, "The State Department Needs Rehab," *Foreign Policy*, 5 March 2018, https://foreignpolicy.com/2018/03/05/the-state-department-needs-rehab/; Hunter, "Rex Tillerson reassigns 'hundreds' of State Department employees to search for Hillary Clinton dirt," DAILY KOS, 8 November 2017, https://mail.google.com/mail/u/0/#inbox/FMfcgxvzLDvPHHQsz jpmftQNndVgLvSL?compose=CllgCKCBBpNzVccMvqqsn VTRSv FrsXBvbQXqBMTslZzJmDMJfzRnmxBwHGMsGqLLWmjcbPtLjJq (all accessed 13 October 2018).

42. Walt, "State Department Needs Rehab"; Nicholas Burns and Ryan C. Crocker, "Dismantling the Foreign Service," *New York Times*, 27 November 2017, https://mail.google.com/mail/u/0/#inbox/FMf cgxvzLDvPHHQbhWLGHMmzkDNjRtlf?compose=CllgCKCBBpNz VccMvqqsnVTRSvFrs XBvbQXqBMTslZzJmDMJfzRnmxBwHGMs GqLLWmjcbPtLjJq (accessed 13 October 2018).

43. Bill Chappell, "'I'm The Only One That Matters,' Trump Says Of State Dept. Job Vacancies," 3 November 2017, https://www.npr.org/sections/thetwo-way/2017/11/03/561797675/im-the-only-one-that-matters-trump-says-of-state-dept-job-vacancies?t=1539522068413 (accessed 13 October 2018); Burns and Crocker, "Dismantling the Foreign Service."

44. On the causes of innocent exaggerated assessments, John H. Herz, "The Security Dilemma in International Relations: Background and Present Problems," *International Relations* (2003), pp. 411–16. On deliberate exaggeration, *Anne H. Cahn, Killing Detente: The Right Attacks the CIA* (University Park, Pa.: Pennsylvania State University Press, 1998); Richard Ned Lebow, "Misconceptions in American Strategic Assessment," *Political Science Quarterly* 97 (Summer 1982), pp. 187–206.

45. Alexander L. George, *Managing U.S.-Soviet Rivalry: Problems of Crisis Prevention* (Boulder, Co.: Westview, 1983) and *U.S.-Soviet Security Cooperation: Achievements, Failures, Lessons* (New York: Oxford University Press, 1988); Aaron M. Hoffman, Building Trust: Overcoming Suspicion in International Conflict (Albany, N.Y.: State University of New York Press, 2006); Šumit Ganguly and Ted Greenwood, eds., *Mending Fences:*

Confidence and Security-Building Measures in South Asia (Boulder, Co.: Westview, 1996); Pál Dunay, *Open Skies: A Cooperative Approach to Military Transparency and Confidence Building* (Geneva: United Nations Institute for Disarmament Research, 2004).

46. Janice Gross Stein, "Prenegotiation in the Arab-Israeli Conflict: The Paradoxes of Success and Failure," *International Journal* 44 (Spring 1989), pp. 327–60 and "The Managed and the Managers: Crisis Prevention in the Middle East," in Gilbert R. Winham, ed., *New Issues in International Crisis Management* (Boulder, Co: Westview 1988), pp. 171–98; David Barton, "The Sinai Peacekeeping Experience: A Verification Paradigm for Europe," *World Armaments and Disarmament: SIPRI Yearbook 1985* (London: Taylor and Francis 1985), pp. 541–62 William Quandt, *Decade of Decisions* (Berkeley: University of California Press, 1977); Brian S. Mandell, "Anatomy of a Confidence-Building Régime: Egyptian-Israeli Security Cooperation, 1973–1979," *International Journal* 45, no. 2 (1990), pp. 202–223.

47. Robert Jervis, *Perception and Misperception in International Politics* (Princeton, NJ: Princeton University Press, 1976), pp. 58–113; Lebow, *Between Peace and War*, chs. 4–5.

48. Robert Service, *End of the Cold War* (London: Pan, 2016), pp. 169–220.

49. Lebow and Stein, *We All Lost the Cold War*, ch. 6.

5

China

Unbridled competition between America and China has serious consequences for regional and international order. These two countries command the world's largest economies, strongest militaries, and most advanced industrial and technological bases. Their relationship is going to determine the shape of world order in this century, especially in the Asia-Pacific region. A military clash between these titans would be calamitous and tragic for the region, if not the world. Even a cold war would be seriously damaging and certainly forestall the possible evolution of China toward more Democratic forms of governance.

America and China have every good reason to live in harmony and benefit themselves and the world by doing so. No territorial disputes divide them the way they did other great power rivalries that led to war. Neither power believes the other to be intent on attacking it. They disagree on many substantive issues, but none that should cause a rupture, and none whose effects cannot be addressed or softened, or even resolved, by goodwill and effective diplomacy. Yet, in both capitals, there are officials and pundits who think that the two most powerful countries of the twenty-first century are on a collision course. Why is this so and what can be done about it?

© The Author(s) 2020
R. N. Lebow, *A Democratic Foreign Policy*,
https://doi.org/10.1007/978-3-030-21519-4_5

Tensions between America and China became more pronounced during the Barack Obama presidency and have accelerated since Donald J. Trump took office in January 2017. In December of that year, the Trump administration published its first National Security Strategy: it designated China as a "competitor" and a "revisionist power." This document frames tensions in the relationship as a "geopolitical competition between free and repressive visions of world order."[1] The administration subsequently released its National Defense Strategy that asserts that China, through its military modernization, "seeks Indo-Pacific regional hegemony in the near-term and displacement of the United States to achieve global preeminence in the future."[2] These views are by no means limited to the Trump inner circle but are widely shared in the national security establishment.

In 2018 the Sino-American relationship underwent a serious downturn. Old tensions over security, especially in the South China Sea, Taiwan, and North Korea, continued to fester. China pressed ahead with island building in the South China Sea, deploying anti-ship and antiaircraft missiles and landing a long-range bomber there. An American admiral fretted that "China is now capable of controlling the South China Sea in all scenarios short of war with the United States."[3] The US military ratcheted up its sea and air patrols, had warships sail close to Chinese islands and B-52 bombers. Beijing froze high-level contact with the pro-independence government in Taiwan, weaned away its diplomatic allies, and began "island-encircling" patrols.[4] In response, the Trump administration tightened its ties with Taiwan. The Congress passed the Taiwan Travel Act, approved two arms sales in less than two years, and considered sending warships through the Taiwan Strait to stare Beijing down.[5] On the Korean Peninsula, despite the reduction of tension partly due to his summit with the North Korean leader Kim Jong-un in June 2018, Trump accused China of thwarting the progress of denuclearization.[6] His administration sanctioned the Chinese military for buying Russian arms, a bewildering punishment that led China to cancel a scheduled session of the Diplomatic and Security Dialogue, a high-level security talk between the two countries.[7]

Meanwhile, new disputes over trade and political interference shot to the top of the American agenda. Holding an antediluvian view on trade, Trump had imposed tariffs on $250 billion Chinese imports by September

2018, all the while threatening to slap levies on all the rest of Chinese imports worth about $267 billion in 2017.[8] In September 2018, he accused China—without evidence—of interfering in the coming midterm congressional elections.[9] His officials, think-tank analysts, and journalists claimed to have found a Chinese government-sponsored attempt at political interference in America.[10] Much of Washington believes itself locked into a struggle for global hegemony with China. Competition with China has become the battle cry; cooperation has been put largely on the back burner.

Equally alarming is a general turn to the worse side of media and elite American attitudes toward China. Few public discussions portray China in a positive light; many see it as an aggressive, illiberal, and authoritarian great power bent on challenging America in Asia and around the world. Calls for smart engagement to reduce tension from a few prominent holdouts in the policy and academic communities are snubbed for their supposed naiveté.[11]

Accommodating China is equated with rewarding bad behavior. Competition, despite the risk of fearmongering and overreaction, is considered a lesser evil. Senior officials in the Trump administration, notably John Bolton, a neoconservative firebrand and Trump's second national security advisor, and Steve Bannon, Trump's former chief strategist, would prefer winding down engagement and ratcheting up confrontation.[12] Henry Kissinger saw "considerable merit" in some of Trump's positions, although he insisted on the importance of conflict management and resolution.[13] Frustration over China is so intense that many—including seasoned "China watchers"—have turned to applaud Trump, if for no other reason than for trying out a new approach of pounding China.[14] Underlying such vexation is a perceived failure to manage the China challenge.

Chinese leaders and analysts watched Washington's anti-China frenzy with increasing alarm. Many were stupefied by the rapid downturn of the relationship. In September 2018, Foreign Minister Wang Yi warned of its "total destruction."[15] In a rare self-reproach for failing to understand Trump's America, the Ministry of Finance organized a think-tank alliance across China's major research institutes to grapple with the new reality.[16] But the perception was already growing that Trump's policies had finally proved that America was adopting a containment strategy toward China. The suspicion of American containment had long lingered in Beijing, and now Trump provided the clincher, although it was not yet the mainstream view or official position.

Nevertheless, the Chinese leadership under President Xi Jinping stiffened its resolve to stand firm and prepare for the worst. In March 2018, when a trade war was still a threat, the Chinese ambassador in Washington responded that "if people want to play tough, we will play tough with them and see who will last longer."[17] After September, when it became a reality, China retaliated with tariffs on $110 billion American imports. Meanwhile, Beijing hunkered down on its industrial policy, the source of many American grievances.[18] Xi began to emphasize indigenous technological innovation and economic self-reliance, signaling that he too was ready for disengagement and rivalry.[19]

Let me be absolutely clear that it takes two to tango. The US may be overreacting to China's political, economic, and military actions, but there is no denying that some of them have been provocative. They include China's offshore territorial claims, and repression of dissent of all kinds. The latter, the Chinese insist, is an internal matter. This may be the case, but control of the Internet, arrest of dissidents and their detention without any meaningful trial, and often violent suppression of Muslims in China's eastern provinces provoke opposition in the West. It also arouses deep distrust of China's regime and fear that a country that treats opposition this way cannot be trusted. So too do efforts by the regime to foster nationalism as a means of legitimacy. China's neighbors and Americans worry that such a strategy, while it promises immediate domestic political rewards, will end up by making the country's leaders prisoners of the very passions they have aroused.

Why Conflict?

If we restrict ourselves to foreign affairs, there are two underlying causes of tensions between China and America. First and most importantly, leaders and peoples of both countries seek self-esteem, as do most peoples of the world. They do so in part through their respective country's standing in the world—and have been encouraged to do so by their leaders. The Sino-American competition is more a clash of egos than of interests. The symbolic nature of the competition makes it more, rather than less, difficult to resolve. Max Weber, the famous turn of the twentieth century sociologist, wrote in the context of Franco-German relations that "nations will sacrifice their interests, but never their honor."[20] It is now apparent to prominent historians of the period that World War I was more about honor than it was about security or material interests.[21] It was also a major component of the Cold War, and perhaps the major one after the 1975 Helsinki Accords recognized the European postwar territorial status quo.[22]

The second principal cause of conflict is the faulty conceptions that leaders and intellectuals in both countries have of their national interests and of each other's motives and foreign policies. Classical realists such as Hans Morgenthau understood that there was never such a thing as "the" national interest, only different and competing formulations. Conceptions of national interest are all subjective and at best serve as a guide for foreign policy—and even then only incompletely. Even if leaders have developed a foreign policy theory guided by some notion of national interest, very few of them will be able to conduct foreign policy without domestic constraints.[23] I contend that the ways in which American and Chinese leaders have formulated their interests in Asia have created unnecessary tensions. There is no fundamental or irresolvable conflict of interests between the two sides, and when such conflict of interests arises, it is more often the result of an inability to derive an enlightened and shrewd understanding of mutual interests from complex and sometimes intense strategic settings.

These conceptions of national interest are rooted in history, confirmed tautologically, and make the other country more rather than less threatening. A prime example on the American side is power transition theory, which encourages the belief, some argue the near certainty, that rising powers always challenge dominant powers for leadership of international society and that this is the major cause of great power wars. There is absolutely no evidence in support of power transition theory—quite the reverse. The history of the last 500 years reveals that dominant powers routinely accommodate rising ones, and the latter seek recognition and accommodation, not dominance achieved by war.[24]

The policies generated by the so-called historical lessons intensify Sino-American tensions, just as they did Soviet-American tensions during the Cold War. Deterrence is another offender. Each side believes it necessary to restrain the other through arms build-ups, deployments, and initiatives intended to display resolve. The consequences are more often the reverse of those intended. In the first instance arms build-ups are invariably interpreted as evidence of offensive, not defensive, intentions. This belief convinces leaders that they need to display resolve lest they be perceived as weak. Deterrence in the Cold War was a principal cause of war-threatening crises between the US and the Soviet Union, and the US and China.[25] As practiced by both sides, it has the potential once again to transform Sino-American relations.

This chapter and a recent book I coauthored with Chinese scholar Feng Zhang are seriously at odds with the conventional wisdom in China and America about how to manage their relationship.[26] We challenge many of the principal strategies both sides have pursued, and not only the ways in which they have been applied. We question the concepts on which these strategies are based, arguing that they are based on superficial learning from the past or false historical lessons. Our critique lays the foundation for an alternative set of conceptions we think more appropriate to Sino-American relations, and whose application would make it possible for both nations to buttress their self-esteem in less threatening ways. In the pages that follow I summarize our argument.

Mutual Misunderstanding

On the American side, the dominant analytical lens, as noted, is "power transition theory." It asserts that war is all but inevitable between a rising, would-be, dominant power and an existing, if declining, one. Its proponents contend that this has always happened in the past and is something akin to a "law" of history. Power transition theory is so sharply at odds with history that at least some of the policymakers, academics, and journalists who flog it do so because it suits their political or economic goals. They use it to justify their Cassandra-like claims to a gullible and frightened public that war is likely, if not inevitable, and that the US should maintain, if not increase, its military efforts to "balance" China in the Pacific.

In China, there are diverse discourses. The dominant one depicts the US as simultaneously engaging with and balancing against China. The moderates focus on the US strategy of engagement and appreciate its contribution to China's integration with international society. They have been losing influence. Most analysts now contend that Washington attempts to balance China's rise to maintain its hegemonic position in the Asia-Pacific. A vocal minority of hardliners, who describe this strategy as "containment," argue that China must develop robust military capabilities and strategic options to confront it. Whatever their policy persuasions, most Chinese observers, including the moderates, believe that there is a structural contradiction in Sino-US relations, in the sense that China's interests as a rising power are bound to come into conflict with America's interests as an established power. They are much influenced by American international relations theories, notably realist and power transition theories. These theories reinforce pessimism in both countries and feed arguments about the utility of coercive strategies for competition and conflict. Such theories are intellectually dubious and dangerous for policy.

Escalating Competition

The Obama administration relegated the China policy to a management issue. Its goal was simply to "preserve key national interests where necessary while sustaining a workable and sustainable relationship with China whenever possible."[27] Under Obama, the China policy was a hodgepodge of reactive and ad-hoc decisions, reflecting a contradictory, disorderly, and confusing assortment of engagement, containment, balancing, competition, and cooperation.[28] To the extent that the Obama administration had a coherent policy, it was motivated by concern for credibility of the US strategic commitments in Asia and sought therefore to reassure its allies. Displays of US resolve only encouraged greater Chinese resolve, especially when Washington was seen to challenge China's regional standing in this era of growing Chinese power and confidence.[29]

Obama's policies also triggered a series of indirect and unintended consequences by stimulating a vigorous Chinese strategy toward countries on its regional periphery.[30] The so-called Belt and Road Initiative and island building in the South China Sea—two of Beijing's most significant moves during the Obama administration—were indirect efforts to relieve its strategic pressures.[31] But they were interpreted by Washington as evidence of Chinese expansionism and its alleged intention to push America out of Asia.[32] Washington thus became all the more keen to check Chinese power. In effect, Sino-American interactions for much of this century have made both countries worse off by agitating Chinese assertiveness and undermining mutual strategic trust. China and America increasingly saw each other as security threats and strategic competitors. This made cooperation on common security challenges less likely and the risk of misjudgments and miscalculations more acute.[33]

American strategists are determined to engage China to dissuade it from seeking hegemony in Asia. The primary means to this end is to "balance" rising Chinese power by increasing the combined power of the US and its allies and partners in the region. American policymakers and analysts in the realist tradition focus on Chinese and American economic and military power. Many sound the tocsin about China's growing and threatening military. China has indeed used some of its wealth to upgrade its military forces, but primarily to provide the capability to deal with sovereignty disputes, as regarding Taiwan and the islands in the East and South China Seas, and to protect its expanding overseas trading interests.[34] The US military alleges that China is developing capabilities to thwart US power projection in the Pacific rim, perhaps with the eventual aim of driving the US out of East Asia and imposing a Chinese hegemony in the region. This is an exaggeration based on a self-serving, mirror image of America's hegemonic strategy.

China's recent military modernization efforts, especially the focus on naval and air power, are consistent with its stated goals of near-seas defense, especially those of protecting its territorial security, sovereignty, and maritime rights. In the South China Sea, China maintains some ambiguity in its positions for strategic and domestic political reasons.[35] This highlights the importance of understanding Chinese leaders' assessments of China's interests in the region and the motives behind their policies. Those interests determine how China will invest its resources and deploy its capabilities.

China's strategic programs are also minimal. Only in recent years has it begun to upgrade its nuclear deterrence force, which now includes road-mobile intercontinental ballistic missiles (ICBMs), improved nuclear-powered ballistic-missile submarines, and multiple independently targetable reentry vehicles (MIRVs)-capable silo-based ICBMs, as well as the ongoing development of hypersonic-glide vehicles and MIRV-capable mobile ICBMs. Nevertheless, it has stuck to the long-time policy of maintaining a "lean and effective" deterrent capability.[36] As of January 2018, its nuclear stockpile includes roughly 280 warheads, and only 40–50 of its ICBMs are capable of targeting the continental US.[37]

By contrast, the US has undertaken significant strategic upgrading since the end of the Cold War. It maintains a stockpile of roughly 6550 warheads as of February 2018. Several hundreds of its land-based ICBMs can hit China, in addition to a range of sea- and air-based missiles and warheads. Trident I missiles were replaced with Trident IIIs with a GPS navigation system and larger warheads. Greater accuracy and larger warheads make them deadlier to Chinese missile silos. Three warheads targeted on each Chinese silo have a 99 percent chance of destroying all of them while killing fewer than 6000 Chinese, with hardly any fallout.[38] If China decides to escalate nuclear competition, fearing that it is losing an effective second-strike deterrent, it will most likely result from US provocations in entrenching its nuclear superiority. The Trump administration's 2018 "Nuclear Posture Review," which calls for a significant modernization of its nuclear forces, is an ominous step that will likely elicit a Chinese response to upgrade its own nuclear forces.[39]

Chinese defense spending grew at double-digit annual rates between 1989 and 2015. Since 2016, however, it has declined to a single-digit rate of around 7–8 percent. In 2016, the US spent $611 billion on its military and China $215 billion on its military.[40] China spends a higher proportion of its GDP on the military than many developed countries at an average of 2 percent between 2008 and 2012. This is a mere fraction of the 4.7 percent spent by the US in the same period.[41] In 2016, China spent 1.9 percent of its GDP on the military, in contrast to the US figure of 3.3 percent.[42] Judging from this comparatively low proportion, China is far from engaging in an arms race with America.

China's military modernization is accelerating rapidly, but still has a long way to go. The much-hyped naval build-up offers a telling example. Its first aircraft carrier, commissioned into the Chinese navy in 2012, is a remodeled Soviet-era Kuznetsov-class carrier, lacked the requisite slingshot technology to launch technologically advanced fighter planes. The second indigenously built carrier, launched in April 2017, also derives from the old Soviet model and will not become operational until 2020.[43] Although a mature carrier force—up to five more carriers are planned—will eventually give China power projection capabilities dwarfing those of its smaller Asian neighbors, the current carriers are more a symbol of national power and a training instrument rather than a combat platform.

The figures of Chinese military spending are debatable, as are Chinese military capabilities more generally. What is indisputable, however, is the fallacy of trying to reason from capabilities to intentions. If any more evidence for this truth is required, one need only look back on attempts to do this with regard to the Soviet Union. Faulty conceptions played a large role in intensifying US-Soviet competition during the Cold War. A constructive US-China relationship in the twenty-first century would require a different, and productive, set of strategic conceptions based on an appropriate mix of deterrence, reassurance, and diplomacy.

The overarching American goal of preserving what it considers its hegemony by limiting Chinese influence in Asia has been in place since the mid-2000s.[44] The Obama administration, in only wanting to sustain a workable relationship with China while upholding the longstanding principle of US leadership, unwittingly inherited the preceding Bush administration's China strategy. Chinese critics viewed the strategy as contradictory because America's pursuit of regional hegemony was at odds with its declaratory policy of welcoming China's rise. US officials saw no contradiction because the strategy was designed to shape China's rise in ways that would not challenge US hegemony. This mismatch between Chinese and American views about the coherence of US strategy helps in part to explain rising bilateral tension.

Yet some officials and analysts want to march in the other direction and appear to have the ear of President Trump. His administration has become more committed to hegemony, more confrontational toward China, and less willing to recognize its legitimate interests in influencing developments in the region. Kurt Campbell, former assistant secretary of state and the State Department official in charge of China, insists that preventing hegemony in the Pacific is no longer enough to achieve American interests. He would try to impose a set of American-sanctioned rules, norms, and institutions that he refers to as "Asia's operating system."[45] He advocates adding to the traditional hub-and-spokes model of America's bilateral alliance system in Asia "a tire that links Asian allies to one another without interfering with their strong ties to the US hub."[46]

The Trump administration appears receptive to Campbell's suggestion of taking a "network approach" to its Asian alliance system without finding a proper place for China in the evolving security order; Beijing is likely to feel further besieged and more uncompromising in safeguarding its perceived interests. Hardline voices decrying US containment will be on the rise, and Beijing will be more compelled to respond assertively and even aggressively. US-China relations during the first two years of the Trump administration manifested these hazards.

Respected American scholars recognize the dangers of such an approach. Tom Christensen points out that even the exaggerated language about a pivot or rebalance could feed into Chinese conspiracy theories about alleged US containment and encirclement.[47] Robert Ross argues that the rebalance "unnecessarily compounds Beijing's insecurities and will only feed China's aggressiveness, undermine regional stability, and decrease the possibility of cooperation between Beijing and Washington."[48] A new US-China *modus vivendi* is needed to transform their relationship, and that requires an effective strategy for competition management and conflict reduction.

Such a strategy should address attempt to reduce or resolve the principal areas of tension between the US and China. In the pages that follow, I identify and address four problem areas: Taiwan, North Korea, maritime disputes, and US alliances in Asia.

Taiwan

Taiwan has been a bone of contention between China and the US since the end of the Chinese civil war of 1946–49 and the proclamation of the People's Republic. Beijing has always insisted that Taiwan is an integral part of China. The Nixon administration, eager to end war in Vietnam and cement a tacit alliance with the PRC against the Soviet Union, recognized China's claim. In the famous Shanghai Communiqué of February 1972, signed at the conclusion of President Nixon's historic visit to China, the US acknowledged the Chinese position that "there is but one China and that Taiwan is a part of China."[49]

Acknowledgment is not the same as endorsement and there is a crucial difference between Washington's "one China" policy and Beijing's "one China" principle. Whereas Beijing claims Taiwan as a part of China whose sole legal government is the PRC, Washington acknowledges this position but has "*not* itself agreed to this position."[50] Believing that the sovereign status of Taiwan is yet to be determined, the US neither confirms nor denies Taiwan's sovereignty.[51] In his 1982 "Six Reassurances" to Taiwan, President Ronald Reagan pledged that the US would not formally recognize Chinese sovereignty over Taiwan as the sovereignty of Taiwan was a question to be decided peacefully by the Chinese themselves.[52]

Beijing insists on honoring the three PRC-US joint communiqués of 1972, 1979, and 1982 as the foundation for conducting bilateral relations and policies toward Taiwan. Washington, especially when under Republican administrations, hews more closely to the Taiwan Relations Act (TRA) of 1979 and Reagan's "Six Reassurances." Maintaining a continuing, if weakened and nonbinding, security commitment to Taiwan as compensation for its loss of official ties, the TRA requires the US "to consider any effort to determine the future of Taiwan by other than peaceful means, including by boycotts or embargoes, a threat to the peace and security of the Western Pacific area and of grave concern to the United States."[53] It authorizes Washington "to provide Taiwan with arms of a defensive character" and "to maintain the capacity of the United States to resist any resort to force or other forms of coercion that would jeopardize the security, or the social or economic system, of the people on Taiwan."[54]

American arms sales to Taiwan are a persistent irritant in US-China relations. So too is the prospect of the US's defense of Taiwan in the event of a PRC attack. China and the US nearly came to blows in the Taiwan Strait crises of 1954–55, 1958, and 1995–96.[55] They could do so again, especially if they fail to moderate their mutual deterrence strategies by effective reassurance and clever diplomacy.[56]

A US concession of ending its defense commitment to Taiwan would mean abandoning deterrence as a strategy for managing cross-Strait tensions. It is neither advisable nor feasible in the current environment. To make it feasible and useful, China would have to demonstrate strategic self-restraint and make a credible commitment to keep Taiwan's political system intact after unification. It has sought to convey such a commitment through the "one country, two systems" proposal since the 1980s. This formula was adopted in Hong Kong when the former British colony reverted to China in 1997, but there is a widespread perception in Taiwan and the US that Beijing has violated the terms of the agreement and is reducing Hong Kong's autonomy. No promise about Taiwan will be seen as credible in Taipei or Washington until such time as Beijing honors its agreement in Hong Kong.

Reassurance by means of trade-offs is the only strategy likely to succeed. This demands mutual concessions from Beijing, Taipei, and Washington. Beijing needs to make a credible commitment to Taiwan's security and autonomy to reassure both Taipei and Washington. Beijing's greatest fear is Taiwan's permanent separation from the mainland and creeping move toward independence.[57] These prospects would defeat the PRC's goal of national unification and call into question the legitimacy of the Communist Party's (CCP) rule of China or at least its competence in a vital area of national policy. Taipei accordingly needs to reassure Beijing by renouncing the goal of de jure independence and by opening itself to unification at some future date on terms acceptable to both sides. Such cross-Strait mutual reassurance would meet the US insistence that the status of Taiwan be resolved in a peaceful manner by both sides of the Taiwan Strait.

Washington in turn needs a new declaratory policy to reassure Beijing that its arms sales are contingent upon the dynamics of cross-Strait relations, that the need for such sales will diminish, and that it will eventually cease with improvement of the Beijing-Taipei relationship. It must further make clear that its defense commitment is conditional upon Taipei's willingness to refrain from moving toward independence. This would represent a significant adjustment of and improvement upon the US-PRC joint communiqués of August 1982, in which the US pledges to "reduce gradually its sales of arms to Taiwan, leading over a period of time to a final resolution."[58]

Continued improvement of cross-Strait relations, including but not limited to the military dimension, is a more realistic and productive criterion for assessing arms sales. Washington could propose to Beijing that it will restrict its arms sales to Taipei if Beijing can place verifiable limits on its military production and deployments against Taiwan and credibly commit not to use force except in the extreme cases of Taipei's declaration of de jure independence or a significant enhancement of the US-Taiwan security relationship, such as the deployment of US forces on the island.[59] Such a move would signal a positive US intention while incentivizing Beijing to improve relations with Taipei.

A declaration of linking its defense commitment to Taipei's restraint on independence would partially resolve America's longstanding "strategic ambiguity" over the prospect of its intervention in a Taiwan conflict.[60] It would reassure Beijing because it provides a new constraint on Taiwan's independence; it would not harm Taipei since Washington has long declared its opposition to Taiwan's independence.[61] Indeed, Washington could go one extra step by reassuring Beijing that Taiwan's independence will not receive its consent and that it would welcome unification peacefully and voluntarily achieved by both sides.[62] Since its Taiwan policy has always been about a peaceful process of settlement between Beijing and Taipei, not any particular outcome of that process, and since it opposes unilateral attempts to change the status quo such as a de jure declaration of independence by Taipei, which will almost certainly mean war across the Strait, such reassurance does not violate the spirit of longstanding US policy.[63] If cross-Strait relations stabilize and improve in the longer term as a result of trilateral reassurance, political and military reconciliation between Beijing and Taipei would deprive Washington of its justification for continued arms sales.

These trade-offs give some indication of how the strategy of reassurance might be used to defuse tension in the Taiwan Strait and promote a peaceful resolution. It is unlikely to result in a "grand bargain" fashion given the degree of mistrust and the complexities in devising and gaining acceptance of such proposals. More feasible is a reciprocal process in the form of contingent, sequential trade-offs and agreements among the three parties through a series of interlocking agreements. Measured success could sustain the momentum of reassurance.[64]

North Korea

Next to Taiwan, the ongoing North Korean nuclear weapons and missile crisis is the other major flashpoint in Sino-American relations. From the early 1990s when the crisis first broke out to 2017 when Trump threatened to "totally destroy North Korea," the risk of a new Korean War never disappeared.[65] Rapprochement between the two Koreas and between the US and North Korea in 2018 brought about a dramatic turn of events. Reassurance is now needed to sustain positive momentum and would have some chance of success.

North Korea's interest in nuclear weapons dates back to the Cold War. The current cycle of crises started in 1992, when Pyongyang was caught pursuing a plutonium-based nuclear weapons program.[66] In the first nuclear crisis of 1992–94, the Clinton administration considered surgical strikes, but the crisis was resolved by former President Carter's personal diplomacy in Pyongyang. In the Agreed Framework of October 1994, North Korea agreed to freeze and eventually dismantle its nuclear weapons program in return for the provision of two light-water reactors, the interim supply of heavy fuel oil, some relaxation of sanctions, and progress in normalizing relations with the US. The implementation of the agreement, however, was constrained by a commitment problem that has plagued the crisis period since the 1990s. The US suspected North Korea of nuclear cheating at an underground facility in 1999. Yet, the Clinton administration's own delay in oil delivery, the easing of sanctions and the construction of the light-water reactors, and its ultimate failure to deliver the promise of normalization reduced Pyongyang's confidence in Washington's commitment to the agreement.

The George W. Bush administration derided the Clinton administration's engagement with North Korea as appeasement and, influenced by neoconservative hawks, chose to aggravate tensions. President Bush was also personally repelled by the North Korea leader Kim Jong-il, whom he regarded as an evil tyrant. President Bush considered negotiations with "rogue regimes" like North Korea as rewarding bad behavior and thus immoral. Agitated by the 11 September 2001 terrorist attacks, he quickly dubbed North Korea a member of the "axis of evil." It was in this context that the second nuclear crisis broke out in October 2002, when Washington confronted Pyongyang with alleged evidence of a clandestine uranium enrichment program. Adopting preemption as a new counter-proliferation strategy, and regarding pressure rather than inducement as the key to altering North Korean behavior, the Bush administration refused to engage in meaningful bilateral negotiations, despite repeated North Korean appeals for talks.

China found itself caught between Pyongyang's escalation and Washington's intransigence. In August 2003, it brokered the Six Party Talks—China, South Korea, Japan, Russia, the US, and North Korea.[67] Two years of painstaking negotiations produced the landmark Joint Statement of September 2005. It committed the parties to a series of quid pro quos, including a North Korean promise to dismantle the nuclear weapons program in return for security guarantees, future steps toward normalization, and economic assistance.

The Obama administration pursued what it called "strategic patience," a combination of sanctions and prospective inducements. Neither deterred nor lured, North Korea accelerated its weapons program by conducting three more nuclear weapons tests—in 2013 and 2016—and launching longer-range road-mobile and submarine-based missiles. By the end of its two terms in office, the Obama administration had realized that "strategic patience" had resulted in much greater North Korean capabilities, estimated at ten or more nuclear weapons. Implicitly acknowledging a colossal failure of American diplomacy across three administrations, it advised the incoming Trump administration that North Korea represented the biggest national security threat to the US.

President Trump took Obama's warning to heart. In 2017, his first year in office, he identified North Korea as the greatest security threat, abandoning "strategic patience" in favor of a strategy of "maximum pressure" through diplomatic and economic sanctions. Despite his threats to destroy North Korea, Trump was open to engagement from the beginning.[68] He praised Kim as "a pretty smart cookie" and repeatedly announced his intention to make a deal.[69]

Trump's deal-making vanity helps to explain his acceptance of an invitation from Kim Jong-un, the North Korean leader since 2012, to a summit meeting. Their encounter in Singapore in June 2018 was historic in that it was the first time a sitting American president had met with a North Korean leader. Trump agreed to halt US-South Korea military exercises but refused to consider reducing the number of American troops in South Korea. The joint statement of the summit called for the "complete denuclearization" of the Korean Peninsula, without providing a timeline or details about how the North would go about relinquishing its weapons.[70] As I write in October 2018, attention is focused on Kim's commitment to completely abandon North Korea's nuclear and missile programs. Kim demands a reciprocal, step-by-step process of mutual concessions. American officials worry that he may be using negotiation to ease sanctions in return for a freeze—not dismantlement—of his nuclear weapons programs. They demand that North Korea move quickly toward denuclearization by submitting an inventory of its nuclear weapons and fissile materials.

Any effective strategy toward North Korea must address the twin problems of coordination and commitment noted in the context of Taiwan. The US continues to prioritize denuclearization and non-proliferation. The Trump administration, pointing out that over 80 percent of North Korean trade goes through China, has urged Beijing to curtail and cut oil and other shipments to North Korea. In a pithy three-sentence statement, China insists on the twin goals of denuclearization and regional peace and stability and prefers dialogue and consultation to coercion and conflict.[71] In principle, China is committed to denuclearization even if it involves some destabilization of North Korea. In practice, China has valued the stability of the Korean Peninsula more than denuclearization for a multitude of historical, political, and economic reasons ranging from the profound to the parochial.[72]

China has made clear its bottom line: whatever the approach to the crisis, it should not result in major instability or military conflict. As the Chinese put it, there should be no war and no chaos (*bu sheng zhan, bu sheng luan*).[73] Beijing wants to maintain a minimum degree of stability on the Korean Peninsula and keep North Korea a friend, however strained that friendship may be. In the conventional Chinese view, a destabilized or a hostile North Korea portends serious trouble. In desperation, it might initiate military action against South Korea, reigniting the Korean War. Alternatively, regime collapse could unleash a flood of refugees on the Chinese border and result in a unified Korean Peninsula under the control the US-South Korea alliance. This is an outcome Beijing averted during the Korean War at the cost of close to one million casualties. A hostile North Korea can wreak havoc now that it has developed nuclear-capable missiles that can be trained on China. A friendly, or at least deferential, North Korea, the conventional wisdom goes, can serve as a strategic buffer against American forces based in South Korea. Thus, in response to the question of whether China would cut off oil supplies to North Korea under American pressure, Chinese elites uniformly answer "no," for that would undermine the goal of stability.[74] According to the Chinese scholar Shi Yinhong, pressured too hard, Beijing could flip the other way, deciding that Washington is the real threat to stability on the peninsula and opposing it more strongly.[75]

The only way to resolve this problem of coordination is for the US and China to bring their goals into convergence on the basis of an enlightened understanding of their respective national interests. The two countries share the goal of denuclearization, but each attaches a different priority to it. Asking the US to emphasize peninsular stability over denuclearization would mean the abandonment of denuclearization as a goal altogether, with the momentous consequences for the nuclear non-proliferation regime. This is not in China's interest either and would be damaging to regional security. China needs to reassure the US and other countries in the region that it is serious about denuclearization. To take this step, it has to be convinced that denuclearization will not destabilize North Korea.

The commitment problem is harder to overcome. Ever since the 1994 Agreed Framework, the US has tried to reassure North Korea that it is not committed to regime change or economic strangulation. The 2005

Joint Statement of the Six Party Talks represents the climax of such reassurance: Washington promised to guarantee Pyongyang's security, normalize political relations, and provide economic assistance, as long as Pyongyang demonstrated its commitment to full denuclearization. The Obama administration even offered to negotiate normalization and a peace treaty without the longstanding precondition that Pyongyang first take steps to curtail its nuclear arsenal.[76] Rex Tillerson, Trump's first secretary of state, declared that the US does not seek regime change or an accelerated reunification of the Korean Peninsula.[77] However, 20 years of diplomatic failure and broken promises, exacerbated by periodic calls of military action from hawks, have significantly reduced the credibility of US commitments. Trump veered from military threats to diplomatic chumminess in 2018, but Kim and his advisors might well have doubted his credibility in view of his impulsive vacillation.

North Korea is even more of a puzzle. Before 2018, it seemed all but certain that it had moved away from accommodation. Its commitment to denuclearize might have been more or less serious before the collapse of the Six Party Talks in 2008. But in 2013, it rolled out the *byungjin* line, which emphasized the simultaneous pursuit of economic development and nuclear weapons. The Kim regime enshrined the pursuit of nuclear weapons in its constitution, thus entrenching its resolve to achieving the status of a full nuclear weapons state.[78] But in April 2018, Kim Jong-un declared that *byungjin* was over and that all efforts would now go to "socialist economic construction." Perhaps he was truly different from his father Kim Jong-il, who used negotiation to stall for time. John Delury argues that Kim Jong-un fits the model of an East Asian strongman who sets his country on the path of economic development.[79] Many Americans, recalling North Korea's failure to honor commitments in the past, remain unconvinced.

It seems likely that North Korea will at most accept a freeze, not complete nuclear dismantlement. If so, direct US-North Korea negotiations over *complete* denuclearization will reach a dead end.[80] Here is where China can play an important role by means of reassurance and commitment. Toward this end Washington needs to address relevant Chinese concerns; the two most significant are the risk of an inadvertent war and the role of the US-South Korea alliance in future Korean contingencies. Washington needs to convince Beijing that it will not unleash a preemptive or preventive war against North Korea.[81] More importantly, it needs to make a credible commitment that can alleviate China's profound and historically generated strategic anxieties about Korea, rooted as they are in the belief that stability on the Korean Peninsula is an essential requirement for China's national security. An irrevocable commitment by the US to withdraw troops from South Korea if Chinese cooperation delivers North Korea's denuclearization would be an important step in assuaging Chinese concerns and making it more willing to cooperate with the US.[82]

For its part, China might offer a kind of "regime security assurance" by committing itself to protect the North Korean regime centered on the Kim family in return for denuclearization. North Korea may have wanted this type of reassurance from the US, which, for political and ideological reasons, is very difficult for Washington to contemplate.[83] China, however, is already positioned to make such an offer by virtue of the 1961 Sino-North Korean alliance treaty. The treaty codifies a de facto Chinese security guarantee to North Korea, and Beijing can clarify the new commitment of regime security by amending its clauses. Although not essential, Chinese reassurance may go one extra step by offering extended deterrence to North Korea in the case of a US invasion or preemptive strike.[84]

North Korea is China's only treaty ally in the world today. It is a Cold War leftover that often embarrasses Beijing. A regime security assurance would constitute a Chinese reassurance to North Korea through an irrevocable commitment and thus a tightening of the alliance. Those Chinese elites who are repelled by North Korea's past intransigence and affronts may find it objectionable. Yet, a closer alliance could be a counterintuitive mechanism for controlling a recalcitrant ally, if it makes possible denuclearization and stability.[85] Indeed, it promises to bring multiple advantages, including placating conservative grievances about abandoning North Korea, satisfying the policy bottom line of maintaining peninsular stability, avoiding the risk of turning North Korea into a hostile country, increasing Chinese influence and leverage over Pyongyang, and burnishing China's reputation as a reliable and responsible ally. The long existence of the Sino-North Korean alliance, the nature of China's authoritarian political system nominally sharing the same communist ideology with North Korea, and the Chinese fear of North Korean collapse give credibility to such a commitment—a level of credibility impossible for the US to attain.

Maritime Disputes and Tensions

Maritime tensions in East Asia involving China and the US operate at three levels: disputes about territorial sovereignty and maritime rights between China and its neighbors, disagreements over freedom of the seas especially concerning US military activities in China's exclusive economic zones (EEZs) and the South China Sea, and geopolitical competition between an established and rising power. Each level impinges on a core aspect of the Asian maritime order critical to the role of the US in the region. Recent Chinese approaches to sovereignty disputes, perceived as coercive by the US and its allies, raise the question of Beijing's commitment to their peaceful resolution in a rules-based order. They also pose challenges to the plausibility and credibility of US security commitments to its Asian allies. Disputes over freedom of military action risk upending the regional security order that the US has dominated since the end of World War II. Maritime strategic competition may bring that dominance to an end. Rising tensions in these areas will harden Sino-US competition in maritime Asia, produce war-threatening incidents and miscalculations, and generate instability and turmoil in regional security.

China has disputes with Japan over the sovereignty of the Diaoyu/Senkaku islands in the East China Sea and with the Philippines, Vietnam, Malaysia, Brunei, and Taiwan over the sovereignty of the South China Sea islands. Each of these sovereignty disputes in turn has significant implications for the distribution of maritime rights, including resource extraction and military activities. The US position on these disputes is principled neutrality: it takes no position on the competing claims but supports the principle that disputes should be resolved peacefully, without coercion, intimidation, threats, or the use of force, and in a manner consistent with international law.[86] China's policy, consistently maintained since the late 1970s and reiterated by a major speech that President Xi gave in July 2013, insists on Chinese sovereignty over the islands but proposes to shelve the disputes in order to pursue common development with other claimant countries.[87]

The US and China have no territorial disputes of their own but differ in their interpretations of and approaches to disputes between China and its neighbors. Similar to its Taiwan policy, the US stresses a peaceful process of dispute settlement without staking out a firm position on the merits of the competing claims or any particular outcome of the disputes. But just as in cross-Strait relations, Beijing accuses Washington of hypocrisy and suspects its "real" intention of siding with other claimant states against China. Chinese elites fault the Obama administration's intervention in the South China Sea disputes and its Asian rebalance strategy for aggravating regional territorial disputes. They attribute Asian maritime tension to the rebalance strategy while minimizing the role of Chinese policy.[88] American policymakers and media criticize Chinese coercion toward its neighbors and lack of a serious commitment to a peaceful resolution of the disputes.[89] And indeed, just as in the case of Taiwan, while Beijing emphasizes its peaceful intention, it has never renounced the use of force as an option to settle disputes. China's preference for peace, says Xi, does not mean the abandonment of legitimate interests, much less the sacrificing of core interests.[90]

The possibility of the Chinese use of force is deeply unsettling for the US. Not only would this affect peace and stability in East Asia, it would also pose major strategic dilemmas for Washington. Two of its treaty allies—Japan and the Philippines—are directly, and sometimes dangerously, embroiled in disputes with China. America's security commitments to Japan are codified in the 1960 US-Japan treaty, and both the Obama and Trump administrations have reaffirmed their defense commitment to the Diaoyu/Senkaku islands. The 1951 US-Philippines treaty commits both parties to meet common dangers in case of "an armed attack in the Pacific Area on either of the Parties." Washington has nevertheless refrained from pledging defense of maritime areas disputed between the Philippines and China, such as the potentially explosive Scarborough Shoal.[91] However, in March 2019, Secretary of State Mike Pompeo came close to extending the defense umbrella to cover a Chinese attack in disputed waters.[92] Miscalculation by either side, not to mention by both sides, could lead to some kind of military confrontation.

A no less agonizing row is over the role of international law in dispute settlement. The US criticizes China for refusing to clarify its legal claims in the South China Sea and for failing to comply with the United Nations Convention on the Law of the Sea (UNCLOS). It supports the Philippines versus China arbitration ruling of July 2016 as the new legal framework that should not only govern the bilateral disputes between these two countries but also find wider applications in the region. Contending that UNCLOS forms only part of the international maritime legal regime, Beijing argues that its claims are also based on customary international law and historic rights and practices not incorporated by UNCLOS. It vehemently opposes the July 2016 arbitration ruling, berating it as a US-backed plot to wipe out Chinese rights in the South China Sea.[93]

The satisfactory and defensible way to manage and resolve Asian maritime territorial disputes is for claimant states to clarify their claims, bring them into line with prevailing international law and norms, and work toward a negotiated settlement based on fair and reciprocal compromise. Chinese approaches to the legal and diplomatic aspects of the East and South China Sea disputes are different. In the East China Sea, China asserts its claims to the Diaoyu/Senkaku islands and hounds Japan for refusing to even acknowledge the existence of the territorial dispute. Since 2012, Beijing has adopted a coercive strategy of asserting administrative control by dispatching coastguard and naval vessels to the area, creating risks of maritime incidents escalating into conflicts.

A peaceful resolution to the dispute requires effective reassurance and diplomacy between Beijing and Tokyo. Washington can contribute given its leverage in the US-Japan relationship. Taking no position on the sovereignty of the Diaoyu/Senkaku islands, the US nevertheless recognizes Japan's de facto jurisdiction over them and extends its security commitment on that basis. In 1971, when the Nixon administration was deliberating a position on the islands, Kissinger considered the State Department's recommendation that the US remain neutral on sovereignty while returning administrative rights to Japan nonsensical and demanded a more neutral position. Even the State Department officials who made this recommendation privately recognized the superiority of Taiwan's—and thus China's—claims. They proposed the contradictory position of neutrality on sovereignty but support for Japanese jurisdiction only because of the bureaucratic need for completing the Okinawa reversion treaty then under negotiation and the strategic need of keeping Japan as an ally.[94]

The US can reassure China of its constructive role in the Sino-Japanese dispute by nudging Japan to acknowledge the existence of the sovereignty dispute and start negotiations with China. It may further propose a quid pro quo between Beijing and Tokyo to settle both the sovereignty dispute and the historic issue—the other festering wound that has damaged the Sino-Japanese relationship since the 1990s.[95] Japan could offer a concession of Chinese sovereignty in return for a Chinese settlement of the historic issue. To allay Japanese concerns about resources and security, China can propose to equitably share resources in the area in conjunction with their negotiation over continental shelf and maritime delimitation in the East China Sea, and to impose limits on its military deployments around the islands. To ease both countries' concerns, they could include in any treaty settling the sovereignty dispute a final Japanese apology of its invasion of China in the spirit of the 1995 apology offered by Prime Minister Tomiichi Murayama. China in return would acknowledge this apology as ending their historical dispute. The resolution of these two conflicts would not only constitute a historic breakthrough in Sino-Japanese relations but herald a new era of East Asian peace and stability.

In encouraging Japan to make such concessions, the US would be engineering its own trade-off with China: negation of its commitment to defend the Diaoyu/Senkaku islands in return for China's strategic restraint in the East China Sea and reconciliation with the US-Japan alliance. The US considers this alliance the cornerstone of East Asian security; China criticizes it as a destabilizing containment tool. A reconciliation between China and the US-Japan alliance through quid-pro-quo reassurance would remove a root cause of East Asian tension and contribute to healthy Sino-Japanese and Sino-US relations at the same time.

China has partially clarified its legal claims in the South China Sea but has deliberately maintained some ambiguity in order to preserve diplomatic flexibility and bargaining leverage in future negotiations.[96] In a July 2016 statement, Beijing claims sovereignty over all South China Sea islands; the internal waters, territorial seas, and contiguous zones based on these islands; any EEZ and continental shelf based on these islands; and historic rights.[97] This statement deploys internationally recognized concepts under the UNCLOS framework, suggesting an effort to enhance legal clarity. Ambiguities nevertheless remain. Does the term "islands" meet the definition of an island given in Article 121 of UNCLOS that enables claim to an EEZ and a continental shelf in addition to territorial sea and a contiguous zone? Or, is the term so loosely used that it also includes "low-tide elevations," which cannot claim territorial sovereignty under UNCLOS unless they are within 12 nautical miles of an island? In claiming the various maritime rights, China leaves the geographical scope of these rights entirely undefined. And on the controversial issue of historic rights, China fails to delimit the geographical boundary of such rights or specify their content.[98]

China is both unwilling and unable to produce complete clarity in its claims, as a national consensus on Chinese claims to the South China Sea is still being debated inside the country.[99] Beijing should reassure regional countries and the US by clarifying its position on the contentious U-shaped line, rejecting it as a national boundary which would make 85 percent of the South China Sea enclosed by China's internal waters under its exclusive sovereign control and jurisdiction.[100] Even so, China's vast claims to maritime rights based on sovereignty over all of the islands would still make its neighbors nervous, fearing that a powerful but impatient China might resort to force to realize these interests.

China would still need to establish the credibility of any promises of restraint in the South China Sea. This could be accomplished through an irrevocable commitment to peaceful management and settlement of disputes. It could take the form of a binding code of conduct to be negotiated between China and the US and perhaps China and the ten Association of Southeast Asian Nations (ASEAN) member states. Toward this end, the US should pledge full support for diplomatic efforts between China and its neighbors—whether bilateral or multilateral—to resolve their outstanding disputes. It should no longer take advantage of the disputes to build regional alignments against China.[101]

A sustained Chinese commitment to peace would lessen its neighbors' fears of its power and reduce the need for the US to bolster military deterrence. The result would be lowered tension, enhanced trust, and greater stability in the region. The disputes themselves will take a long time to resolve, necessitating careful management in the interim. But a region-wide reassurance through a commitment to peace and restraint between China and its neighbors and a US commitment to diplomacy rather than deterrence will stabilize the interim situation, creating a favorable environment for the eventual settlement of the disputes. As a salutary by-product for the US, it would freeze the vexed question of whether its alliance commitments would help its allies deter China or encourage their risk-taking or brinksmanship behavior in their disputes with China.

The US Alliance System in Asia

The US alliance system in Asia was a product of early Cold War rivalry between the US and the Soviet Union. The US negotiated five bilateral alliances with the Philippines (1951), Australia (1951), Japan (1951), South Korea (1953), and Thailand (1954) respectively. These pacts led to the so-called hub-and-spokes bilateral alliance system, with the US as the "hub" and its regional allies as separate "spokes." The system has proved remarkably resilient, able to strengthen itself in the post-Cold War era despite the disappearance of the communist threat that was its original *raison d'état*. American scholars argue that it reflects a bargain whereby the US provides security protection and access to American markets, technology, and resources within an open world economy, while America's allies provide support for US leadership.[102] By providing public goods to the region in terms of military security, economic openness, and political stability, it allegedly contributes to peace and progress in East Asia.[103]

Tensions between China and the US alliance system center on three issues. First, while America touts the stabilizing benefits of its alliance system, China sees it as a thinly veiled, anti-China tool of encirclement or containment and an unfortunate relic of the Cold War. Second, the US finds value in the alliance system as a hedge against China. Perceived Chinese assertiveness in territorial disputes with Japan and the Philippines has generated a mounting sense of an American need to buttress its strategic credibility by further strengthening the alliance system. Third, untamed rivalry between China and the US alliance system risks plunging Asia into a new competition reminiscent of the Cold War.

Whether reconciliation and accommodation can be achieved between the respective security orders of China and the US will determine Asia's strategic future. Reassurance strategies on both sides are necessary to address the Chinese fear of encirclement and the American one of a rising, seemingly aggressive China. Only then can there be accommodation between Chinese and American security orders.

China maintains a principled opposition to the US alliance system in Asia, but its attitudes and strategies have undergone subtle changes. For a time following the end of the Cold War, some Chinese elites developed a reluctant appreciation of the system's contribution to Asian security, especially in containing the haunted specter of Japanese militarism. Watching the progressive strengthening of the US-Japan alliance, however, they increasingly come to view it "as more of a security impediment than security facilitator."[104] At the same time, Beijing has developed a sophisticated appreciation of its limits and constraints. The US did not come to the aid of the Philippines during the 2012 Scarborough Shoal incident, after which China seized control of the area. Nor did it try to prevent China's island building after 2014. Beijing finds some satisfaction in its ability to withstand pressure from the US alliance system.

Having accepted coexistence with the system, China focuses on managing a tense relationship with it. Bemoaning its still-limited role in regional security, it hopes to create more strategic space in the institutional architecture of East Asian security. With respect to the US alliance system, China's goal is to reduce its exclusivity by preventing its further tightening. The exclusivity of the system suggests a US intention to squeeze China's strategic influence. It also produces the pernicious effect of indiscriminately channeling all of China's tensions with either the US or its separate allies to the alliance system, even though they may only concern bilateral matters between China and individual countries in the system, not the system as a whole. The US alliance system thus risks magnifying strategic tensions in Asia by turning individual disputes between China and its neighbors into a region-wide contest between Chinese and American security orders.[105]

A US strategy of giving China some institutional space in its alliance system can ease the Chinese fear of exclusion and encirclement. Such reassurance through limited security regimes can draw on Asia's burgeoning "minilateralism"—multilateral security cooperation among small groups of states informally pursuing common security interests.[106] So far, these institutional practices are confined to arrangements among US treaty allies and security partners, such as US-Japan-Australia, US-Japan-India, and US-Japan-Australia-India strategic dialogues. It would, however, be counterproductive to make the new minilateralism directed against China as the US alliance system has been. In fact, an opening minilateralism can usefully serve as a strategic bridge between China and the US alliance system. Bringing China in will both satisfy its desire for a greater strategic role and achieve the larger purpose of building trust and reducing tensions in the region. China, for its part, need not unduly fear exclusion, for Asia's complex security architecture means that some space can always be found to offset challenging initiatives from the US alliance system.[107]

Among the five US alliances in Asia, the US-Japan alliance gnaws at China the most. A trilateral US-Japan-China minilateral strategic dialogue to address all three countries' concerns about East Asian security is thus a promising first step. Such an idea has been broached before but has never had a life of its own due to mistrust and tensions in both Sino-Japanese and Sino-US relations. It must be taken more seriously now. The US bears no small responsibility in promoting Japan's reconciliation with China and other Asian neighbors.[108] For 70 years, its exclusive alliance with Japan and the penchant for controlling Japan's strategic choice have undercut the motivation for Japan and the region to reconcile and build trust with one another.[109]

The US alliance system, with the US–Japan alliance as its cornerstone, is an organic part of Asia's security landscape. The crumbling of this alliance, with the possible consequence of an independent and assertive Japan-seeking nuclear weapons, would not be in China's best interest.[110] But it would also not be in America's best interest to tighten it further. The closer it becomes, the more expansive America's commitments, the greater its credibility worries, and the more onerous its security burden. The US needs to give more agency to regional allies and partners in providing for their own security. Capable of standing up to China collectively when necessary, Asian countries do not always need America at the forefront.[111]

Decrying the US alliance system as an anachronistic relic offensive to contemporary realities, China proclaims an opposing strategy of partnership diplomacy. President Xi announced in a 2015 speech that a new approach of "dialogue not confrontation, partnership not alliance" must be developed to build "global partnership relationships." China's new security concept of "common, comprehensive, cooperative, and sustainable security" must replace all forms of Cold War mentality.[112] In practice, China is slowly and cautiously building up a regional order conducive to its interests and centered on itself. China is now member to a dozen regional institutions, including ASEAN+1, ASEAN+3, the ASEAN Regional Forum, the Conference on Interaction and Confidence-Building Measures in Asia (CICA), the Shanghai Cooperation Organisation (SCO), the East Asia Summit (EAS), the Regional Comprehensive Economic Partnership (RCEP), the Asian Infrastructure Investment Bank (AIIB), and the ASEAN-China Defense Ministers' Informal Meeting (ACDMIM). In the ASEAN-centered institutions of ASEAN+1, ASEAN+3, the EAS, RCEP, and the ACDMIM, China acknowledges ASEAN centrality and plays a supporting and facilitating role. In CICA, the SCO, and the AIIB, however, it seeks a central, if not dominant, role, and challenges US influence accordingly. Xi's 2014 speech to CICA, in which he called for Asian approaches to Asian problems, was read by many as a call to exclude the US and assert a greater role for China. A more significant strategy is the "Belt and Road Initiative," a massive infrastructure building and economic cooperation program across Eurasia and beyond. These Chinese initiatives feed the speculation that "a semi-hierarchical arrangement with individual states or subregions tied to Beijing as the central hub" is emerging in Asia.[113]

America's longstanding order in Asia confronts an emerging China that also seeks to impose a hierarchical order. The American order is predominantly security focused, although economic openness is also a major aspect of it. Traditionally composed of a series of bilateral relationships centered on the US, it is increasingly taking on "networking" characteristics as a result of closer security cooperation among the "spokes." Having renounced alliances as a security strategy since the 1980s, China's order building is predominantly economy focused. While capitalizing on its economic strength to orient the regional agenda toward development, it nevertheless wants to expand its security influence through partnership diplomacy, institution building, and a more proactive security policy.

The US should consider reassurance strategies to ameliorate competition and promote accommodation between the Chinese and American orders. One is based on security regimes and the other on authority sharing. Reassurance through security regimes can draw on active institutionalism that is already an integral part of the regional security architecture. China and the US could moderate their competition in the ASEAN-centered multilateral institutional framework, credited by so many scholars and officials as a major contributor to regional stability and development in the post-Cold War era.[114] ASEAN-centered institutionalism, especially the ASEAN Regional Forum, the EAS, and the series of enlarged ASEAN foreign and defense ministers' meetings, has created an indispensable diplomatic platform that regularly brings all regional powers together. As the only party trusted by all regional countries, ASEAN is uniquely positioned to provide a neutral geopolitical platform for great power engagement, playing "a kind of 'lubricating' role by 'softening' the interactions among the great powers."[115] In helping to soothe competition and promote reconciliation, ASEAN is a felicitous strategic cushion between the Chinese and American orders.

Reassurance through authority sharing is based on insights from both Western and Chinese traditions in statecraft and is especially useful in light of the hierarchical qualities of the American and Chinese orders in Asia. A surprising parallel exists between ancient Greek and traditional Chinese conceptions of ordering relations between great and lesser political units. Drawing on Homeric portrayals of honor, Greeks developed the concept of *hēgemonia*. Our contemporary idea of hegemony derives but is different from this concept, as hegemony suggests domination through material power.[116] *Hēgemonia* described an honorific status conferred on a leading power because of the services it has provided to the community. It confers a right to lead, based on the expectation that this leadership will continue to benefit the community as a whole. *Hēgemonia* represents a clientalist approach to politics: the powerful gain honor in return for providing practical benefits to the weak. The latter willingly accept their inferior status in return for economic and security benefits and the constraints such an arrangement imposes on the powerful.

Clientalist relationships are hierarchical. Its principle of fairness requires rule packages associated with different statuses in the hierarchies. The higher the status, the greater the honor and privileges, but also the more demanding the role and its rules. Clientalist hierarchies are designed to restrain selfishness and its consequences by embedding actors with resources in a social order that requires them to protect and support those who are less advantaged and feel shame if they do not meet their responsibilities. Robust clientalist hierarchies satisfy the spirit of those with high status and the security and appetites of those with low status.[117]

Imperial China drew on Confucian ethics to develop a similar concept of *wangdao*, literally meaning "the kingly way" but more usefully translated as "humane authority," to describe clientalist relations hierarchically centered on the centrality and authority of the Chinese emperor.[118] The purpose of such hierarchy was to promote a universal ethical world order based on Confucian propriety and underpinned by China's relational authority. In its ideal form, it should provide political, economic, and security benefits for all units involved in such a Sino-centric order.[119] Like *hēgemonia*, *wangdao* confers the right to lead, but only if the powerful leads by providing benefit to the community as a whole.

Both the Greek concept of *hēgemonia* and the Chinese concept of *wangdao* denote legitimate leadership based on clientalist authority relationships. As such they can be shared by great powers in search of accommodation and cooperation—unlike hegemony based on material power. Both the US and China should reject hegemony as a strategic goal and instead focus on *hēgemonia* or *wangdao*. As long as they share their *hēgemonia* or *wangdao* in Asia and maintain their respective rule packages in relationships with regional countries, no conflict should arise between the two countries or their respective networks of alliances and partnerships in the region. For the US, this means discharging its responsibilities to its regional allies and partners while encouraging them to improve relations with China. For China, it means doubling down on its neighborhood policy by improving relations with neighboring countries without compelling them to choose between Beijing and Washington. Rather than a binary strategy dividing Asia between Chinese-led and US-led spheres of influence or opposing blocks, a common *hēgemonial wangdao* strategy leads to an intermeshing community of regional countries friendly to both powers—or, in the words of President Xi, "a circle of friends common to both countries."[120]

Moreover, sharing authority in this way can be practiced on a global scale, with both countries seeking honor—that is, the respect of others and the influence it confers—in a cooperative, even collaborative manner. Acting this way, China and the US would both gain influence and reduce tensions between them, while collectively contributing to global governance. Indeed, that would be the ideal for the most important bilateral relationship in the twenty-first century.

Conclusion

Several caveats are in order. Conflict management is no silver bullet. Even the most sophisticated and best-coordinated strategies can fail, and for multiple reasons. Target leaders can be obtuse to signals, miscalculate the costs and risks of cooperation or competition, subordinate avoidance or resolution to other foreign and domestic goals, or correctly conclude that continued competition is in their national or political interest. Leaders attempting to reduce tensions can miscalculate the effects of their initiatives on key foreign or domestic constituencies. Many conflicts are simply not ready for serious amelioration, let alone resolution, because leaders do not have sufficient authority or control over their governments or armed forces, fear losing control if they appear weak or compromising, or believe the risks and costs of any move toward peace greater than those of enduring the status quo. Good prospects for Sino-American relations will present themselves over time, but timing and overcoming domestic and organizational constraints will still be essential.

Strategies of conflict management generally take time to produce positive effects. General deterrence aims to discourage an adversary in the long term from considering the use of force as a viable option, and immediate deterrence to prevent a specific use of force when a challenge appears likely or imminent. Ideally, the two strategies work together to prevent challenges, but also to convince adversarial leaders that the military option is fruitless and that their national and political interests are best served by some kind of accommodation. When successful, deterrence can not only forestall armed conflict but also provide an incentive for adversaries to seek accommodation. Reassurance and diplomacy also take time but have the potential to produce more rapid results.

This empirical reality further highlights the importance of context. The most sophisticated and cleverly applied strategy of conflict management can fail when adversarial leaders are unreceptive or fearful of the consequences of grasping the olive branch. Less sophisticated and cleverly applied strategies can succeed when they are well disposed to accommodation. As the old song has it, it takes two to tango. Leaders on both sides must be open to accommodation and willing to accept some of the risks movement in this direction is likely to involve.

We must distinguish conflict management from conflict resolution. Conflict management is a general term applied to efforts to keep strategic competition contained. This can mean preventing its military escalation (e.g., the use of armed force or development, the deployment of new weapons, or the forward deployment of existing weapons) or political escalation that extends existing competition to new regions or participants. The goal for the Sino-American relationship is conflict management in the short term but also conflict resolution in the longer run.

My final point is a conceptual one. Any perspective is merely a starting point for a narrative that builds in context. This assumption informs my holistic strategy of competition management based on a judicious combination of deterrence, reassurance, and diplomacy. I cannot provide rigid guidelines about how they should be combined or which areas of tension should be addressed first. Leaders can assess the relative importance of contentious issues and decide the order in which they should be addressed. There is no general rule because behavior and outcomes are ultimately determined by context.

Notes

1. President of the United States, "National Security Strategy of the United States of America" (Washington, DC: The White House, 2017), pp. 25, 45.

2. United States Department of Defense, "Summary of the 2018 National Defense Strategy of the United States of America: Sharpening the American Military's Competitive Edge" (Washington, DC: Office of the Secretary of Defense, 2018), p. 2.

3. Hannah Beech, "China's Sea Control Is a Done Deal, 'Short of War with the U.S.,'" *New York Times*, September 20, 2018, https://www.nytimes.com/2018/09/20/world/asia/south-china-sea-navy.html (accessed 30 September 2018).

4. *The Economist*, "China Is Getting Tougher on Taiwan," January 18, 2018, https://www.economist.com/china/2018/01/18/china-is-getting-tougher-on-taiwan (accessed 1 October 2018).

5. Phil Stewart and Idrees Ali, "At Delicate Moment, U.S. Weighs Warship Passage through Taiwan Strait," *Reuters*, June 5, 2018, https://www.reuters.com/article/us-usa-taiwan-military-exclusive/exclusive-at-delicate-moment-us-weighs-warship-passage-through-taiwan-strait-idUSKCN1J030R (access 30 September 2018).

6. Mark Landler, "Trump Accuses China of Undermining Diplomacy with North Korea," *New York Times*, August 29, 2018, https://www.nytimes.com/2018/08/29/us/politics/trump-mattis-north-korea.html (accessed 30 September 2018).

7. Jane Perlez, "China Cancels High-Level Security Talks with the U.S." *New York Times*, September 30, 2018, https://www.nytimes.com/2018/09/30/world/asia/china-us-security-mattis.html (accessed 1 October 2018).

8. Jim Tankersley and Keith Bradsher, "Trump Hits China with Tariffs on $200 Billion in Goods, Escalating Trade War," *New York Times*, September 17, 2018, https://www.nytimes.com/2018/09/17/us/politics/trump-china-tariffs-trade.html (accessed 30 September 2018).

9. Mark Landler, "Trump Accuses China of Interfering in Midterm Elections," *New York Times*, September 26, 2018, https://www.nytimes.com/2018/09/26/world/asia/trump-china-election.html (accessed 3 October 2018).

10. The White House, "Background Briefing by a Senior Administration Official on Chinese Interference," New York, September 26, 2018; Thomas G. Mahnken, and Toshi Yoshihara, "Countering Comprehensive Coercion: Competitive Strategies Against Authoritarian Political Warfare" (Washington, DC: Center for Strategic and Budgetary Assessments, 2018); Josh Rogin, "China's Interference in U.S. Politics Is Just Beginning," *Washington Post*, September 20, 2018, https://www.washingtonpost.com/opinions/global-opinions/chinas-interference-in-us-politics-is-just-beginning/2018/09/20/2b462558-bd0f-11e8-8792-78719177250f_story.html?noredirect=on&utm_term=.a3471d09bb7d (accessed 29 September 2018).

11. Jeffrey Bader, "U.S.-China Relations: Is It Time to End the Engagement?" (Washington, DC: The Brookings Institution, 2018).

12. CNBC, "CNBC Exclusive: CNBC's Michelle Caruso-Cabrera Interviews Steve Bannon From CNBC Institutional Investor Delivering Alpha Conference," New York, July 18, 2018, https://www.cnbc.com/2018/07/18/cnbc-exclusive-cnbcs-michelle-caruso-cabrera-interviews-steve-bannon.html (accessed 30 September 2018).

13. Henry Kissinger and J. Stapleton Roy, "'The Key Problem of Our Time': A Conversation with Henry Kissinger on Sino-U.S. Relations," New York, September 20, 2810, https://www.wilsoncenter.org/article/the-key-problem-our-time-conversation-henry-kissinger-sino-us-relations (accessed 30 September 2018).

14. John Pomfret, "As China-U.S. Feud Enters Uncharted Territory, Beijing Can Only Blame Itself," *Washington Post*, September 26, 2018, https://www.washingtonpost.com/news/global-opinions/wp/2018/09/26/as-china-u-s-feud-enters-uncharted-territory-beijing-can-only-blame-itself/?noredirect=on&utm_term=.423ed74fe08d (accessed 29 September 2018).

15. Teddy Ng, "Cold War Mentality Will Harm US-China Relations, Top Diplomat Warns Kissinger," *South China Morning Post*, September 26, 2018, https://www.scmp.com/news/china/diplomacy/article/2165775/cold-war-mentality-will-harm-us-china-relations-top-diplomat (accessed 29 September 2018).

16. Kristin Huang, "China Sets Up Think Tank Alliance to Better Understand US as Trade War Continues," *South China Morning Post*, July 17, 2018, https://www.scmp.com/news/china/diplomacy-defence/article/2155678/china-sets-think-tank-alliance-better-understand-us (accessed 1 October 2018).

17. *The Economist*, "America's Trade Strategy Has Many Risks and Few Upsides," March 28, 2018, https://www.economist.com/news/finance-and-economics/21739726-it-undermining-rules-based-trade-order-and-could-start-series (accessed 2 April 2018).

18. Barry Naughton, "Economic Policy under Trade War Conditions: Can China Move Beyond Tit for Tat?" *China Leadership Monitor*, No. 57 (Fall 2018), pp. 1–12.

19. Javier C. Hernández, "For Xi Jinping, Beijing a Man of the People Means Looking the Part," *New York Times*, September 28, 2018, https://www.nytimes.com/2018/09/28/world/asia/xi-jinping-china-propaganda.html (accessed 29 September 2018).

20. Max Weber, *Economy and Society: An Outline of Interpretive Sociology*, 2 vols. Guenther Roth and Claus Wittich, eds. (Berkeley: University of California Press, 1978), I, pp. 909–11.

21. For a review of this literature, Richard Ned Lebow, "What Can International Relations Theory Learn from the Origins of World War I?" *International Relations*, 28, no. 4 (2014), pp. 387–411, and "World War I: Recent Historical Scholarship and IR Theory?" *International Relations*, 28, no. 2 (2014), pp. 245–50.

22. Richard Ned Lebow, *A Cultural Theory of International Relations* (Cambridge: Cambridge University Press, 2008), ch. 9.

23. Richard Ned Lebow, The Tragic Vision of Politics: Ethics, Interests and Orders (Cambridge: Cambridge University Press, 2003).

24. Richard Ned Lebow and Benjamin A. Valentino, "Lost in Transition: A Critique of Power Transition Theories," *International Relations*, 23, no. 3 (2009), pp. 389–410; Richard Ned Lebow and Daniel Tompkins, "The Thucydides Claptrap," *Washington Monthly*, June 2016.

25. Richard Ned Lebow and Janice Gross Stein, We All Lost the Cold War (Princeton: Princeton University Press, 1994); Jian Chen, *Mao's China and the Cold War: Beijing and the Taiwan Strait Crisis of 1958* (Chapel Hill, N.C.: University of North Carolina Press, 2001), ch. 7.

26. Feng Zhang and Richard Ned Lebow, *Taming American-Chinese Rivalry* (under review).

27. Kurt M. Campbell, *The Pivot; The Future of American Statecraft in Asia* (Boston: Little Brown, 2016), p. 232.

28. Yuan Peng, "Zhongguo wei lishi nanti xunzhao xin da'an" [China Is Seeking a New Answer to a Historically Difficult Question], *Caokao Xiaoxi* [Reference News], http://www.guancha.cn/YuanPeng/2016_08_31_372956_s.shtml (accessed 29 March 2018).

29. Author's interview with Ministry of Foreign Affairs official, Beijing, September 9, 2016.
30. Wang, "Guodu kuozhang," p. 17.
31. Feng Zhang, "Challenge Accepted: China's Response to the US Rebalance to the Asia-Pacific," *Security Challenges* 12, no. 3 (2016), pp. 45–60.
32. Yuan, "Zhongguo wei lishi nanti xunzhao xin da'an."
33. Yang Jiemian, "US Rebalance to Asia-Pacific and Sino-US Relations," speech to the Boao Forum for Asia's Strategic Planning Workshop, October 15, 2016, http://mp.weixin.qq.com/s?__biz=MzAwODc2M DY2Nw==&mid=2247484038&idx=2&sn=277c9f5425b8da0afaadb b5dbfeeea37&chksm=9b68beb2ac1f37a4caf5360bbcf802494432ad2 b451c49e3e4fbe007bca556f21b440d10bca8&scene=0&from=group message&isappinstalled=0#wechat redirect (accessed October 26, 2016).
34. David M. Lampton, *Three Faces of Chinese Power: Might, Money, and Mind* (Berkeley: University of California Press, 2008), pp. 37–76.
35. Feng Zhang, "Chinese Thinking on the South China Sea and the Future of Regional Security," *Political Science Quarterly* 132, no. 3 (2017), pp. 435–66.
36. Eric Heginbotham, Michael S. Chase, Jacob L. Heim, Bonny Lin, Mark R. Cozad, Lyle J. Morris, Christopher P. Twomey, Forrest E. Morgan, Michael Nixon, Cristina L. Garafola, and Samuel K. Berkowitz, *China's Evolving Nuclear Deterrent: Major Drivers and Issues for the United States* (Santa Monica, CA: Rand, 2017), p. xi.
37. Arms Control Association, "Arms Control and Proliferation Profile: China," https://www.armscontrol.org/factsheets/chinaprofile#nw (accessed 30 September 2018).
38. Arms Control Association, "US Nuclear Modernization Programs," August 2012, http://www.armscontrol.org/factsheets/USNuclear Modernization (accessed February 16, 2013).
39. United State Department of Defense, "Nuclear Posture Review" (Washington, DC: Office of the Secretary of Defense, 2018).
40. Stockholm International Peace Research Institute, "The Top 10 Military Spenders," *SIPRI Yearbook 2011: Armaments, Disarmament and International Security* (Oxford: Oxford University Press, 2011), p. 9; "Military Expenditure by Country, in Constant (2015) US$m., 1988– 1996, 1997–2006, 2007–2016," SIPRI Military Expenditure Database,

https://www.sipri.org/sites/default/files/Milex-constant-2015-USD. pdf (accessed March 18, 2018).

41. "Military Expenditure (% of GDP)," World Bank Data, http://data. worldbank.org/indicator/MS.MIL.XPND.GD.ZS (accessed February 8, 2013).

42. "Data for All Countries from 1988–2016 as a Share of GDP," SIPRI Military Expenditure Database, https://www.sipri.org/sites/default/ files/Milex-constant-2015-USD.pdf (accessed March 18, 2018).

43. Sebastien Roblin, "The Real Reason the World Needs to Pay Attention to China's Growing Aircraft Carrier Fleet," *National Interest*, May 1, 2017, http://nationalinterest.org/blog/the-buzz/the-real-reason-the-world-needs-pay-attention-chinas-growing-20406 (accessed May 8, 2017).

44. Silove, "The Pivot before the Pivot."

45. Campbell, *The Pivot*, p. 150.

46. Ibid., p. 206.

47. Thomas J. Christensen, "Obama and Asia: Confronting the China Challenge," *Foreign Affairs* 94, no. 5 (2015), pp. 28–36, at p. 29; Christensen, *The China Challenge*, pp. 250–1.

48. Robert S. Ross, "The Problem with the Pivot," *Foreign Affairs*, November/December 2012, https://www.foreignaffairs.com/articles/ asia/2012-11-01/problem-pivot (accessed 20 October 2018).

49. For the text of the document, see Kerry Dumbaugh, "Taiwan: Texts of the Taiwan Relations Act, the U.S.-China Communiques, and the 'Six Assurances'" (Washington, DC: Congressional Research Service, 1998).

50. John J. Tkacik, "Donald Trump Has Disrupted Years of Broken Taiwan Policy," *The National Interest*, December 5, 2016, emphasis in original, http://nationalinterest.org/feature/donald-trump-has-disrupted-years-broken-taiwan-policy-18609 (accessed January 3, 2018). See also Nancy Bernkopf Tucker, "Strategic Ambiguity or Strategic Clarity?" in Nancy Bernkopf Tucker, ed., *Dangerous Strait: The U.S.-Taiwan-China Crisis* (New York: Columbia University Press, 2005), pp. 186–211, at p. 209; Richard C. Bush, *Untying the Knot: Making Peace in the Taiwan Strait* (Washington, DC: Brookings Institution Press, 2005), p. 90; Shelley Rigger, *Why Taiwan Matters: Small Island, Global Powerhouse* (Lanham, MD: Rowman & Littlefield, 2011), p. 180.

51. Bush, *Untying the Knot*, p. 254.

52. The text is in Dumbaugh, "Taiwan."

53. On the TRA's defense comment as modest and nonbinding, see Bush, *Untying the Knot*, pp. 22, 110.
54. Dumbaugh, "Taiwan," P. 2.
55. Allen S. Whiting, "China's Use of Force, 1950–96, and Taiwan," *International Security* 26, no. 2 (2001), pp. 103–31.
56. Nancy Bernkopf Tucker and Bonnie Glaser, "Should the United States Abandon Taiwan?" *Washington Quarterly* 34, no. 4 (2011), pp. 23–37, at p. 23.
57. Bush, *Uncharted Strait*, p. 7.
58. Dumbaugh, "Taiwan," p. 17.
59. Michael D. Swaine, "The Real Challenge in the Pacific: A Response to 'How to Deter China,'" *Foreign Affairs* 94, no. 3 (2015), pp. 145–53, at p. 150.
60. Tucker, "Strategic Ambiguity or Strategic Clarity?"; Bush, *Untying the Knot*, pp. 255–6; Rigger, *Why Taiwan Matters*, p. 181.
61. Bush, *Uncharted Strait*, p. 18.
62. Swaine, "Trouble in Taiwan," p. 43.
63. On the process-centered nature of US policy, see Bush, *Uncharted Strait*, p. 214; Rigger, *Why Taiwan Matters*, p. 193.
64. Bush, *Untying the Knot*, p. 10; Bush, *Uncharted Strait*, p. 72.
65. Peter Baker and Rick Gladstone, "With Combative Style and Epithets, Trump Takes America First to the U.N.," *New York Times*, September 19, 2017, https://www.nytimes.com/2017/09/19/world/trump-un-north-korea-iran.html (accessed 1 October 2018).
66. The account of the North Korean nuclear crisis draws on Leon V. Sigal, *Disarming Strangers: Nuclear Diplomacy with North Korea* (Princeton, NJ: Princeton University Press, 1999); Charles L. Pritchard, *Failed Diplomacy: The Tragic Story of How North Korea Got the Bomb* (Washington, DC: Brookings Institution Press, 2007); Mike Chinoy, *Meltdown: The Inside Story of the North Korean Nuclear Crisis* (New York: St. Martin's, 2009); Victor Cha, *The Impossible State: North Korea, Past and Future* (New York: Vintage, 2012).
67. Pritchard, *Failed Diplomacy*, p. 97.
68. Peter Baker and Rick Gladstone, "With Combative Style and Epithets, Trump Takes America First to the U.N.," *New York Times*, September 19, 2017.
69. Josh Mitchell and Eric Morath, "Trump Leaves Open Possibility of Military Action against North Korea," *Wall Street Journal*, April 30, 2017.

70. Mark Landler, "The Trump-Kim Summit Was Unprecedented, but the Statement Was Vague," *New York Times*, June 12, 2018, https://www.nytimes.com/2018/06/12/world/asia/north-korea-summit.html (accessed 1 October 2018).

71. Wang Yi, "Xiwang gefang lengjing panduan xingshi, zuochu mingzhi xuanze" [I Hope All Parties Judge the Situation Coolly and Make Wise Choices], March 18, 2017, http://www.fmprc.gov.cn/web/zyxw/t1446819.shtml (accessed January 9, 2018); see also Fu Ying, "The Korean Nuclear Issue: Past, Present, and Future: A Chinese Perspective" (Washington, DC: John L. Thornton China Center at Brookings, 2017), p. 23.

72. Cha, *The Impossible State*, pp. 342–45.

73. Yao Yunzhu, Zhang Tuosheng, Zhao Xiaozhuo, Lyu Jinghua, and Li Chen, "China-US Military Relations: Evolution, Prospect, and Recommendations," in Fu and Wang, *China-US Relations*, pp. 122–80, at p. 136.

74. Author's interview with Chinese officials and scholars, Beijing, December 2017.

75. Simon Denyer, "China's Korea Policy 'in Tatters' as Both North and South Defy Sanctions," *Washington Post*, April 17, 2017.

76. Alastair Gale and Carol E. Lee, "U.S. Agreed to North Korea Peace Talks before Latest Nuclear Test," *Wall Street Journal*, February 21, 2016.

77. David E. Sanger, "Trump on North Korea: Tactic? 'Madman Theory'? Or Just Mixed Messages," *New York Times*, April 28, 2017.

78. Haggard and Noland, *Hard Target*, p. 7.

79. John Delury, "Kim Jong-un Has a Dream. The U.S. Should Help Him Realize It," *New York Times*, September 21, 2018, https://www.nytimes.com/2018/09/21/opinion/kim-jong-un-moon-economic-development-north-korea-denuclearization.html (accessed 1 October 2018).

80. Henry A. Kissinger, "How to Resolve the North Korea Crisis," *Wall Street Journal*, August 11, 2017; Stephen Krasner, "A Least Worst Option on North Korea," *Lawfare*, May 15, 2017, https://lawfareblog.com/least-worst-option-north-korea (accessed January 12, 2018).

81. On the danger of war as a result of the Trump administration's combative rhetoric, see Sagan, "The Korean Missile Crisis."

82. As the crisis escalated in 2017, more analysts have called on the US to make such an offer. See, for example, Yasuhiro Izumikawa, "Acting on the North Korea Playbook: Japan's Responses to North Korea's Provocations," *Asia Policy* 23, January (2017), pp. 90–6, at p. 96; Krasner, "A Least Worst Option on North Korea."
83. Cha, *The Impossible State*, p. 304.
84. Philip Bobbitt, "What to do about North Korea," *Lawfare*, December 18, 2017, https://www.lawfareblog.com/what-do-about-north-korea (accessed January 12, 2018).
85. Victor Cha argues that an alliance becomes potentially a powerful instrument for a great power to control its smaller ally if the alliance relationship is asymmetrical and unequal. Victor D. Cha, *Powerplay: The Origins of the American Alliance System in Asia* (Princeton, NJ: Princeton University Press, 2016), p. 30.
86. Ronald O'Rourke, "Maritime Territorial and Exclusive Economic Zone (EEZ) Disputes Involving China: Issues for Congress" (Washington, DC: Congressional Research Service, 2017).
87. Xi Jinping, "Tuidong haiyang qiangguo jianshe" [Building a Maritime Great Power], July 30, 2013, http://jhsjk.people.cn/article/22402107 (accessed January 15, 2018).
88. Zhu, Huang, and Hu, "Competing Perspectives between China and the United States," p. 79.
89. Michael J. Green, Kathleen H. Hicks, Zack Cooper, John Schaus, and Jake Douglas, *Countering Coercion in Maritime Asia: The Theory and Practice of Gray Zone Deterrence* (Washington, DC: Center for Strategic and International Studies, 2017).
90. Xi, "Building a Maritime Great Power."
91. For the text of these treaties concerning the US defense commitments, see O'Rourke, "Maritime Territorial and Exclusive Economic Zone (EEZ) Disputes," pp. 61–2.
92. John Reed, "Pompeo warns China on Philippines 'threat,'" *Financial Times*, 2–3 March 2019, p. 7.
93. Feng Zhang, "Assessing China's Response to the South China Sea Arbitration Ruling," *Australian Journal of International Affairs* 71, no. 4 (2017), pp. 440–59.
94. Richard McGregor, *Asia's Reckoning: The Struggle for Global Dominance* (London: Allen Lane, 2017), pp. 67–8.
95. Ibid.

96. Zhang, "Assessing China's Response," p. 450.

97. Government of the People's Republic of China, "Zhonghua renmin gongheguo zhengfu guanyu zai nanhai de lingtu zhuquan he haiyang quanyi de shengming" [Statement of the Government of the People's Republic of China on China's territorial sovereignty and maritime rights and interests in the South China Sea], July 12, 2016, http://www.mfa.gov.cn/nanhai/chn/snhwtlcwj/t1380021.htm (accessed January 16, 2018).

98. Zhang, "Assessing China's Response," p. 450.

99. Feng Zhang, "Chinese Thinking on the South China Sea and the Future of Regional Security," *Political Science Quarterly* 132, no. 3 (2017), pp. 435–66.

100. On the U-shaped line, see Zhiguo Gao and Bing Bing Jia, "The Nine-Dash Line in the South China Sea: History, Status, and Implications," *American Journal of International Law* 107, no. 1 (2013), pp. 98–123; Chris P. C. Chung, "Drawing the U-Shaped Line: China's Claim in the South China Sea, 1946–1974," *Modern China* 42, no. 1 (2016), pp. 38–72.

101. Wu Xinbo and Michael Green, "Regional Security Roles and Challenges," in Nina Hachigian, ed., *Debating China: The US–China Relationship in Ten Conversations* (Oxford: Oxford University Press, 2014), pp. 198–220, at p. 204.

102. G. John Ikenberry, *Liberal Leviathan: The Origins, Crisis, and Transformation of the American World Order* (Princeton, NJ: Princeton University Press, 2011), pp. 208–9.

103. Victor D. Cha, "Complex Patchworks: US Alliances as Part of Asia's Regional Architecture," *Asia Policy* 11, January (2011), pp. 27–50, at p. 41.

104. Zhou Fangyin, "The U.S. Alliance System in Asia: A Chinese Perspective," *Asian Politics & Policy* 8, no. 1 (2016), pp. 207–18, at p. 208.

105. Feng Zhang interview, Beijing, June 2017.

106. William T. Tow, "The Trilateral Strategic Dialogue, Minilateralism, and Asia-Pacific Order Building," in Yuki Tatsumi, ed., *US–Japan–Australia Security Cooperation: Prospects and Challenges* (Washington, DC: Stimson Center, 2015), pp. 23–36.

107. Cha, *Powerplay*, p. 216.

108. Goldstein, *Meeting China Halfway*, pp. 226–27.
109. Cha, *Powerplay*, p. 204.
110. Art, "The United States and the Rise of China," p. 385.
111. Michael Beckley, "The Emerging Military Balance in East Asia: How China's Neighbors Can Check Chinese Naval Expansion," *International Security* 42, no. 2 (2017), pp. 78–119.
112. Xi Jinping, "Xi Jinping zai di qishijie lianheguo dahui yibanxing bianlun shi de jianghua" [Remarks at the Seventieth United Nations General Assembly], New York, September 28, 2015, http://news.xinhuanet.com/world/2015-09/29/c_1116703645.htm (accessed January 20, 2018).
113. Cha, *Powerplay*, p. 204.
114. Amitav Acharya, *Constructing a Security Community in Southeast Asia: ASEAN and the Problem of Regional Order*, 2nd ed. (London: Routledge, 2009).
115. Kishore Mahbubani and Jeffrey Sng, *The ASEAN Miracle: A Catalyst for Peace* (Singapore: NUS Press, 2017), p. 101.
116. Simon Reich and Richard Ned Lebow, *Good-Bye Hegemony! Power and Influence in the Global System* (Princeton, NJ: Princeton University Press, 2014); Richard Ned Lebow and Robert Kelly, "Thucydides and Hegemony: Athens and the United States," *Review of International Studies* 27, no. 4 (2001), pp. 593–609.
117. Richard Ned Lebow, *A Cultural Theory of International Relations* (Cambridge: Cambridge University Press, 2008), pp. 64, 84.
118. Yan Xuetong, *Ancient Chinese Thought, Modern Chinese Power*, eds. Daniel A. Bell and Sun Zhe, transl. Edmund Ryden (Princeton, NJ: Princeton University Press, 2011).
119. Feng Zhang, *Chinese Hegemony: Grand Strategy and International Institutions in East Asian History* (Stanford, CA: Stanford University Press, 2015).
120. Xi Jinping, "Wei goujian zhongmei xinxing daguo guanxi er buxie nuli" [Persistently Working Toward a New Model of Sino-US Major Country Relationship], Beijing, June 6, 2016, http://jhsjk.people.cn/article/28416143 (accessed January 22, 2018).

6

Democracy and the Rule of Law

President Donald Trump's cozying up to dictators makes almost daily head-lines. He seems comfortable with and anxious to please such strongmen as Vladimir Putin of Russia, Rodrigo Duterte of the Philippines, Crown Prince Mohammed bin Salman of Saudi Arabia, and Kim Jong-un of North Korea. Rather than condemning their violence, he validates it—as he did violent neo-Nazi demonstrators in Charlottesville, Virginia. He praised Republican Representative Greg Gianforte, who violently assaulted a *Guardian* reporter at a rally.[1] In October 2018, the world was treated to photos of Trump embracing the Saudi ambassador and publicly accepting his explanation that "rogue killers" had broken into the Saudi embassy in Turkey and dismembered dissident journalist Jamal Khashoggi.[2] Under enormous pressure, Trump backed away from his outright support for the Saudi regime but defended his action with reference to a $100 million arms deal with the US.[3] Like many Trump claims, the arms deal and the American jobs it would generate turned out to be fictitious.[4] When his lies were exposed, Trump accused the media of being "enemies of the people"—a phrase taken out of the Soviet and Chinese communist playbooks.[5]

Trump has always acted as a bully in his personal and professional life and appears to feel more at home—as we all do—with people like himself.

© The Author(s) 2020
R. N. Lebow, *A Democratic Foreign Policy*,
https://doi.org/10.1007/978-3-030-21519-4_6

He seems to revel in the friendship and seeming support of dictators. There is also some suspicion—as yet unsubstantiated—that he owes favors to Putin and the Saudis for earlier financial backing. Whatever the explanation, there can be no doubt that Trump has little regard or respect for democratic values, practices, or leaders and has attempted to reorient domestic and foreign policy away from them. When he took his oath of office, he knew little to nothing about the constitution and workings of the American government and seems to have thought he was elected dictator and could run the country the way he did his real estate business. There is little evidence that Trump's approach to government has changed in the two years in which he has been in power.[6]

Trump is unlike any previous holder of his office, as are many of his policies. So it is comforting to think that he and they are aberrations that will disappear if and when he is replaced by a more responsible president. In this chapter I argue that Trump's deplorable excesses are not so much novel in kind as they are in degree. Previous presidents, Democratic and Republican alike, have supported right-wing dictatorships and their leaders, undermined and even toppled democratic governments, and have sold arms to the most retrograde regimes knowing they would use them against their neighbors or own people for the most nefarious of purposes. If Trump is the most disliked and disrespected president in the eyes of non-Americans, America as a whole has suffered a precipitous loss of standing and respect by virtue of the policies noted above and some of the interventions or coups associated with them. Anger and dismay at Trump and his behavior should not blind us to the deeper, endemic, and ultimately self-defeating pattern in US foreign policy.

The same is true for the rule of law. The cornerstone of democracy is respect for law that allows governmental and private institutions to function but also limits their power and makes them to varying degrees transparent and responsible to those of whom they govern through elections and legal challenges. Democracy also requires equal treatment of all citizens before the law, and fair access to citizenship and the ballot box, an impartial and fair judiciary, and governmental and legal tolerance of civil society and its institutions, especially the media. To function effectively, a democracy must have not only laws but people who respect and comply voluntarily with them. Laws are only enforceable when 90 percent or more of those subject to them obey them. Think about Prohibition in the 1930s or present-day speed limits on the highway. No alcohol beyond 3.2 percent beer was the law, but people drank like fish. Today's 65 miles per hour speed limits on highways in many states mean that in most jurisdictions you can drive up to 74 without getting ticketed. Police and politicians would meet a fierce outcry if they pulled over and fined people driving 66 mph.

Most of us obey laws out of habit, but if we stop and think about it we recognize the value of compliance. Laws make behavior predictable, facilitating everyday life, as well as commerce, trade, education, and a host of other activities. In democracies, they protect people in a myriad of ways, which is why there is an outcry when they are abused. In the US, the greatest violations were always against African-Americans. They were legally slaves for the first 70 years of the Republic's existence and segregated in education and housing for much of the twentieth century. They are still subject to de facto discrimination in school, shopping, employment, and perhaps most blatantly so in stop-and-searches on streets and highways.[7] In democracies, unfair laws can be challenged, violations of the law publicized, and sometimes corrected.

As we all know, fair laws, fair enforcement, and voluntary compliance remain an ideal. There is always a gap between theory and practice even in the most robust democracies. In 2017, a total of 987 people were shot dead by police, and 788 people in the first nine months of 2018.[8] There can be little doubt that many of the police responsible for these shootings are breaking state and federal laws and will continue to do so as long as juries refuse to convict policemen of murder in circumstances where violence was clearly unjustified. African-American and Hispanic men, teenagers, and children were killed by police in greater numbers than their proportion of the population. Of the 788 people shot dead by police up to October 2018, 250 of the victims, or 31.7 percent, were either Black or Hispanic. These groups represent only 24.5 percent of the population.

Democracies always struggle to live up to their norms and laws. Leadership is crucial in this regard, as it was in facilitating greater civil rights for African-Americans, women, and other minorities. Courts were helpful, but the biggest breakthrough came in the form of legislation shepherded through the Congress by President Lyndon Johnson. President

Trump and his administration have been marching in the other direction. Trump encourages racists and neo-Nazis. In the towns nestled in Oregon's south Willamette Valley, neo-Nazis and assorted other far-right actors have been operating in the open throughout the Trump era—hate crimes in the area have doubled in the year following the 2016 election.[9] In October 2018, Trump intensified Republican efforts to frame the midterm elections as a battle over immigration and race, warning that "unknown Middle Easterners" were marching toward the border with Mexico. He and Republican candidates hold Democrats responsible for unfettered immigration and violent crime and have attacked minority candidates and minorities more generally in nakedly racial terms.[10] Many people believe that dotted lines connect the president to the pipe bombs mailed to prominent politicians and George Soros and the murderous assault on Pittsburgh's Tree of Life Synagogue in October 2018.

President Trump's outright lies, encouragement of racism and violence, gutting of enforcement of rights for ordinary people, and appointment of unqualified people to federal courts threaten democracy in fundamental ways.[11] In the words of pro-Republican columnist David Brooks, "He's challenged basic norms of honesty, decency, compassion and moral conduct. He unabashedly exploits rifts in American society."[12] American democracy is likely to survive, but only if the electorate returns to office representatives, senators, and presidents committed to the rule of law. Regional and international societies are much less robust. They are more easily unsettled by rogue leaders and states. Trump's opposition to the European Union (EU), free trade agreements, longstanding alliances, international law and norms, and, worse still, his explicit support for dictators and states that violate them can destabilize these orders and make his fear of a chaotic, disordered world self-fulfilling. Historical analogies can be misleading or overstated, but it is well within reason to identify parallels with the 1930s where dictators, often supporting one another, resorted to lies and violence to gain and maintain power and then to destroy regional orders by subversion, threats, and war.

Here too it would be reassuring to know that Trump was a radical departure from past presidents. And indeed he is. His goals are destructive of regional and international order, his rhetoric is unrestrained and often downright confrontational, and his foreign policy is unrelievedly unilateral. But there is precedent for this behavior. Previous administrations have violated international law and norms in pursuit of short-term, ill-considered gains, insisted on special privileges for America, and cozied up to some of the worst postwar dictatorships, even supplying them with economic and military aid.

Trump is more an extreme expression of past policies than he is a pioneer of new ones. He is not initiating, but accelerating, a process by which the US seeks to gain advantages by placing itself above and beyond the law.

I document these claims so far as space permits and show just how counterproductive, if not self-defeating, these policies have been. American interests are enabled and sustained by robust regional and international orders and it is in the country's interest to strengthen international norms and laws, not to violate and erode them. I conclude the chapter by returning to tragedy and Thucydides' account of the collapse of the Athenian Empire. It offers sobering insights into the explanation for, and likely outcome of, America's increasingly unilateral approach to the world.

Friend or Foe of Democracy?

In August 1941, President Franklin D. Roosevelt and British Prime Minister Winston Churchill held a secret meeting in Placentia Bay, off the coast of Newfoundland. Together they wrote what came to be known as the Atlantic Charter. Although America had not yet entered the war, it declared the goals of Atlantic allies: no territorial aggrandizement; no territorial changes made against the wishes of the people (self-determination); restoration of self-government to those deprived of it; reduction of trade restrictions; global cooperation to secure better economic and social conditions for all; freedom from fear and want; freedom of the seas; and abandonment of the use of force, as well as disarmament of aggressor nations. Supporters of the Atlantic Charter signed the declaration by the United Nations on 1 January 1942, which became the basis for the United Nations, created at the end of the war in 1945.[13]

The Charter was a sophisticated mix of self-interest and idealism. It aspired to open the world up to American trade and investment, and at a time when local production was everywhere depressed because of wartime damage and exigencies. It reaffirmed self-determination—and here Roosevelt had British, French, Portuguese, and Spanish colonies in mind, not only countries to be liberated from German, Italian, and Japanese occupation. Freedom from fear and want was a radical agenda that required not only self-rule but economic assistance. Disarmament of aggressor nations and the abandonment of force were equally radical, and the latter, which harked back to the idealism of the 1920s, would certainly require some supranational authority.

Roosevelt died in April 1945 and the Truman administration had a mixed record in implementing the principles of the Charter. It made a series of policy choices at the high point of American power and prestige that would shape American policy throughout the Cold War. Some of these choices were consistent with the Charter and aimed at rebuilding war-ravaged countries and strengthening Democratic forces within them. The occupation and Democratic restructuring of Japan and Germany were notable accomplishments in this regard as was the Marshall Plan.

The Marshall Plan (officially, the European Recovery Program) was an American initiative to aid Western Europe, in which the US gave over $12 billion (nearly $100 billion in today's dollars) in economic assistance from 1948 through 1952 to help rebuild Western European economies. It encouraged the removal of trade barriers and many internal regulations, modernization of industry and business procedures, and trade union membership. It was intended to strengthen Democratic forces in Western Europe, prevent the spread of communism, and create markets for American goods.[14] Self-interest and idealism combined in a way they would in few postwar initiatives.

In other domains, the Truman administration made trade-offs between the commitment to democratization and freedom of domestic choice on the one hand and their opposition to the Soviet Union and communism on the other. The de-Nazification of Germany was put on hold and former Nazis allowed to hold political office, judgeships, university posts, and important positions in business. Implementation was lukewarm once the Cold War began and the program was terminated in 1951. The Nuremberg trials were quietly shelved so as not to antagonize any further the German population. The US actively intervened in European domestic politics, funding anti-communist unions and political parties and anti-communist propaganda. The American, British, and French occupation sectors of Germany were given a common currency and then united to form the Federal Republic of Germany, which was then rearmed and incorporated into the NATO alliance.[15]

American leaders, advisors, and much of the media came to view the world in stark binary terms: as a Manichean struggle of good and evil between the West and communism. Communism was regarded as monolithic and expansionist. It had to be opposed by military as well as political means and the US began a military build-up that would accelerate at various times during the Cold War. This was accompanied by political hysteria that led to witch hunts against domestic communists and blacklisting in Hollywood and television.[16]

Outside of Europe the US did an about-face on colonialism. Many liberation movements were communist affiliated or at least left wing in their politics and the widespread belief of communism as a worldwide conspiracy prompted the US government to aid European countries attempting to reimpose colonial rule by force in Africa and Asia. In Vietnam, the Americans provided the airlift for French troops to return to the country where they and their puppet regime met with intense resistance. The US gradually became drawn into the conflict. It supplied the French military with arms and some American generals wanted to use atom bombs to stave off French defeat at Dien Bien Phu in 1954. Following the French surrender, the US used the 1954 Geneva Conference to prevent a full communist takeover of Vietnam. The collapsing French Empire in Southeast Asia was divided into four states: North and South Vietnam, Laos, and Cambodia. A general election was to be held in Vietnam in 1956 and the two countries reunified.

Recognizing that the communists were likely to win in the South, the US prevented any such election and reunification from taking place. President Eisenhower and Secretary of State John Foster Dulles increased military and political aid to the regime in the south that they had inherited from the French. Under President Kennedy, this commitment would escalate to include more American military advisors, the beginnings of a destructive herbicidal program, and support for a bloody coup against unpopular and ineffective southern leader, Ngo Dinh Diem. President

Lyndon B. Johnson would carry out air strikes against the North, commit US troops to the South, and, in effect, begin a full-scale war against the Viet Cong in the South and an aerial war against the North. President Richard Nixon and his National Security Advisor, then Secretary of State Henry Kissinger, would extend the war to Cambodia.[17]

The Department of Defense estimated that the Vietnam War cost approximately $168 billion (over a trillion in 2018 dollars).[18] It resulted in 58,220 Americans dead, 153,303 wounded, and 1643 missing. After the war, more than 70,000 Vietnam veterans committed suicide and another 700,000 suffered psychological trauma.[19] As for Vietnamese military and civilian casualties, estimate vary from a low American academic estimate of 1.3 million, an official North Vietnamese estimate of upwards of 2 million, and a high estimate of 3 million made by the *British Medical Journal*.[20]

Vietnam was America's longest, most expensive, and most costly—in terms of lives—Cold War intervention. It ended in abject and total failure. Ironically the worst-case scenarios that motivated American intervention never came to pass. Southeast Asia did not fall like dominos to "the communists." Neither the Soviet Union nor China began to doubt US resolve. The monolithic nature of communism was decisively disproven when communist China went to war with communist Vietnam. And Vietnam as a whole has been transformed into almost the kind of country President Johnson and his advisors hoped the South might be. It has a communist government to be sure, but one that is committed to the territorial status quo, does not attempt to subvert its neighbors, and is development oriented and has a largely capitalist economy. It is open to foreign visitors and investment and is legitimate in the eyes of most of its citizens. The Vietnam War was fought for naught.

There were numerous other American anti-Democratic interventions and coup attempts, some of them against popularly elected governments. In 1949, under US President Harry Truman, a coup overthrew an elected parliamentary government in Syria, which had delayed approving an oil pipeline requested by US international business interests.[21] In 1953, the CIA, with President Eisenhower's authorization, helped Mohammad Reza Pahlavi of Iran remove the democratically elected Prime Minister Mohammed Mosaddegh.[22] In 1954, the CIA deposed the democratically elected President Jacobo Árbenz of Guatemala.[23] In 1962, the CIA armed Cuban exiles and with US military support landed them at the Bay of Pigs in an abortive attempt to overthrow Cuban President Fidel Castro. In 1965, in the Johnson administration, the US invaded the Dominican Republic.[24,25] In 1970, President Richard Nixon ordered the CIA to cooperate with Chilean generals to depose the popular and freely elected Marxist President of Chile, Salvador Allende.[26] In 1975, the Church Committee Senate investigation revealed that the US had begun covert intervention in Chile from as early as 1962.[27] Under President Reagan, the CIA supported the Contra rebels in Nicaragua against the elected Sandinista government.[28] In 1986, the US bombed Libya in response to Libyan involvement in international terrorism.[29] A 2016 study found that the US intervened in 81 foreign elections between 1946 and 2000, with the majority of those being through covert, rather than overt, action.[30]

To be fair, the US has also intervened in support of democracy on occasion, to repel invasions of Korea and Kuwait, and to remove dictators, as in Libya and Iraq. Even successful interventions and coups did not necessarily advance American interests, and often did the reverse. In Korea, as noted, it tempted, perhaps compelled, the Truman administration to invade the North, triggering off a costly and stalemated war. The Gulf War succeeded in expelling Iraq from Kuwait, but allowed Saddam's still functioning army to wage genocidal wars against opponents of his regime. It encouraged a groundswell on the American right in support for what would prove a second, and disastrous war to remove Saddam from power and occupy Iraq. The Libyan intervention, conducted with European NATO partners, also succeeded in its short-term goal of a removing an unpalatable dictator, but created conditions of near anarchy, triggered large-scale violence among competing factions for power, and encouraged wave after wave of refugees to Europe.

Seemingly more successful interventions and coups often created longer-term problems for the US. Iran provides a classic illustration. The 1953 coup placed Mohammed Reza Pahlevi in power, who declared himself Shahanshah (King of Kings) and ruled with an increasingly iron hand until overthrown in the revolution of February 1979. Pahlevi became the US cat's-paw in the region as he bought billions of dollars' worth of US weapons, opened his country to US businesses, and with Washington's connivance, sought to become the dominant power in the Gulf region. The US helped Iran create its nuclear program starting in 1957 by giving Iran its first nuclear reactor and nuclear fuel and after 1967 by providing Iran with weapons grade enriched uranium.[31] Iran's nuclear program would come back to haunt Washington when its Islamic regime sought to build nuclear weapons. So too would the close political relationship between Pahlevi and the US. In Iranian eyes, he was regarded, if not as a puppet of the US, certainly as someone who did their bidding. Public opinion also connected the US, perhaps incorrectly, with Pahlevi's hated secret police. American leaders never spoke out against it or condemned its brutal interventions in the country's domestic life. The US was widely hated by the persecuted opposition. Not surprisingly, the country's new "supreme ruler" Ayatollah Ruhollah Khomeini, condemned the US as "The Great Satan" and authorized the takeover of the US embassy by radical students in November 1979.[32]

In 1945 the US was the most admired country in the world. It was seen as a liberator by people in Europe and Asia and a beacon of democracy and source of generosity in a war-ravaged world. A decade later that reputation was badly tarnished. In the struggle against communism, America aligned itself with the declining colonial powers in Africa and Asia, supported right-wing dictators around the world, backed Apartheid South Africa, and tried to impose de facto imperial rule on Central and South America. For many in the developing world, its support of Democratic Israel was also anathema. Its reputation was further damaged by involvement in multiple coup attempts and interventions, in none of which could Washington effectively mask its involvement. In subsequent decades its standing declined further. There was an upward bump at the end of the Cold War, especially in Eastern Europe, but that did not last long, and respect for the US declined precipitously with the invasions of Afghanistan and Iraq. The standing of the US rose in the Obama administration but plummeted again under Trump.

The US seems to have learned little from what should have been a series of reinforcing lessons from its coups and interventions. Instead, a self-descriptive script is played out again and again. During the Cold War, whenever a *A* left-wing leader came to power, often as the result of an election. American business interests feared increased taxation or ending of sweetheart deals that were the product of corrupt deals with American-supported leaders. They would press the panic button and claim, generally without evidence, that the new leader was a communist, agent of the Soviet Union, or extreme nationalist inimical to American interests. Otherwise reasonable reporters, academics, and policymakers repeatedly gave credence to these claims. The right-wing media manufactured evidence in support and the testimony of ambitious local politicians or generals hoping to gain power at home backed by American money or military action. In the post-Cold War era the charge is linked to religious extremists and terrorists. As often as not American leaders respond positively to calls and the CIA steps up efforts at subversion and the military to intervene.

Post-coup or intervention rulers are invariably hailed as progressive and a breath of fresh air for their country. In 1954 the *New York Times* rejoiced after the Iranian coup that "Oil is flowing again into the free markets of the world," Mosaddegh, the overthrown leader was "where he belongs—in jail," and Iran under Shah Pahlevi was open to "new and auspicious horizons."[33] A year later, the *Atlantic Monthly* hailed the Shah as "an articulate and positive force."[34] In Iraq, Saddam Hussein, who came to power in 1979, was perceived by American leaders as a strongman who might help offset Iranian power in the region. During the Iran-Iraq War (1980–88), the US supplied him with weapons and intelligence and turned a blind eye to his efforts to develop chemical weapons and the use of poison gas against Kurdish villagers. Relations with Iraq were cordial until Saddam's invasion of Kuwait in 1990.[35] The monster cultivated and encouraged by the US became sufficiently emboldened to act in a way that his erstwhile supporter could not tolerate.

This adulation is also offered to leaders not put into power by Western coups or bayonets. Up until the 2011 NATO intervention in Libya, Seif al-Islam el-Gaddafi, son of Libya's dictator, was hailed as a liberalizing modernizer by prominent members of the Anglo-American establishment. Former British Prime Minister Tony Blair spoke favorably of his largely plagiarized and ghost-written doctoral thesis at the London School of Economics.[36] This illusion remained until the Berlin nightclub bombing of 1986 for the US and for Britain until Gaddafi sought to suppress by violence opponents of the regime during the Arab Spring uprisings. British-educated Syrian President Bashar al-Assad and his British-born wife were initially described in the Western media as committed modernizers. As the Arab Spring got underway in 2011, *Vogue* published a fawning profile of Ms. Assad, depicting her as "the very freshest and most magnetic of first ladies."[37]

The most recent example of this misplaced enthusiasm is the American response to the accession of Crown Prince Mohammed bin Salman of Saudi Arabia. He was almost uniformly praised by investors and journalists. In the *Atlantic*, Editor Jeffrey Goldberg proclaimed that he and his wife were "wildly democratic" and that his rise to power would equal the collapse of the Soviet Union in its impact! Writing in the *Washington Post*, David Ignatius wrote that the prince, who let Saudi women drive, sing in public, and join sports teams, would usher in "a more modern, more entrepreneurial, less hidebound and more youth-oriented society."[38]

Prince Charming quickly revealed his true nature. He went to war in Yemen to suppress the Houthi rebels. His indiscriminate bombing and naval blockade of that country has put its entire population at risk of disease and starvation.[39] The CIA concluded that he was behind the murder and dismembering of critical journalist Jamal Khashoggi in October 2018 in the Saudi embassy in Istanbul, Turkey.[40] *Vogue* did its best to scrub the story from the Internet once Assad was exposed as a cold hearted killer willing to use barrel bombs and poison gas against his own people. Bin Salman's erstwhile cheerleaders, including President Trump, are doing their best to distance themselves from him.

As in China, Vietnam, and Iran, there is inevitably a price to pay for such public association with leaders who oppress their own citizens. American intervention in China's civil war and backing of Chiang Kai-shek created mistrust and antagonism between the victorious communists and the US in the aftermath of their 1949 triumph on the mainland. It encouraged the perceived need in Beijing to intervene in Korea—where the US suffered 128,000 casualties—and poisoned relations between the two countries for three decades. Intervention in Indochina also had negative long-term consequences, including tremendous loss of US prestige. Support for the Shah's Iran made its successor government anti-US. Interventions in Afghanistan and Iraq further damaged US prestige, standing, and influence, destabilized the region, facilitated the rise of ISIS, encouraged terrorism, and made the US more dependent on Saudi Arabia. Washington's backing of the Saudi royal family has already begun to have negative consequences, which could become more dramatic if and when the current regime loses power.

Rule of Law

At the First Hague Peace Conference in 1899, the US delegate, Andrew Dickson White, the founder of Cornell University, pushed for the creation of the Permanent Court of Arbitration and persuaded Andrew Carnegie to build the monumental Peace Palace at The Hague as its home. At the Second Hague Conference in 1907, Secretary of State Elihu Root urged that future international conflicts be resolved by a court of professional jurists, an idea realized when the Permanent Court of International Justice was established in 1920. Woodrow Wilson conceived of the League of Nations and Franklin Delano Roosevelt the United Nations. Both presidents were committed to the rule of law and wanted to make international relations resemble domestic relations between Democratic states more closely.

Roosevelt and his advisors recognized that law to be effective must be enforceable. For that to happen, states and peoples had to see the law as in their interest. Only then could coalitions of status-quo powers, acting with the authorization of appropriate regional and international organizations, successfully isolate violators and enforce legal commitments. The Atlantic Charter and postwar treaties extended laws and commitments beyond the economic realm to economic and physical security and human rights. In the early postwar era American governments initiated and backed a series of measures to extend and strengthen international law, create institutions to foster development and address economic shocks, and encouraged regional organizations that fostered economic and security cooperation. The US was an active and enthusiastic supporter of early steps toward European integration.

During much of the Cold War, but more so during and after the Reagan administration, the US underwent a reversal in its approach to the rule of law. It has opposed and refused to sign important treaties and routinely violated international law in pursuit of short-term, often ill-considered interests. This obstruction and violation has been close to across the board and has affected war and intervention, arms control, economics, and human rights.[41] Diminishing respect for international law can be linked to the rise of the US as a military power after World War II, to the domination of US foreign policy by realists who emphasize

US military might and the right to use it to advance national interests. American leaders and their spokespersons have consistently claimed special privileges in this regard by virtue of their self-proclaimed status as a hegemon.

Since the end of the Cold War, the US has increasingly violated international law or resisted its extension. Among other things, it invaded Iraq in defiance of the UN Security Council, resorted to torture, secret detention of suspected terrorists without trial, Guantanamo rendition of others to third countries where they could more readily be tortured, tried to derail and refused to sign treaties banning land mines, ignored or undermined international efforts to limit climate change, and made repeated efforts to weaken international institutions by violating their rules.[42]

Torture is without doubt the most egregious violation of domestic and international law, although not responsible for nearly as many deaths as invasions, bombing, and illegal drone attacks in the Middle East and Africa. Washington had earlier been responsible for torture indirectly through its support of authoritarian regimes in Iran, Vietnam, Egypt, and Central and South America. The US military trained special local military and security forces in these countries and provided them with up-to-date equipment to combat domestic opponents. By 1971, it had trained more than a million policemen in 47 nations, including 85,000 in South Vietnam and 100,000 in Brazil.[43]

After invading Afghanistan and Iraq, the military flew people of interest to Guantanamo, where they would not be subject to US laws, had no access to counsel, and could be waterboarded and sleep deprived to soften them up for interrogation. The CIA arranged for other suspects to be "rendered" to foreign prisons, or "black sites," even more beyond the reach of any court or legal authority. With the outlawing of piracy and slavery, abolition of torture had long been a priority of international law. In 1984, the U.N. General Assembly unanimously adopted the Convention Against Torture, which Washington only signed a decade later. In 1995, in the shadow of President Clinton's signing of the convention, CIA agents kidnapped terror suspects in the Balkans, some of them Egyptian nationals, and sent them to Cairo to be interrogated by a regime that routinely used extreme forms of torture. Former CIA director George Tenet testified that in the years before 9/11, the CIA sent some

70 individuals to foreign countries by means of "extraordinary rendition," a procedure explicitly outlawed by Article 3 of the Convention Against Torture.[44]

President Obama's most questionable behavior was the extended use of drone missile strikes against suspected terrorists. Obama authorized ten times as many strikes as his predecessor, President Bush, and an increasing number of them in countries where the US was not engaged in combat. Some of these attacks were not authorized by local governments. Obama instituted new procedures to make drone use more transparent, reduce civilian damage, and compensate innocent victims or their families. Many international lawyers nevertheless thought his use of drones a violation of international law on the grounds that extra-judicial of civilians has been unlawful since the late eighteenth century.[45] Critics have also objected to the collateral damage drones cause, with some estimates claiming that nine children have been killed for every one targeted adult.[46]

President Donald Trump accelerated the use of drone attacks and has been more flagrant in his violations of international law than any of his predecessors, with his military actions in Syria, "zero tolerance" immigration policy, unilateral sanctions against Iran, and separation of children from their parents along the Mexican border.[47] In October 2018, the UN Commission of Inquiry on Syria crimes held the US culpable of transgressing international humanitarian law when it launched airstrikes the year before on a school in Syria that killed at least 150 civilians. The investigators rejected the claims of the US military that 30 ISIS fighters had been targeted and killed in the attack.[48]

Trump removed the US from participation in trade and security treaties. He dumped the North American Free Trade Area Treaty (NAFTA), only, under pressure from businesses, to negotiate a new agreement with Canada—Mexico was excluded—that was more or less similar. He has repeatedly threatened to pull out of the deal the US and Europeans painstakingly negotiated with Iran to halt its development of nuclear weapons. Most recently, he has withdrawn from the Intermediate-Range Nuclear Forces Treaty, signed in 1987 by Ronald Reagan and Mikhail Gorbachev. He did so, egged on by National Security Advisor John Bolton, on the grounds that the Russians were violating the treaty.[49]

Russian Deputy Foreign Minister Sergei Ryabkov condemned Trump's withdrawal from 1987 Intermediate-Range Nuclear Forces Treaty (INF) "as a very dangerous step." Mikhail Gorbachev, Soviet general secretary at the time it was signed, worried that "it would undermine all the efforts made by the leaders of the USSR and USA to achieve nuclear disarmament."[50] The Treaty bans land-based missiles with a range of 500–5500 kilometers. It was an important step toward an 85 percent reduction in the nuclear weapons of the two superpowers. Republicans Senators Rand Paul and Bob Corker also worried about the consequences of unilateral termination. Paul told Fox News that it would be "a big, big mistake to flippantly get out of this historic agreement."[51] Trump's ambassador to NATO threw further fuel on the fire by warning Russia that if it did not terminate development of its new cruise missile, the US would "take out" the missile.[52] The INF Treaty is not the first victim of American desire to free itself from treaty obligations and limitations. In 2002, the US withdrew from the Antiballistic Missile Treaty and, in 2018, from the Iran nuclear deal. According to Gorbachev, the Trump administration, by withdrawing from two important international agreements "has in effect taken the initiative in destroying the entire system of international treaties and accords that served as the underlying foundation for peace and security following World War II."[53]

Nazi jurist Carl Schmitt infamously declared that "The sovereign is he who decides on the exception."[54] Powerful states could and would determine which laws they would obey or violate. His claim made a mockery of international law and was strenuously opposed by American lawyers inside and outside of government. Well before 9/11, but dramatically so in its aftermath, the US conforms more and more in practice to Schmitt's account of international law. It has justified repeated claims for special privileges and exclusions on the basis of its claim to be a hegemon. It has used the War on Terror, which poses at worst a limited threat to American security, as the excuse for a widening scope of illegal behavior that includes illegal killings, often at the cost of considerable collateral damage; incarceration without charges, trail, or access to legal counsel; drone surveillance and air strikes over countries who have not given permission to enter their air space; and protection of all those involved in these extralegal activities on the grounds of national security.

Tragedy Redux

I noted earlier that Thucydides structures his account of the Archidamian and Peloponnesian Wars as a tragedy. Athens commits a double *hamartia* —a Homeric word that originally meant missing the mark in archery and later came to describe major miscalculations. It responds positively to Corcrya's plea for an alliance, setting in motion a chain of events that make its expectation of war with Sparta self-fulfilling. Two decades later the assembly foolishly votes to invade Sicily, sends an expedition against Syracuse whose destruction sets the stage of Athens' defeat and loss of empire. Power has gone to the head of its leaders and people. They think they can violate international norms with impunity, control others successfully through bribes and threats, and extend their empire without limits. They prove their own worst enemies and are defeated by their hubris.

Thucydides described his account as a gift for all time because he expected history to repeat itself in the most general kind of way. The powerful, whether individuals or political units, would confuse themselves with gods, become convinced of their invulnerability, ignore conventional norms and restraints in search of money, power, or sex, and ultimately meet their comeuppance. Tragedy may be an art form, but it is also a description of life.

Modern international relations validate Thucydides' pessimistic expectations. Spain under Philip II, France under Louis XIV and Napoleon, Germany under Kaiser Wilhelm and Hitler, all followed the trajectory of Athens. They became powerful, expanded, increasingly violated the conventions of the day, expanded to the point where they seriously threatened others, and fatally overextended themselves through their military commitments.

Postwar American behavior conforms in large part to this pattern. Americans believe they and their way of life is superior to all others, and that other people recognize this, envy them, and would emulate them given half the chance. Through trade and investment, but also by means of violence, they extended their formal and informal "empire" in the course of the nineteenth and twentieth centuries and continued to do so after 1945. Like the Athenians, they repeatedly use force to overthrow leaders who might prove inimical to their political or economic interests and maintained pliant leaders in power. They retained democracy at home while often preventing its development abroad, or even snuffing it out when it was too independent. They overextended themselves militarily in Vietnam, Afghanistan, and Iraq, although they were so powerful relative to other states that they managed to survive these disasters without being bled white. Their power, prestige, and influence nevertheless suffered. Rather than retrenching, they responded by acting even more aggressively.

Athenian prestige and standing were the result in the first instance of its courageous stand against Persia. Athens repelled the Persian invasion and liberated the rest of Greece but over time imposed its own yoke over those it liberated. It exploited their resources by using money intended for the common defense to enrich its own citizens and beautify its city. The US makes its own citizens bear the financial burden for its bloated military. However, it exploits its allies, and the rest of the world, by borrowing from them to sustain a higher living standard than it could otherwise afford.

Athenian democracy remained institutionally robust but became corrupted from within. Demagogues replaced responsible leaders, appealed to the baser instincts of the people, encouraged what today would be called fake news, and used their offices to advance their economic and political interests at the expense of the state. The most transparent, self-serving, and psychologically disturbed politician—Alcibiades—became the most revered by the least educated part of the people. Here too there is an uncanny resemblance with the US.

Under its most responsible leader, Pericles, Athens pursued its most unrealistic foreign policy by attacking powerful and peaceful Syracuse, the dominant city of Sicily. It could easily have continued to live at peace with it and profited from even closer trading relations. The final chapter of America's bid for hegemony has yet to be written.

Notes

1. Brian Kass, "Amid the scandal over a missing Saudi journalist, Trump applauds violence against American ones," *Washington Post*, 19 October 2018, https://www.washingtonpost.com/news/democracy-

post/wp/2018/10/19/amid-the-scandal-over-a-missing-saudi-jour-nalist-trump-applauds-violence-against-american-ones/?utm_term=.cbe37e281f3e (accessed 20 October 2018).

2. Agence France Presse, "Donald Trump says he finds Saudi explanation of Khashoggi death 'credible,'" *Guardian*. 20 October 2018, https://www.theguardian.com/world/2018/oct/20/donald-trump-says-he-finds-saudi-explanation-of-khashoggi-death-credible (accessed 20 October 2018).

3. Julian Borger, Martin Chulov, Patrick Wintour, "Trump announces Jamal Khashoggi investigation but says he won't halt Saudi arms sales," *Guardian*, 11 October 2018, https://www.theguardian.com/world/2018/oct/11/jamal-khashoggi-saudi-arabia-under-pressure-from-trump-administration (accessed 20 October 2018).

4. Steve Benen, "Trump points to dubious arms deal to excuse Saudi Arabia," MSNBC, 12 October 2018, http://www.msnbc.com/rachel-maddow-show/trump-points-dubious-arms-deal-excuse-saudi-arabia; Associated Press, "AP FACT CHECK: Trump Inflates Jobs Impact of Saudi Arms Deal," *New York Times*, 20 October 2018, https://www.nytimes.com/aponline/2018/10/20/us/politics/ap-us-fact-check-week.html (both accessed 20 October 2018); Paul Krugman, "Arms and the Very Bad Men," *New York Times*, 23 October 1018, https://www.nytimes.com/2018/10/22/opinion/khashoggi-saudi-trump-arms-sales.html?action=click&module=Opinion&pgtype=Homepage (accessed 23 October 2018).

5. Krugman, "Arms and the Very Bad Men."

6. Bob Woodward, *Fear: Trump in the White House* (New York: Simon & Schuster, 2018).

7. Michelle Singletary, "Shopping while black. African Americans continue to face retail racism," *Washington Post*, 17 May, 2018, https://www.washingtonpost.com/news/get-there/wp/2018/05/17/shopping-while-black-african-americans-continue-to-face-retail-racism/?utm_term=.bd4f0596fd2c; Kim Soffen, "The big question about why police pull over so many black drivers," *Washington Post*, 8 July 2018, https://www.washingtonpost.com/news/wonk/wp/2016/07/08/the-big-question-about-why-police-pull-over-so-many-black-drivers/?utm_term=.251d322e58c2; Stanford Open Policing Project, "Findings," 2018, https://openpolicing.stanford.edu/findings/ (all accessed 23 October 2018).

8. "Fatal Force," *Washington Post*, 1 October 2018, https://www.washingtonpost.com/graphics/2018/national/police-shootings-2018/; Statista,

"Number of people shot to death by the police in the United States in 2017–2018, as of October, by race," October 2018, https://www.statista.com/statistics/585152/people-shot-to-death-by-us-police-by-race/ (both accessed 23 October 2018).

9. Jason Wilson, "'This is evil at work': how should a small town react to neo-Nazis?," *Guardian*, 23 October 2018, https://www.theguardian.com/world/2018/oct/23/this-is-evil-at-work-how-should-a-small-town-react-to-neo-nazis (accessed 23 October 2018).

10. Alexander Burns and Astead W. Herndon, "Trump and G.O.P. Candidates Escalate Race and Fear as Election Ploys," *New York Times*, 23 October 2018, https://www.nytimes.com/2018/10/22/us/politics/republicans-race-divisions-elections-caravan.html?action=click&module=Top%20Stories&pgtype=Homepage; Editorial Board, "Donald Trump Is Lyin' Up a Storm," *New York Times*, 22 October 2018, https://www.nytimes.com/2018/10/22/opinion/editorials/transgender-trump-lies-midterm-election.html?action=click&module=Opinion&pgtype=Homepage (both accessed 23 October 2018).

11. Alexander Burns and Astead W. Herndon, "Trump and G.O.P. Candidates Escalate Race and Fear as Election Ploys," *New York Times*, 22 October 2018, https://www.nytimes.com/2018/10/22/us/politics/republicans-race-divisions-elections-caravan.html?action=click&module=Top%20Stories&pgtype=Homepage (accessed 24 October 2018).

12. David Brooks, "The Materialist Party," *New York Times*, 22 October, https://www.nytimes.com/2018/10/22/opinion/midterms-democrats-health-care.html?action=click&module=Opinion&pgtype=Homepage (accessed 24 October 2018).

13. Douglas G. Brinkley and David Facey-Crowther, eds., *The Atlantic Charter* (Basingstoke: Palgrave Macmillan, 1994).

14. Martin Schain, ed., *The Marshall Plan Fifty Years Later* (New York: Palgrave Macmillan, 2001); Michael J. Hogan, *The Marshall Plan: America, Britain, and the Reconstruction of Western Europe, 1947–1952* (New York: Cambridge University Press, 1987).

15. Konrad H Jarausch, *After Hitler: Recivilizing Germans, 1945–1995* (Oxford: Oxford University Press, 2006); Dennis L. Bark and David R. Gress, *A History of West Germany* Vol 1: *From Shadow to Substance, 1945–1963* (Cambridge: Cambridge University Press, 2011); Richard Bessel, *Germany 1945: From War to Peace* (New York: Simon and Schuster, 2012); Camilo Erlichman and Christopher Knowles, eds., *Transforming Occupation in the Western Zones of Germany: Politics, Everyday Life and*

Social Interactions, 1945–55 (London: Bloomsbury, 2018); Frederick Taylor, *Exorcising Hitler: The Occupation and Denazification of Germany* (London: Bloomsbury, 2011).

16. David Caute, The *Great Fear: The Anti-Communist Purge Under Truman and Eisenhower* (New York: Simon & Schuster, 1978); Ted Morgan, *Reds: McCarthyism in Twentieth-Century America* (New York: Random House, 2004).

17. See Chap. 3 for references.

18. Alan Rohn, "How Much Did the Vietnam War Cost?" *Vietnam War*, https://thevietnamwar.info/how-much-vietnam-war-cost/ (accessed 24 October 2018).

19. Ibid.; Wikipedia, "Vietnam Casualties," https://en.wikipedia.org/wiki/Vietnam_War_casualties (accessed 24 October 2018).

20. Wikipedia, Vietnam Casualties," citing estimates by Guenter Lewy, the North Vietnamese government, and the British Medical Journal.

21. Hugh Wilford, *America's Great Game: The CIA's Secret Arabists and the Making of the Modern Middle East* (New York: Basic Books, 2013).

22. James Bill, *The Eagle and the Lion: The Tragedy of American-Iranian Relations* (New Haven: Yale University Press, 1988); David Crist, *The Twilight War: The Secret History of America's Thirty-Year Conflict with Iran* (New York: Penguin, 2012); Nicholas Cullather, *Secret History: The CIA's Classified Account of Its Operations in Guatemala, 1952–1954* (Stanford: Stanford University Press, 2006).

23. William Blum, *Killing Hope: US Military and CIA Interventions Since World War II* (London: Zed Books, 2003), ch. 10.

24. Ibid., ch. 29; Noel Maurer, *The Empire Trap: The Rise and Fall of U.S. Intervention to Protect American Property Overseas, 1893–2013* (Princeton: Princeton University Press, 2013), ch. 5.

25. Peter Wyden, *Bay of Pigs—The Untold Story* (New York: Simon and Schuster, 1979); Trumbull Higgins, *The Perfect Failure: Kennedy, Eisenhower, and the CIA at the Bay of Pigs* (New York: Norton, 2008).

26. Peter Kornbluh, *The Pinochet File: A Declassified Dossier on Atrocity and Accountability* (New York: New Press, 2003).

27. Select Committee to Study Governmental Operations (Church Committee), "Alleged Assassination Plots Involving Foreign Leaders" (Washington, D.C.: Government Printing Office, 1975), pp. 246–247 and 250–254.

28. Glenn Garvin, *Everybody Had His Own Gringo: The CIA and the Contras* (Washington, D.C.: Brassey's, 1992); International Court of Justice (IV)

(1986) "Case concerning Military and Paramilitary Activities in and Against Nicaragua (Nicaragua v. United States Of America), Vol. IV—Pleadings, Oral arguments, Documents," https://web.archive.org/web/20111202063640/http://www.icj-cij.org/docket/files/70/9619.pdf (accessed 25 October 2018).

29. Robert E. Venkus, *Raid On Qaddafi* (New York: St. Martin's Press, 1992); David B. Cohen and Chris J. Dolan, "Revisiting El Dorado Canyon: Terrorism, the Reagan Administration, and the 1986 Bombing of Libya," *White House Studies* 5, no. 2 (2005), pp. 153–175.

30. Dov Levin, "When the Great Power Gets A Vote: The Effects of Great Power Electoral Interventions on Election Results," International Studies Quarterly 60, No. 2, (2016), pp. 189–202.

31. National Public Radio, "Born in the USA: How America Created Iran's Nuclear Program," 18 September 2015, https://www.npr.org/sections/parallels/2015/09/18/440567960/born-in-the-u-s-a-how-america-created-irans-nuclear-program; Sam Roe, "An atomic threat made in America," *Chicago Tribune*, 28 January 2007.

32. Bill, *Eagle and the Lion*; Crist, *Twilight War*; Barbara Slavin, *Bitter Friends, Bosom Enemies: Iran, the US, and the Twisted Path to Confrontation* (New York: St. Martin's Press, 2007).

33. Pankaj Mishra, "The Enduring Fantasy of the Modernizing Autocrat," *New York Times*, 25 October 2018, https://www.nytimes.com/2018/10/25/opinion/autocrats-prince-mohammed-saudi-arabia.html (accessed 25 October 2018).

34. Ibid.

35. Karan Makiya, *Republic of Fear: The Politics of Modern Iraq*, rev. ed. (Berkeley and Los Angeles: University of California Press, 1998); Bryan R. Gibson, *Sold Out? US Foreign Policy, Iraq, the Kurds, and the Cold War* (London: Palgrave Macmillan, 2015); Andrew Cockburn, Saddam Hussein: An American Obsession (London: Verso, 2002).

36. Thomas Harding, "Libya: secret documents link Tony Blair to Gaddafi son Saif al-Islam and his suspect thesis," *Telegraph*, 5 September 2011, https://www.telegraph.co.uk/news/worldnews/africaandindianocean/libya/8740464/Libya-secret-documents-link-Tony-Blair-to-Gaddafi-son-Saif-al-Islam-and-his-suspect-thesis.htm; Stuart Hughes, "LSE criticised for links with Gaddafi regime in Libya," BBC, 30 November 2011, https://www.bbc.co.uk/news/education-15966132; Wikipedia, "London School of Economics Gaddafi links," 20 June 2018, https://en.wikipedia.org/wiki/London_School_of_Economics_Gaddafi_links (all accessed 26 October 2018).

37. Max Fisher, "The Only Remaining Online Copy of Vogue's Asma al-Assad Profile," *Atlantic*, 3 January 2012, https://www.theatlantic.com/international/archive/2012/01/the-only-remaining-online-copy-of-vogues-asma-al-assad-profile/250753/ (accessed 26 October 2018); Mishra, "Enduring Fantasy of the Modernizing Autocrat."

38. Mishra, "Enduring Fantasy of the Modernizing Autocrat."

39. Hannah Summers, "Yemen on brink of 'world's worst famine in 100 years' if war continues," *Guardian*, 15 October 2018, https://www.theguardian.com/global-development/2018/oct/15/yemen-on-brink-worst-famine-100-years-un (accessed 26 October 2018).

40. BBC, "Jamal Khashoggi: All you need to know about Saudi journalist's death," 25 October 2018, https://www.bbc.co.uk/news/world-europe-45812399 (accessed 25 October 2018); Julian E. Barnes, "C.I.A. Concludes That Saudi Crown Prince Ordered Khashoggi Killed," *New York Times*, 16 November 2018, https://www.nytimes.com/2018/11/16/us/politics/cia-saudi-crown-prince-khashoggi.html (accessed 18 November 2018).

41. Jon Frapppier, "Above the Law: Violations of International Law by the U.S. Government from Truman to Reagan," *Crime and Social Justice*, No. 21/22 (1984), pp. 1–36.

42. Mary Ellen O'Connell, *The Power and Purpose of International Law* (Oxford: Oxford University Press, 2008); Alfred W. McCoy, "You Must Follow International Law (Unless You're America)," *Nation*, 24 February 2015, https://www.thenation.com/article/you-must-follow-international-law-unless-youre-america/ (accessed 26 October 2018).

43. McCoy, "You Must Follow International Law"; Aziz Z. Huq, "Extraordinary Rendition and the Wages of Hypocrisy," *World Policy Journal* 23, no. 1 (2006), pp. 25–35.

44. "Transcript of Testimony of George J. Tenet, Updated April 14, 2004," *Wall Street Journal*, 29 October 2018, https://www.wsj.com/articles/SB108195905693082548 (accessed 29 October 2018); McCoy, "You Must Follow International Law."

45. Hina Shamsi, "Death Without Due Process," American Civil Liberties Union, 3 March 2014, https://www.aclu.org/blog/national-security/targeted-killing/death-without-due-process (accessed 23 February 2019); Ben Jones, "Despite Obama's New Executive Order, U.S. Drone Policy May Still Violate International Law," *Washington Post*, 10 July 2016, https://www.washingtonpost.com/news/monkey-cage/wp/2016/07/07/

obamas-new-executive-order-on-drones-means-the-u-s-may-still-violate-international-law/?noredirect=on&utm_term=.c5e8a3ea847d (accessed 29 October 2018); Jeremy Scahill, *The Assassination Complex: Inside the Government's Secret Drone Warfare Program* (New York: Simon & Schuster, 2016).

46. Anna Goppel, *Killing Terrorists. A Moral and Legal Analysis* (Berlin: De Gruyter), pp. 2–13; Clive Stafford Smith, "Who's getting killed today? Terror, Tuesday, the US Disposition Matrix and a modern history of state-sponsored assassination," *Times Literary Supplement*, 30 June 2017, pp. 3–5.

47. American Society of International Law, "International Law and the Trump Administration: An Online Series," 2018, https://www.asil.org/trump; Gholamali Khoshroo, "Trump's sanctions against Iran are a clear breach of international law," 8 August 2018, https://www.theguardian.com/commentisfree/2018/aug/08/donald-trump-sanctions-iran-international-law; Juliam Black, "Trump Administration's Family Separation Policy Violates International Law." INTLWGRRLS, 8 June 2018, https://ilg2.org/2018/06/10/trump-administrations-family-separation-policy-violates-international-law/ (all accessed 29 October 2018).

48. Edward Hunt, "UN: US Attack on Syrian Civilians Violated International Law," *Lobe Log*, 13 March 2018, https://lobelog.com/un-us-attack-on-syrian-civilians-violated-international-law/ (accessed 28 October 2018).

49. Anne Gearan, Paul Sonne and Carol Morello, "U.S. to withdraw from nuclear arms control treaty with Russia, raising fears of a new arms race," *Washington Post*, 1 February 2019, https://www.washingtonpost.com/world/national-security/us-to-withdraw-from-nuclear-arms-control-treaty-with-russia-says-russian-violations-render-the-cold-war-agreement-moot/2019/02/01/84dc0db6-261f-11e9-ad53-824486280311_story.html?utm_term=.e972dd0a4711 (accessed 23 February 2019).

50. Andrew Roth, "Ditching nuclear arms treaty would be dangerous step, Russia warns US," *Guardian*, 21 October, https://www.theguardian.com/world/2018/oct/21/cold-war-weapons-treaty-inf-russia-us-donald-trump; Mikhail Gorbachev, "Mikhail Gorbachev: A New Nuclear Arms Race Has Begun," *New York Times*, 25 October 2018, https://www.nytimes.com/2018/10/25/opinion/mikhail-gorbachev-inf-treaty-trump-nuclear-arms.html (both accessed 25 October 2018).

51. Ibid.

52. Michael Birnbaum and Paul Sonne, "Trump's ambassador to NATO sets off diplomatic incident with a nuclear edge," *Washington Post*, 2 October 2018, https://www.washingtonpost.com/ (accessed 25 October 2018).
53. Gorbachev, "Mikhail Gorbachev."
54. Carl Schmitt, *Political Theology* (Chicago: University of Chicago Press, 2005 [1922]), p. 45.

7

The National Interest

Realists foreground the national interest as the benchmark for intelligent foreign policy. They are certainly correct in thinking that there should be some general principles in terms of which policy is formulated and against which the goals it seeks and the means used to achieve them can be evaluated. In their absence policies are more likely to be formulated from a short-term perspective, in response to inappropriate criteria like organizational concerns and special interests, and more likely to be implemented in ways that have the potential to embarrass the country.

This said, the concept of the national interest is a deeply problematic one. Many realists think they know what it is and support or criticize policies on this basis. Their judgments are arbitrary because there is no objective way of formulating the national interest. Any conception of it inevitably—and quite properly—reflects the values and goals of those proposing it. As people differ in their values and goals, at best, their conceptions of the national interest are logical expressions of their commitments and may or may not constitute realistic guidelines for policy. Given the often pronounced differences among people, there will be contrasting understandings of the national interest. In practice these formulations constitute rationalizations to advance and defend particular political

© The Author(s) 2020
R. N. Lebow, *A Democratic Foreign Policy*,
https://doi.org/10.1007/978-3-030-21519-4_7

projects. If we define America as an immigrant nation whose openness to and assimilation of hard-working and upwardly mobile newcomers is the primary source of national strength and pride, we are encouraged to construct the national interest in a manner supportive of continuing immigration. If we attribute American success to the values and practices of the white Northern-European stock that constituted a majority of the population from the settlement until quite recently, we will define the national interest very differently and probably attempt to restrict immigration and citizenship.

As the above example suggests, formulations of the national interest are inward looking. People are primarily concerned with their own life worlds and values and want the country to reflect and support them. They are more alert and attentive to perceived domestic threats than foreign ones and want their elected representatives to address these threats. This is not to suggest that there are no foreign threats, and very occasionally they are grave enough to warrant priority. The last time this occurred in the US was before and during World War II, where the growing power of the German-Italian-Japanese axis threatened the territorial status quo on a worldwide basis, the survival of democratic governments in Europe, and if successful, the independence of the US. Cold Warriors made similar claims from 1947 until the collapse of the Soviet Union in 1991.

Many realists stand the national interest on its head when they proclaim that foreign or security interests are paramount and have first claim on our attention and resources. Many further assert, again without merit, that the national interest should be above party politics. Some, like former Ambassador George F. Kennan, claim that its formulation should be left in the hands of professionals.[1] This is a conceptual error because, the rarest and gravest security threats aside, the national interest is properly about our domestic values and goals. Domestic concerns override foreign ones, and foreign policy should respond to these goals, not the other way around. It is also enormously arrogant because it suggests some elite should have the rights to determine our foreign policy goals and implement them—often behind closed doors. Finally, it is unacceptable because it prompts policies and resource allocations that are for the most part inimical to the goals most Americans seek.

The Cold War, the so-called War on Terror, and current hysteria about China illustrate these problems all too well. They allowed foreign and defense policy to be hijacked by a group of people and industries who stood to profit politically or economically from acute conflict and the threat of war it raised. When they were able to impose their definition of the national interest on the country, opposition to it came close to being branded as treason, and in the McCarthy era certainly was. Foregrounding security and exaggerating the threat posed by the Soviet Union during the Cold War, Iraq in its aftermath, and today, terrorism, and China, is to make a claim for directing resources away from social and infrastructure spending and toward the military and security establishment. Formulations of the national interest are not arcane statements of interest only to scholars and specialists in foreign policy; they have profound practical implications for how much we pay in taxes and where our tax dollars go.

Threat assessments within and outside the government are critical for resource allocation. During the Cold War, and arguably even more now, non-profit organizations, many of them supported by defense contractors or right-wing sources, produced alarming threat assessments. They also sponsored speakers to advocate their point of view and lobbied Congress and other influential people to gain support for defense spending. The same process occurs within government. When I was a scholar-in-residence in the Central Intelligence Agency in the Carter administration, I observed first-hand how strategic assessments of the Soviet Union were prepared. They invariably incorporated worst-case analyses (e.g., everything would go right for them and badly for us when it came to weapons, trajectories, warheads). Not surprisingly, methods and analyses of this kind greatly exaggerated the Soviet threat. The military in turn flogged these estimates behind closed doors in the House of Representatives to shake loose the sugar plums they desired from the congressional budget tree.[2] After the Cold War it became evident that the Soviet Union had done the same.[3]

Any progressive Democratic government needs to wrest control of threat assessments from those with parochial interests in propagating self-serving formulations. They need to encourage a meaningful discussion about the national interest. Toward this end political leaders and those who advise them must give some serious thought themselves to what they think constitutes the national interest. This is important for three reasons.

First, as noted, to stimulate public debate. Debate is an essential requirement of democracy, but debate about the national interest needs an important catalyst. In recent years the most active propagators of it have been white nationalists on the Internet. Their growing influence needs to be offset, if not negated, and this is only possible by open, tolerant discussion in the mainstream print, television, and social media.

Second, policymakers and their advisors need to free themselves from the glib, ill-considered, conceptually and empirically questionable assumptions of the national security establishment. It is the dominant discourse and widely shared across the political spectrum. George H. W. Bush, Bill Clinton, George Bush, Hilary Clinton, and Barrack Obama all operated in terms of its assumptions. Hilary Clinton is a true believer in American hegemony, big military budgets, and drop-of-the-hat military interventions. George Bush and Obama were largely ignorant of foreign and defense policy when they assumed office and were socialized into thinking and acting in terms of the assumptions and goal of the national security establishment. There is a striking parallel here to Lyndon Johnson, who felt in his gut that intervention in Vietnam was not in his or the country's interest but lacked the self-confidence to oppose the men who had considerable foreign policy experience and appeared to have won the Cuban missile crisis. The next Democratic president—and especially one committed to domestic reform—must not be captured, as his predecessors were, by the national security establishment.

Finally, leaders and their advisors must stimulate public debate to build support for policies at odds with traditional ones. Starving the military beast—even putting it on a mild diet—will meet enormous opposition from large corporations and smaller businesses who drank at the Pentagon and Homeland Security's troughs. They and their congressional allies and right-wing think tanks and journalists will produce papers, talking points, speeches and advertisements, and engage in extensive lobbying to show how the country's security will suffer if these budgets are cut. Their campaigns for defense spending will rival the conservative Republican and healthcare industry's assault on the Patient Protection and Affordable Care Act (Obamacare). Cuts in the military and Homeland Security budgets will need a compelling rationale and it will inevitably rest on a different set of assumptions than those accepted by those who push for even more military spending. People accept and reject arguments largely on the basis of their assumptions and the people making them. So any move to cut military spending must be preceded by an attempt to educate the electorate not only about the costs and dangers of a military the size of ours but about ways of looking at our country and the world that make them receptive to the idea of these budget cuts.

Just how do we think about the national interest? As I noted there is no "correct" formulation of the national interest, only ones consistent with the values and goals of those who construct them. So the first step is to think about our values and goals. What kind of country do we want? How do we preserve and nurture what we think good about it? What foreign threats are there to these values and goals, and how do we best protect ourselves against them? Formulations of the national interest and policies intended to serve it must meet the additional test of being practical. They must be politically feasible at home and have some reasonable chance of success abroad. For this latter reason, any formulation of the national interest must be conscious and respectful of the interests of other nations. It must be made compatible as far as possible with those with whom we have close associations. It should also take into account the interests of other states, even adversaries with whom it is better to live in peace.

Values

My starting point is democracy because it is a value in its own right and enables most, if not all, of the other values in my list. Democracy is notoriously hard to define but certainly includes a set of institutions and procedures (e.g., free and frequent elections, independent judiciary, trial by jury, free press, and federalism), and various norms that sustain them. The latter are critical because some authoritarian regimes, the Soviet Union for one, had all the trappings of democracy, including a written constitution, elections, judiciary, federalism, but these documents and institutions were a public relations façade. Democratic institutions only serve their intended ends when the norms on which they rest are internalized and honored by government officials and the wider citizenry. We accordingly need to protect and foster these norms, but this is not the task of government.

Bad leaders and corrupt officials, however, can do much to undermine them, as many of us believe the current president is doing.

The survival of democracy at home is very much connected to the success of democracy abroad. This linkage, as previously noted, was recognized in the Atlantic Charter and, in theory, became a central goal of postwar American foreign policy. In practice, it was honored more in the breech as successive administrations, Democratic and Republican alike, supported right-wing dictatorships around the world and intervened, directly or indirectly, to prevent or overthrow left-leaning governments. Early postwar efforts to democratize Germany and Japan were, by contrast, notable successes even if de-Nazification was halted and former Nazis were allowed to occupy prominent positions in politics, the judiciary, and business. American efforts fared less well in Italy because Washington was willing to ally itself openly with the Christian Democrats because they opposed communism.

Despite their mixed postwar record, American leaders and most members of the national security establishment took for granted that a primary American interest was the preservation of democracy in Western Europe. Successive presidents supported the European project as a means toward this end and after the Cold War and collapse of the Soviet Union encouraged democratization in Eastern Europe and successor states to the USSR. Americans belatedly came to the recognition that democracy was also important all along the Pacific Rim and supported its emergence consolidation in South Korea, Taiwan, and Southeast Asia.

The reasons for this support are practical as well as ideological. America benefits in numerous ways for a world in which other powerful states are also democracies. Such states, by definition, share more in common with America than their non-democratic *D*emocratic counterparts. These common interests make them more likely to adopt similar positions on a range of political, economic, security, and humanitarian issues. This in turn facilitates collaboration with them. Democracies encourage the exchange of people and ideas, build respect and tolerance across borders, and reduce or eliminate the possibility of war between and among such states. These interactions create a sense of shared destiny and community and predisposition to come to one another's aid. Friends count in international relations and democratic states are our closest friends.

For all of these reasons it was terribly short-sighted of Cold War administrations to spurn Democratic movements and leaders in favor of right-wing, authoritarian regimes. The argument in favor one of so-called *Realpolitk* maintains that ethics are irrelevant to foreign policy, even a hindrance, and that their support of these unpalatable regimes was necessary during the Cold War to oppose communism. Politicians like Henry Kissinger and scholars like John Gaddis prefigured Donald Trump in their desire to collaborate with the Soviet Union against Europeans. They were keen to recognize and sustain Soviet domination of Eastern Europe and suppression of dissent throughout the region because they believed that a condominium with the Soviet Union was in America's best interest.[4]

This is a real irony here. We gave up the real benefits of supporting democracy for the putative benefits of supporting dictatorships and these expected benefits rarely, if ever, materialized. Most authoritarian regimes took American economic and military aid, often using the latter against their own citizens. Some behaved in aggressive ways—Taiwan vis-à-vis China in the 1950s, Turkey in Cyprus in the 1960s and 1970s, Pakistan more recently in its support of terrorists; actions directly inimical to American interests. None of these countries were really needed to check the Soviet Union. The US gave up the high ground by supporting these regimes and got little to nothing in return. Egypt is a quintessential example. In 1973 Nixon and Kissinger sought successfully to separate it from its reliance on the Soviet Union and encouraged Sadat and his successors to become dependent on American aid. Under the dictator Hosni Mubarak, in power from 1981 to 2011, a high percentage of the $2 billion yearly aid from the US went directly into private pockets. Mubarak adhered to the Camp David accords but fostered a culture of vicious anti-Semitism, looked the other way when fundamentalists attacked Christian Copts, used violence and mass terror against his domestic opponents. He was totally unresponsive to American requests for domestic reform.[5]

The Trump administration has marched double-time away from support for democracy in favor of dictators. The president is clearly drawn to strong men for many reasons, but the national interest does not figure among them.[6] He has also distanced himself from democratic leaders, saying nasty and often factually incorrect things about them and the European Union. Some of his closest advisors and former advisors are hand-in-glove with the Alt Right and European nationalists, many of them overtly racist and neo-Nazi, who seek to destroy the EU by having their countries secede. This alignment is directly contrary to the national interest.

The US should be supportive of democracy everywhere, and regional projects that attempt to transcend historical rivalries encourage trade and deal collectively with security and other issues like immigration. It should not sacrifice these commitments for the sake of imagined gains. The past 70 years had demonstrated that the benefits of supporting right-wing dictatorships are entirely illusory. They are also costly, as the US generally becomes the enemy of successor regimes that overthrow dictators with whom it was closely associated. The conflict with Iran is arguably entirely attributable to this phenomenon.

Support for democracy prompts the corollary of opposition to racism and extreme nationalism abroad. This is important for foreign and domestic reasons. Regimes of this kind are more likely to seek closer ties with one another and with Vladimir Putin of Russia, as have Hungary's Orban, the Five Star Movement in Italy, Erdogan in Turkey, and Marine Le Pen's Front National in France. Their collective goal is to weaken democracy everywhere and escape, at home and abroad, from the norms and constraints it imposes. These movements and governments are increasingly linked and mutually supportive. The Alt Right has close ties to racist groups in Europe; Nigel Farage of Britain is a frequent visitor to the US, and Steve Bannon goes to Europe in efforts to create a common front of right-wing nationalist groups.[7]

At home, the Alt Right and related white nationalist and racist groups threaten serious disruption in the coded or even open calls—for violence against Jews, Muslims, and immigrants. In 2018, in the aftermath of the shootings at Pittsburgh's Tree of Life Synagogue, the Anti-Defamation League reported that anti-Semitic incidents had risen in the previous nine months by a whopping 60 percent.[8] Dutch Prime Minister Mark Rutte compared his country to "a fragile vase" held by 17 million ordinary and exceptional citizens who "do not only want a good life for themselves and those around them, but also want to contribute to the happiness of others." Fighting over the vase or gripping it too tight threatens to break. This is the danger posed by violence and anti-Democratic yearnings of the right and some evangelicals.[9]

Equality: I consider equality another fundamental American value. It includes equality before the law, equal access to education, employment, and opportunities for upward mobility. America has always been the land of opportunity and proud of it. Much progress has been made in removing barriers to equality for Catholics, Jews, African-Americans, other minorities, and women, but here too the Trump administration has done its best to turn back the clock. It has sought to undermine gender equality, deny healthcare to poor people or those with preexisting conditions, supported measures that unfairly keep people—many of them poor or minorities—from voting, limit the rights of accused to counsel and fair trials, and reduce enforcement of laws intended to promote racial equality. His speeches appear to embrace, and have certainly encouraged, neo-Nazis, white supremacists, and other racists responsible for violence against Blacks, Muslims, Jews, and immigrants. He wants fewer immigrants from "shithole" countries and more from places like Norway.[10] Senator Lindsey Graham, to whom Trump made this remark, had the courage and presence of mind to reply; "Time out. … A lot of us come from shitholes."[11]

The competing principal of justice to equality is fairness. Its core claim is that those who contribute the most to society should get the most rewards. It was the traditional justification for elitist hierarchies in the premodern era. Equality is far and away the preferred principle of justice in America.[12] Since the 1970s surveys and experiments have been carried out in diverse domains (e.g., business, pensions, healthcare), with individuals and small groups, and with people of different gender, age, class, and nationalities. They indicate that the triumph of the principle of equality is far from total. Americans opt for equality in making certain kinds of distributions, but for fairness (generally called equity by experimenters) in making others.[13] Depending on what is at stake, they may go with a different principle. An everyday example is a group of friends paying the bill in restaurants. They generally opt for tab splitting, but not if there is big variation in what people have consumed.

A number of other studies have people make society-wide rather than individual distributions. When asked if "the fairest way of distributing wealth and income would be to give everyone an equal share," about one-third of Americans concur. This percentage drops markedly when people are presented with a statement to the effect that "under a fair economic system people with more ability would earn higher salaries."[14] On the whole Americans consider fairness the most applicable principle to income distribution. However, they also think equality germane because they favor income distributions less unequal than they are in practice.[15] Occupation turns out to be the single most important variable; people favor greater rewards for those in high-status professions.[16] However, a 2016 Gallup poll found that 63 percent of Americans think that rich Americans pay too little in taxes, down from a high of 77 percent in the 1990s.[17]

The 2016 presidential election was very revealing with respect to equality and fairness. Hilary Clinton couched and defended most of her campaign promises in terms of equality and spoke to and about people who have been traditionally at a disadvantage: African-Americans, other minorities, women, immigrants, and the gay community. Donald Trump repeatedly deployed the language of fairness with respect to domestic and foreign policy. His campaign slogan "Make America Great Again" when elaborated on the campaign trail meant restoration of the white, male, Protestant hierarchy at home, on the grounds that they made the country great, and restoration of America's position as top dog on the world stage.[18]

Trade-offs among these principles of justice are always possible but difficult to make and defend politically, and some people or groups are left unhappy. Trump and Republicans more generally favor fairness in domestic and foreign affairs. They support "tax reform," a codeword for reducing taxes for the wealthy, which increases inequality in income distribution. Democrats are more likely to support higher taxes for the wealthy and use some of this income for the redistribution of wealth through social programs. This is the major difference between the two parties and pits fairness against equality.

Equality and fairness also have implications for foreign policy. Trump's understanding of "Make American Great Again" is a more extreme version of the national security establishment's assertion of hegemony. Trump envisages America as close to a world dictator whom others should obey and somehow define their interests in ways that do not clash with ours. It is even more unattainable and dangerous that the pursuit of hegemony. Both goals rest on the principle of fairness, although neither is a "fair" enactment of that principle. Supporters of hegemony claim that the US makes sacrifices in order to provide and sustain security and economic wellbeing to the rest of the world. It is a self-proclaimed Atlas holding up the globe. In practice, I have shown, it is nothing close to a hegemon, its interventions are often against the interest of global security, and its economic policies are exploitative.

The principle of fairness has always been central to international affairs. Great powers—a status that achieved something of legal recognition at the 1815 Congress of Vienna—receive honor and special privileges in return for assuming the responsibility of maintaining international society and its ordering principles.[19] The United Nations, established in 1945, enshrined this principle in its Charter with the creation of the Security Council. Its permanent members, five states deemed to be great powers, were given responsibility for the security of the world. Many subsequent international organizations, like the Group of Five, established in 1970, continue this principle. The Group of Five was later expanded to seven and eight, to include the largest economies of the world, countries that assumed responsibility for the maintenance of economic order.[20] Equality has also become increasingly important in international relations. The General Assembly of the United Nations includes all members and each has one vote. Some nations want the Security Council to be enlarged to include developing nations and nations of the southern hemisphere. The Group of Five evolved and in the current century has come to describe the five largest emerging economies of the world: Brazil, China, India, Mexico, and South Africa.[21]

In practice, hierarchy and even more so the imposition of a more rigid hierarchy with the US at the top have become increasingly indefensible. International hierarchy is widely regarded as an atavism: an attitude and structure from the past that is long past its use-by date. Even those countries like Brazil, Japan, India, and Germany, who seek permanent seats on the Security Council, advance their claims for hierarchy—superior status and privileges vis-à-vis their neighbors—in the language of equality.[22] The US needs to follow suit in lieu of its until-now blatant use of the language of hierarchy. American proponents of hegemony claim that it is widely valued and welcomed by others. This is another self-propagated myth. Others put up with, work around, attempt to finesse, or attempt to exploit American power for their parochial ends. The only people happy with American claims of hegemony are dictators who receive billions in US aid and do little to nothing in return.

The language of leadership is more than a rhetorical matter. It reflects beliefs about how the world should be ordered and run. I will return to this question at the end of the chapter, when I take up the question of America's proper role in the world. I make the case for a more multilateral approach and one in which key security and economic responsibilities are more diffused among major and even minor actors. Paradoxically, the US, I contend, will end up wielding more influence this way, although influence is limited to projects for which there is wide support.

Immigration: Openness to newcomers is another time-honored American value, although it has been controversial since the mid-nineteenth century. The nativists know-nothings of the 1850s felt threatened by Irish Catholic newcomers. The populists of the 1890s mobilized political support from the rural poor on the basis of tirades against Blacks and Jews. Immigration laws were put into place in the Johnson-Reed Act of 1924 that sought to exclude Asians and limit immigration of so-called inferior racial types of southern and eastern Europe. The right wing continues this tradition with Muslims, Central and South Americans, and anyone with a dark skin is the focus of its irrational hostility. It finds validation in Donald Trump's promises to build a wall along the Mexican border, ban visits and immigration from certain Muslim countries, and do away with the constitutional guarantee of birthright citizenship.

The current swing against immigration defies economic logic, as it does in Britain and countries of Eastern Europe where it has become increasingly important, if not the hottest political issue. In the US and Europe people greatly exaggerate the percentage of the immigrant population and falsely believe that immigrants take jobs from native workers. Trump and other nativists encourage them to believe—falsely again—that immigrants are disproportionately responsible for crimes.[23]

Immigration is a longstanding American practice, and contrary to the claims of Trump and nativists it is what has made America great. Immigrants have swelled the population over the centuries and made the US and Canada different from most of Europe and Japan, where aging and declining populations do not bode well for their economic future. Immigrants have not only provided a good percentage of the American labor force over the last several centuries, they have contributed in major ways to the country's economic, scientific, medical, and cultural development. Immigration is the national rite of passage and efforts to stem it, or limit it to those with white skin, challenge a fundamental value of America. Trump's opposition to immigration became the centerpiece of his appeal to nativist voters. He promised a wall with Mexico to stop immigrants from crossing. His early efforts to ban immigrants from certain Muslim countries by executive order was initially overturned by the federal courts and had to be reformulated and narrowed to make it acceptable.[24] After the 2018 midterm elections, Trump announced new rules that assume his authority to deny asylum to virtually any migrant who crosses the American border.[25]

The Trump administration's measures against immigrants, most of them of questionable legality, must be reversed. Here too, a responsible administration needs to strike a balance between our tradition as an immigrant country and the current wave of popular opposition to immigration. Much of this opposition is a product of the earlier economic recession and fake news that exaggerates numbers of immigrants and falsely claims that they take jobs from Americans, and are more responsible for crimes and terrorism. The public needs to be educated about the facts, especially about the economic benefits of immigration, but also reassured that immigrants and asylees will be properly vetted.

The US has long supported free trade and it has been in the American interest. So too are the many bi- and multilateral agreements that facilitate trade and investment and the flow of ideas and people. Trump not only opposes free trade but has pulled out of existing agreements, including NAFTA (North American Free Trade Agreement) that governs relations with our closest neighbors, Mexico and Canada. It was renegotiated, as was a separate agreement with Mexico, and Trump was all but prevented by his advisors from canceling KORUS (US-South Korea Free Trade Agreement), regarded as essential for economic, political, and security reasons.[26] Returning from the G-20 summit in Hamburg in July 2017, Trump edited a speech and inserted the words: "Trade is bad."[27] In effect, Trump and his economic nationalist advisors are hostile to any country that has a favorable trade balance with America. South Korea was a target and China even more so.[28]

The Trump-initiated trade war with China seriously affected the world economy and was damaging to American consumers and many American businesses, especially those who rely on overseas production.[29] The Chinese imposed tariffs on American goods, Trump imposed more tariffs on China, and they retaliated in turn. We are at the early stages of this conflict as I write, but its effects are already being felt in the agricultural sector. China has all but stopped buying soybeans from the US—purchases were down by 94 percent in 2018—and those soybeans harvested are being left to rot in silos in the Middle West.[30] The Trump administration has had to provide subsidies to farmers, which adds to the deficit, and, ironically, this is covered by foreign borrowing, principally from China.

In January 2017, Trump pulled the US out of the Trans-Pacific Partnership, negotiated by previous administration. Trade agreements and rule-setting now go on in the Pacific without US participation or influence. Eleven Pacific countries have joined the Comprehensive and Progressive Agreement for Tran-Pacific Partnership; the most recent member is Australia. The most immediate impact for the US is selling products of all kinds to Japan as members of the partnership alone receive tariff cuts. In the longer term, US intellectual property rights will suffer. Rules that American pharmaceutical companies lobbied heavily for, and with success, have now been dropped. Something similar is likely to happen in Europe, where Google, Facebook, and other IT companies benefit greatly from US clout in rule making.[31]

International law: As noted in the previous chapter, Republican and Democratic administrations throughout the twentieth century have declared their support for international law and defined this commitment as central to American security and economic interests. They have also routinely violated international law and failed to sign on to important treaties like the international criminal court and the Paris climate accord. The US appears to want its cake and eat it too. It routinely condemns states for violating international law as it pertains to trade, money laundering, human rights, intellectual property, and other domains. Yet, successive administrations have felt free to violate international law as it suits their convenience. In earlier chapters I highlighted some of the most important of these violations. This duplicity is not lost on foreign audiences and does nothing to enhance international law or respect for the US.

American violations of international law are for the most part an abuse of its power. Successive administrations since Ronald Reagan have routinely chosen to violate international law or not sign on to treaties when they think it will limit their freedom in any way. The US opposed the landmines treaty, for example, because it could only think of the benefits of its own munitions of this kind planted along the Demilitarized Zone (DMZ) in Korea. It did the same with the International Criminal Court of Justice, not wanting it to have any possible jurisdiction over American citizens. If everyone acted this way, there would be no international law and everyone would be poorer and more insecure. On the whole, the US, like other democracies, would be better off adhering to the law, not seeking exceptions, often by fiat, and acting to make international law more robust. Most other democracies act accordingly.

Finally, we come to the question of truth. There is an old adage that a diplomat is an honest man who lies for his country. Most diplomats would reject this characterization outright. They depend very much on their reputation and that of their country's for telling the truth—even when it is uncomfortable. To be sure, they do their best to soften uncomfortable truths and to put the best spin on all events, statements, and policies. The US has increasingly played fast and loose with the truth in its public statements and diplomacy. This does not speak well of the country and undermines its influence—once again in pursuit of often ill-considered short-term interests.

President Trump is not known for his commitment to the truth. In the course of his first 650 days in office, that is, up to October 2018, he had made more than 6400 false or misleading claims.[32] This is an average of 30 whoppers a day! Most of these "misstatements" pertained to domestic affairs, but not his numerous tweets and speeches during the 2018 off-year election campaign about an alleged caravan of Central Americans snaking its way through Mexico where Democrats would welcome them at the American border.[33] He ordered units of the Army to reinforce the border and to shoot illegal immigrants, if necessary—a promise the Army not so quietly made known was contrary to its rules of engagement.[34] Trump's fictions play well with a certain segment of the electorate but not at all with foreign governments and opinion. Trump's ill-considered tweets, about such matters as dumping NATO, attacking North Korea, and support for dictators around the world give the US a reputation for unilateral behavior, often at odds with existing laws and norms, as well as unreliability and lack of predictability. None of these perceptions enhance American influence but rather diminish it.

Trump's behavior is extreme in this and other ways but is useful for this reason in highlighting the differences between the kinds of behavior that is in the country's interest and that which is distinctly opposed. It is not enough for a future president to avoid the excesses of Trump and return to the patterned behavior of the national security establishment. He or she must depart from their practices as well and reorient American foreign policy in a more fundamental manner. In the conclusion I will suggests some of the ways in which this might be done.

Threats

Threats like values are subjective in nature. Our values and the projects to which they support or give rise determine what we consider a threat. The Alt Right and Trump regard immigrants as a threat because they are seen to challenge white Protestant dominance in America. So too is free trade because they frame economics in old-style mercantilist terms where countries compete for trade and markets, a notion no respected economist would accept. For libertarians and isolationists alliances and other foreign entanglements are anathema because they can drag the US into wars that are contrary to the national interest. Libertarians also oppose all kinds of government programs because they are seen as wasteful and undue interference in the freedoms of citizens. Members of the national security establishment favor an active, if not interventionist, foreign policy. This is because they frame threats to the US largely in terms of security and see them as emanating from foreign actors. At present they are focused on Russia and China.

Tragedy teaches us that great powers are their own worst enemies. I have tried to document the wisdom of this insight in the course of the book. Throughout the Cold War the US has unquestionably behaved this way. It expended a lot of blood and treasure in the Vietnam War and even more in maintaining its vast nuclear and conventional land, sea, and air-based arsenals. Defenders of this profligacy insist this war was necessary to protect against the Soviet Union, and further contend that Reagan's arms build-up, especially his Strategic Defense Initiative (Star Wars) brought that conflict to an end. There is no evidence in support of these claims.[35] They can be dismissed as early and successful examples of fake news.

Russia and China: American interests conflict with those of both countries in some important respects. However, they also coincide and do so more fundamentally than they diverge. Both countries are just as keen to avoid any kind of continental war or military contest with the US as Washington is *are* with them. The US, Russia, and China share many economic interests. Russia is a net exporter of energy and raw materials to the West, especially to Western Europe. China trades with the world, and US-China trade in 2017 amounted to $636 billion. The US trade deficit with China was $375 billion because US exports to China were only $130 billion while imports from China were $506 billion. From America, China imported $16 billion in commercial aircraft, $12 billion in soybeans, and $10 billion in autos.[36] China is also the largest creditor of the US; in 2017 the Treasury estimated that it held at least $1.2 trillion of US debt. It is in everyone's interest to maintain and even expand these relationships.[37]

I do not have space to address the various substantive disputes the US has with these nations. With regard to Russia, Americans worry about Putin's commitments to make it once again a great power and a country that must be listened to on a range of international issues. Some believe that his use of force in the "near abroad," including Ukraine, might presage further use of force in the Baltic. Others worry more about China, its aggressiveness regarding islets disputed with Vietnam, the Philippines, and Japan, and its growing military capability. This is not the place to discuss Russian and Chinese ambitions other than to say it is always difficult to fathom the motives of foreign actors but very easy to project one's fear on to them. It is also true that countries rarely speak in single voices; there are generally multiple voices with different takes on foreign affairs that compete for influence. What I will speak to are appropriate ways of responding to countries that may be envisaged as adversaries, but with whom there are powerful reasons to work out some kind of modus vivendi.

One of my goals in the chapters on deterrence and China was to show how overreliance on this coercive strategy during the Cold War made conflict more likely and to argue it was having the same effect today with regard to China. Deterrence prompts target states to apply worst-case analysis to the motives of their adversary, almost invariably exaggerating their evil intentions and plans. Leaders who are targets of deterrence do not want to appear weak lest they be taken advantage of by their adversary. They may act in ways that unintentionally appear to confirm worst-case analysis. Those advocating military build-ups and deterrence and compellence are generally oversensitive to threats and insufficiently attentive—or even blind—to their costs.

The arms race was largely initiated and sustained by the US, which consistently outspent the Soviet Union. There is no evidence that the Soviet Union ever considered attacking the US or its allies. Both sides prepared for war and frequently updated their war plans but did so in large part because they feared the intentions of the other.[38] The "security dilemma" drove the arms race far more than the search for unilateral advantage, although that too played a part. What is indisputable is that leaders on both sides were fearful of any kind of a war between them. As the Cuban missile crisis indicated, they were prepared to back down at considerable cost to themselves to preserve the peace.

The military lessons of the Cold War are clear but political, and military leaders seem not to have learned them. They have defined Russia and China as threats and are responding to them the same way they did to the Soviet Union. As noted earlier, deterrence has the potential to be provocative and to make more, rather than less, likely the kinds of challenges it seeks to prevent. This is precisely what happened in the Cold War, where I offered the Berlin and Cuban missile crises as examples. Deterrence needs to be practiced in the most moderate way, with a careful eye out for the kinds of deployments and associated rhetoric that are more likely to provoke than restrain. It needs to be yoked to strategies of reassurance that seek to reduce perception of hostile intent and those of diplomacy that attempt to resolve or finesse substantive differences between would-be adversaries.

Donald Trump withdrew from the 1988 Soviet-American treaty eliminating intermediate and short-range missiles from Europe. The treaty was a giant step in the reassurance and ending of the Cold War. Withdrawal has the potential to trigger a new arms race and encourage the kind of worst-case analysis that led to Cold War crises. Mikhail Gorbachev, who signed the treaty for the Soviet Union, insists that whatever compliance problems there are can be overcome through diplomacy and should be given the dangers that will certainly arise for any unilateral exit from an arms control treaty. It will threaten the arms control regime in general and stimulate further militarization of international affairs.[39] Trump's successor must find a way of managing relations with Russia and of preserving arms control agreements that promote transparency and restraint.

Terrorism: American media pundits and some academics asserted that we lived in a different world after the terror attacks of 9/11. To the extent this is true; the US has made it so. The terrorist attacks were emotionally shocking, in large part because of the targets selected and the ease with which they were attacked. The American response was in no way proportional to the challenge but a gross overreaction. Terrorism on this kind of limited scale is best treated as a police matter, at home and abroad. Good intelligence, surveillance, and arrest of those planning or responsible for terrorist acts are generally the best course of action. Even when effective, it still leaves countries vulnerable to terrorist attacks, as the recent experience of Britain, France, and Germany demonstrate. This is inevitable as there is no solution to the threat of terrorism. The best countries can do is attempt to limit its effects and reduce in the longer term the incentives of the disenchanted to resort to it.

The US pursued a strategy all out of proportion to the threat. The so-called War on Terror justified draconian policies at home and abroad. It was allegedly the reason for invading Afghanistan, although surprisingly little effort was made by American forces in that country to hunt down Osama bin Laden. The Bush administration offered it quite duplicitously as a justification for the follow-on invasion of Iraq, along with the equally false claim that Saddam had weapons of mass destruction. It provides the raison d'être for continuing drone strikes in a spreading number of countries. Successive administrations have argued that these actions were necessary to protect the American homeland from terrorism. A compelling argument can be made that they have made the US and its allies more vulnerable.

In the post-9/11 era, conventional wisdom holds that the jihadist threat is foreign. But 84 percent of terrorist attacks on American territory since 9/11 have been carried out by US citizens.[40] Most of them were white Christians, as was the case of the 2018 pipe bomb mailings to a number of elected officials and George Soros and the deadly attack on the Tree of Life Synagogue in Pittsburgh. Efforts to limit immigration, especially from Muslim countries, have little to no impact as terrorism is overwhelmingly homegrown. The War on Terrorism has played into the hands of the nativist right, even though they are largely responsible for the majority of attacks against individuals, governmental buildings, and places of worship. It has allowed the government to intrude into many areas of American life, infringe civil liberties in important ways, and impose largely ineffective but time-consuming constraints on the transfer of money. It has also justified huge expenditure on security, much of which has gone to security-focused businesses, and is responsible for the new, bloated, and largely ineffective Department of Homeland Security. The War on Terror is estimated to have added $2 trillion to the national debt as of 2018.[41]

For all these reasons a new administration needs to rethink the country's approach to terrorism. The so-called War on Terrorism should be terminated and expenditure on it dramatically reduced. Greater efforts should be made to study and gain intelligence on domestic nativist terrorism. Even though it is the dominant source of terrorism, state and federal governments have largely ignored the threat, adopting an attitude the New York Times describes as "willful indifference."[42] The real source of terrorist attacks in America needs to be publicized, and police and other efforts be made to address it.

The invasions of Afghanistan and Iraq were the most dramatic and counterproductive expressions of the War on Terrorism. The US has drawn down most of its forces in both countries but is still deeply involved. As early as 2005 hawkish analysts in conservative think tanks began writing about the "Long War" and how it could be won. West Point's Combating Terrorism Center has produced monographs on the subject, as has the RAND Corporation.[43] These analysts envisage a war lasting another 10, even 20 years with continuing US participation. In November 2018, Donald Trump appointed retired Army General John Abizaid as ambassador to Saudi Arabia. Abizaid is a proponent of "the Long War," as, of course, are the Saudis, desperate to keep the US military engaged with its adversaries. Michael O'Hanlon of the Brookings Foundation insists that we must stay the course in Afghanistan and Iraq, as ISIS and other terrorists would get stronger if we withdrew.[44] These wars are lost; the US loses influence every day it continues to engage in them, and even more as a result of its more recent involvement in Yemen. A long war that continues to bleed the US of blood and treasure is also a threat to democracy at home.

Environment: In the opinion of almost all serious climate scientists, the greatest threat to our physical security and way of life is global warming.[45] Increasing carbon dioxide in the atmosphere has already led to rising sea levels, more acute storms of all kinds, and warmer temperatures that are beginning to wreak havoc with ecosystems. In my home state of New Hampshire, the moose are dying off because the ticks that feed on their blood are not being killed off by cold winters. There is no doubt that much of the change in carbon dioxide levels is human in origin, and that its consequences will be catastrophic if these levels are not reduced. Coastal cities like Baltimore, Miami, and New Orleans risk inundation, if not total drowning, the heartland will suffer major crop failures, and California will face far more serious droughts and fires.[46] The Fourth Annual National Climate Assessment—an official coordinated publication of US government climate scientists and agencies—estimates that by the end of the century the economy would suffer by as much as 10 percent from the effects of climate change.[47]

The US has recognized this danger when Obama was President. Under Trump it has declined participation in almost all international efforts to grapple with climate change. Governments, especially Republican-led ones, have listened to ignorant corporate naysayers instead of well-informed scientists. These businesses—not at all representative of the business community as a whole—prefer short-term profits to long-term survival. They indulge their owners and shareholders at the expense of future generations. As with earlier corporate denial and then initial opposition to legislation to reverse the hole in the ozone layer, they greatly exaggerate the costs of reversing carbon dioxide levels in the atmosphere.[48]

The Trump administration has taken this ostrich-like policy to a new level. Scott Pruitt, Trump's first administrator of the Environmental

Protection Agency, publicly denied climate change. He weakened the Obama-era program that would shift energy production away from coal, one of the major sources of heat-trapping carbon dioxide in the atmosphere. The EPA are currently loosening standards for how companies discard coal ash, and in the face of evidence that it is spilling into waterways in North Carolina following Hurricane Florence. They are freezing mandates that new cars use less gasoline and expel fewer pollutants into the air and are reducing the limits on methane gas released during oil refining. The EPA is also rejecting science that shows some pesticides make people sick.[49] In 2016 the EPA removed all information on climate change from its website, allegedly for an "update," but nothing has been posted since.[50] In Katowice, Poland, at the 2018 environmental conference, the US proved hostile to almost every positive initiative to reduce carbon emissions. At times, the US played the spoiler. Trump officials gave a presentation promoting fossil fuels and American negotiators joined envoys from Russia, Saudi Arabia, and Kuwait—all major oil producers—in refusing to accept landmark report documenting the even greater than expected impacts of a rise of 1.5 °C in the temperature.[51]

The Global Carbon Project found US emissions likely to rise 2.5 percent in 2018. The Center for Energy and Environmental Policy Research at the Massachusetts Institute of Technology reports that emissions are also on the rise in China and India. Matters are likely to get worse, not better, says Deputy Director Michael Mehling. But it will take time to shoe because Trump's rollback of domestic climate policies "have a considerable lead time before you can actually see their reflection in physical emission trends."[52] Unless a new administration introduces severe measures, there is no way that the US will achieve the pledge made by the Obama administration in the run-up to the Paris climate agreement to reduce its greenhouse gas emissions by 26–28 percent below 2005 levels by the year 2025.

The national interest demands that the next administration treat climate change as seriously as Germany and Scandinavia. It must end favors given to the coal and oil industries at the expense of the health and economic interests of citizens. It must take the lead in proposing, enacting, and enforcing international measures that will halt, and better yet, reduce the levels of carbon dioxide in the atmosphere. It must do the same for pollutants that are the by-product of industrial processes and gasoline powered automobiles and trucks. Taking the lead in environmental protection is very much in the interests of the country and its citizens, and is also a problem that cannot be addressed only at the national level.

Financial Times correspondent Simon Kuper offers eminently reasonable suggestions for how the US might win public support for cutting carbon emission.[53] Leaders should talk about "Green Growth," not saving the planet. Egged on by energy businesses and their well-heeled propaganda machines, Western societies again and again choose growth over cutting carbon emissions and environmental protection. People need to be convinced that they can have both, and they can. The International Labor Organization predicts that going green would generate 18 million more new jobs than it destroys by 2030.[54] The Congressional Budget Office is less optimistic but still predicts an increase in jobs created over those lost.[55]

Governments also need to find the right messages and messengers.[56] As businesses do to sell their products, they need to tailor messages to different key audiences. People are interested in different things and put high priorities on protecting them. These audiences must be identified and approached with messengers credible to them who make a compelling case for cutting carbon emissions to protect that which is of interest to them. These messages and messengers will be different when targeting say hunting enthusiasts versus gardeners.

Leaders should stop predicting doomsday. It encourages denial. Psychologist Irving Janis discovered that when warned about impending disaster people take these warnings seriously to the degree that they believe action on their part can avert them. Reports of rising waters and the danger of flooding produce volunteers to fill sandbags. By contrast, warnings of tornados or nuclear war—situations in which people feel helpless—lead to denial and even anger at the messengers.[57] Political messages about the environment must stress what individual people can do to have real effect.

Government policies must do the same. Leaders should talk about "carbon dividends" not "carbon tax." Elke Weber reports that when the provincial government of British Columbia did this and to hand over these dividends directly to its citizens, support for their policy turned positive within 15 months.[58] Government should talk less about saving whales and future generations and more about benefitting today's population. People care more about themselves than they do about others, even when they are their descendants. For the same reason, governments would be well-advised to talk about current disasters rather than future ones.

Governments should turn the tables on climate change deniers. They should ignore them, as arguing against them gives them undeserved attention and legitimacy. They should tell a popular, anti-elitist story that stresses upon how sheiks and oil companies profit at the expense of everyone else. They should talk about "climate change" and not "global warming," as it is both more accurate and makes it more difficult for deniers to offer cold snaps and snowstorms as counterevidence. Finally, governments must make serious efforts to help those who have lost their jobs or job prospects to the new, greener economy.

Environment is only one of the areas in which US national interests need to be addressed at the regional and international levels. This is true of efforts to forestall nuclear war, prevent proliferation, promote nuclear disarmament, and prevent famines and the spread of deadly pathogens, all of which depend on collective understandings and actions. The national interest in many respects transcends the limits of our nation or any other and must incorporate the perspectives and interests of a number of states. The attempt to go it alone, or dictate policies to others, is patently self-defeating.

Economics: The wellbeing of the country depends on economic growth and high employment. Equally important are the kinds of jobs that are available, their level of compensation and security, degree of on-the-job safety, benefits including pensions and healthcare, and access to good jobs where people already reside. Many of these conditions were taken for granted by American workers for most of the postwar decades. This is no longer the case; each of these conditions are more difficult to fulfill as manufacturing jobs have been exported, many full-time positions reduced to part-time ones, pensions and other benefits dramatically cut, and remuneration in many remaining jobs no longer provides any real increase in income.

Some of these changes were all but inevitable as the rest of the world began to industrialize and with labor and other costs that made it attractive for American businesses to move production offshore. However, Americans had choices, and many of those that they made exacerbated the problem. They led to a country in which the gap between rich and poor has grown markedly because a significant percentage of added wealth goes to a small minority of already well-off people.[59] Chief among the policies responsible for this disturbing phenomenon has been the decades-long effort by businesses, with the support of Congress and conservative courts, to weaken unions, if not undermine them as far as possible. Neoliberalism and its questionable belief in the benefits of deregulation at home and the so-called Washington Consensus abroad is another cause of inequality.[60] Democratic presidents, notably Bill Clinton, have been captured by neo-liberal economic advisors as their Republican counterparts.

A Post Non-hegemonic World

Hegemony, or more properly, the illusion of hegemony, was not necessary to produce the more positive developments of the postwar era.[61] Washington can properly take credit for keeping South Korea independent and helped to democratize and rebuild Western Europe and Japan after the war. The Cold War would have ended in due course without all the American expenditure of blood and treasure. The Soviet Union collapsed because of its own internal contradictions, greatly aggravated by a heavy-handed authoritarian regime and command economy. Undoubtedly, the growth of international trade and the dropping of tariff barriers were facilitated by American policy, but it may have developed even faster and more effectively in the absence of US abuses of the system it helped to create. The spread of democracy in Latin America and East Central Europe did not require active intervention by the US, although American democracy offered, at least initially, an attractive role model. War avoidance among the major powers had very little to do with US deterrence and alliances as it was largely the result of widescale fear of war in the aftermath of World War II. Nuclear weapons, I have argued, intensified the perceived horror of war but also aggravated the insecurities of both superpowers and China. American arrogance about being the "indispensable nation" is unjustified.

Less is often more. The US overextending itself; arrogated responsibility for political and economic order; demanded special privileges; treated other states as second-class citizens of world society; intervened regularly in the political, economic, and military means in the affairs of others; and exploited the order it helped to create and was allegedly committed to preserving for selfish economic ends. All these actions undermined American influence and account for the paradox I noted at the outset of this book: that the US is the greatest power the world has ever seen but is less and less able to persuade others to do what it wants. Rather, it increasingly relies on bribes and coercion, and without notable success. This process has reached its most extreme manifestation to date under the presidency of Donald Trump, but it is an outgrowth of a trend long underway and intensified after the end of the Cold War under Democratic and Republican administrations alike.

The focus on power and hegemony obscures the ways in which international society has been evolving. My critique of hegemony can nevertheless provide insight into these changes. By identifying the ways in which hegemony is thought to make global order possible, we can disaggregate these functions from the role and ask if it is possible to fill them in other ways. This is an eminently feasible and more realistic task in today's world.

The first responsibility of hegemony is the normative task of *agenda setting*. Much of what liberals conceive as leadership is the capacity to shape the policy agenda of global institutions or ad-hoc coalitions.[62] It requires knowledge and manipulation of appropriate discourses.[63] It also requires insight into how other actors define their interests, what they identify as problems, and what responses they consider appropriate. In contrast to the realist emphasis on material power, agenda setting emphasizes persuasion over coercion. It brings about collective action through effective appeals to shared values and norms. Power is important but understood as embedded in institutional and normative structures. Normative influence is heavily dependent on political skill, and all the more so in a world in which so many, if not most, important initiatives are multilateral.

Effective agenda setting requires the adoption of proposed measures in the context of multilateral venues that are designed for negotiation.

Simple advocacy of a policy, even at the negotiating table, is not a sufficient litmus test. Persuasion relies as much on the legitimacy of the proposal as on the sticks and carrots of material power. At the end of World War II and in its immediate aftermath, the US set the agenda for most of the developed world. Since the end of the Cold War, the US has been a major opponent of progressive international measures of all kind, from the international court of justice, to the treaty banning landmines to the responsibility to protect civilians in conflict zones.

The problem of civilian protection offers a telling example of how agenda setting works. Norway, far from being a great power, nevertheless played an important role in the promotion of the concept of civilian protection. In the 1990s, the Norwegian government awarded funds to the Peace Research Institute of Oslo (PRIO) to think through the concept and what would be required to implement it.[64] In the UN, Norway worked with middle powers like Canada to promote human security. The Norwegians focused much of their efforts on promoting the "responsibility to protect" (R2P) doctrine in collaboration with other states and NGOs, including the Brussels-based International Crisis Group. R2P inverts the traditional realist focus on sovereignty and the rights of states by stressing their responsibility to protect civilians or be subject to the prospect of multilateral intervention.[65] By 2001, the R2P initiative had gained significant momentum and won the unstinting support of then Secretary General Kofi Annan.[66] By 2005, the language of the R2P doctrine was embraced by the UN as consistent with Chapters VI and VIII of the UN Charter. At that time, over 150 world leaders adopted R2P, legitimating the use of force through multilateral intervention initiatives sanctioned by the UN Security Council.[67] The Obama administration, which like its predecessor, the Bush administration, opposed R2P, but given its wide international support had to grit its teeth, accept it, and make it part of its *National Security Strategy*, issued in 2010.[68] Good diplomacy and legitimacy trumped power.

The second constituent of hegemony is economic management. In the post-hegemonic era this function is primarily *custodial*. Custodianship entails the management of risk through market signaling (information passed, intentionally or not, among market participants) and intergovernmental negotiations in a variety of venues. The intent, according to

Charles Kindleberger, the father of hegemonic stability theory, is to stabilize and undergird the functions of the global economic system.[69] His formulation became foundational for his realist and liberal successors as they seek to justify the global need for continued American hegemony.[70] However, America has either willingly contravened, or is increasingly incapable of performing, these functions.

The US routinely transgresses the principle of free trade. President Trump has been the most egregious offender, rejecting the North American Free Trade Agreement (NAFTA), coercing Canada into renegotiating the treaty, and far more threatening to international stability, waging an escalating trade war with China. American unilateralism and abuses go back to 1973 and the Nixon administration's closing of the "gold window." It shook the foundations of the global economic order by unilaterally ending the convertibility of the dollar. The US subsequently exploited its dominant economic position by borrowing vast sums of money and at times running high rates of inflation that it would not have been possible for any other country to do without encountering sanctions.[71] Chinese and Japanese investors subsidize American consumers. The US has been a regular exploiter, rather than provider, of public goods. It was responsible for the 2008 Great Recession through lax financial regulation. During the Vietnam War and the Great Recession, Washington's exploitation of its position destabilized existing patterns of global finance.[72] The image of American "hegemony" as characterized by a broader, enlightened conception of self-interest is sharply contradicted by short-sighted, self-serving, unilateral American behavior.

American borrowing took the form of the issuance of US Treasury bills. By October 2018, the US Treasury Department estimated that China's holding of US Treasury bills had reached $1.78 trillion, making it the largest foreign lender.[73] Japan's holdings amounted to $1.30 trillion.[74] The total foreign holdings of US Treasury debt stood at $6.25 trillion and the entire national debt had reached $20.25 billion.[75] The pace of borrowing has accelerated in the last few years without much evidence of it being invested in infrastructure or other forms of investment. The US relies on China's willingness to hold on to these Treasury bills and maintain the value of the dollar and, by doing so, to avoid defaulting on payment of its public debt. Only the US could carry such debt without having to embark on stringent budget cuts imposed by multilateral organizations such as the International Monetary Fund, other national governments, or private bankers. American behavior has become increasingly feckless and destabilizing, and far from propping up the financial system as lender of last resort, the US has emerged as its primary borrower and an increasingly irresponsible one.

For the time being the global economic system functions, for better or worse, without a responsible leader. Leadership, economic management, and security provisions are no longer interrelated. Key management functions—providing market liquidity, reinforcing open trading patterns, market and currency stability, and reinforcing patterns of economic development—take place without a hegemon. Divorced from the concept of hegemony, these functions are best described as "custodianship."

The third element of hegemony is *sponsorship*. It encompasses enforcement of rules, norms, agreements, and decision-making processes as well as the maintenance of security to enhance trade and finance.[76] Liberals and realists consistently maintain that only hegemons can provide such enforcement because of their preponderance of material power. They assume that American hegemony is legitimate in the eyes of other important actors who welcome its leadership and enforcement as beneficial to global stability and their national interests. When empirical support is mustered for these claims, the foreign voices invariably cited are conservative politicians in allied states or authoritarian leaders who benefit personally from US backing. During the Cold War, German conservatives welcomed US leadership as a means of offsetting Soviet power and of constraining Social Democratic opponents. Leaders of South Korea, Taiwan, South Vietnam, the Philippines, Iran, Egypt, and various Latin American states were, to varying degrees, dependent on US military and foreign aid and happy to say in public what Washington wanted to hear to keep these dollars flowing. Their opponents regarded US influence as regressive as it supported regimes opposed to democracy and human rights.

There has been a noticeable decline in pleas for US leadership since the end of the Cold War, and as noted earlier, a corresponding increase in opposition to US military and economic initiatives. Since the Iraq War, the US has undergone a shift in its profile from a status quo to a revisionist power.[77] A BBC World Service poll dated 3 July 2017 revealed increasingly negative views of the US, rising to majorities, are now found in several of its NATO allies, including the UK (up from 42 to 64 percent), Spain (44 to 67 percent), France (41 to 56 percent), and Turkey (36 to 64 percent). Negative opinion has also sharply risen in Latin American nations Mexico (up from 41 to 59 percent), and Peru (29 to 49 percent). In Russia, negative views of the US have also increased from 55 to 64 percent.[78] This and other surveys indicate that the US is not perceived as acting in the interests of the international community. Whatever legitimacy its leadership once had has significantly eroded as publics around the world are particularly worried about the way in which the US uses its military power.[79]

Leadership and legitimacy are closely connected, and enforcement clearly depends on the latter. In situations where US efforts at enforcement have been seen as legitimate (e.g., Korea, the First Gulf War), international support has been forthcoming, and with it, backing by relevant regional and international organizations, notably the UN Security Council. Key to the legitimacy of enforcement has been a common perception of threat but also a commitment on Washington's part to limit its military action in pursuit of a consensus. It often requires collaborative decisions concerning processes of implementation as well. The Truman administration won support for the liberation of South Korea, but not the invasion of the North, and George H.W. Bush for the liberation of Kuwait, but not the overthrow of Saddam Hussein. When George W. Bush insisted on the invasion of Iraq with the goal of removing Saddam, he was unable to gain support from NATO or the UN. When the administration went to war in the absence of international institutional support, it had to cobble together a coalition based largely on bribes and threats. Its subsequent decline in standing was precipitous, and this began before the insurgency in Iraq.

The theoretical and policy lessons of these experiences are straightforward. Material power is a necessary but insufficient condition for enforcement. The latter depends on legitimacy, an important component of influence. In its absence, even successful enforcement—as defined by Washington—will not be perceived as such by other states, and possibly as aggrandizement as the Iraq invasion was by public opinion in France, Germany, Canada, and Japan. Such perceptions undermine legitimacy and make future enforcement more difficult.

The functions of agenda setting, custodianship, and sponsorship overlap in part. All confer advantages to states that perform them and to the community at large. They require consultation, bargaining, and consensus, but also reflect competition and jockeying for influence among powerful states. We neither suggest there is, nor should be, a division of labor in the global system. Decisions to perform these functions are driven by cultural conceptions, domestic politics, and consideration of national self-interest. Within limits, powerful actors generally attempt to exert what degrees of influence they can. This will depend in part on the nature of their resources but also the priorities they establish and their legitimacy in the eyes of other actors. They are also affected by domestic and international constraints and opportunities.

All three functions of hegemony require contingent forms of influence rather than the blunt exercise of power. Their application is becoming increasingly diffused among states, rather than concentrated in the hands of a hegemon. These functions are performed by multiple states, sometimes in collaboration with non-state actors. Global governance practices are sharply at odds with the formulations of realists and liberals alike. Western Europeans have made consistent efforts to extend their normative influence by promoting agendas well beyond those with which they are traditionally associated. These include environmental and human rights initiatives, but also security issues and corporate regulation. Asian states, most notably China, have increasingly assumed a custodial role, albeit embryonic at this point, quite at odds with the neo-mercantilist or rising military power depiction of realists.

It is time for the US to adjust is goals and methods to a world in which hegemony is impossible and counterproductive if it could be achieved, in which power must be masked to be used effectively and can only be done so in pursuit of objectives accepted as legitimate by other actors. American leaders need to lead in different ways than they have in the past but also be prepared to follow. This approach to the world is more sophisticated and more appropriate to contemporary conditions and ultimately will gain more respect and influence than crude assertions of power.

Notes

1. George F. Kennan, *The Kennan Diaries* (New York: Norton David Greenberg, "US Cold War Policy Was Designed by a Bigot," *New Republic*, 20 April 2014), p. 393; https://newrepublic.com/article/117174/george-f-kennans-diaries-reviewed (accessed 2 November 2018).
2. Richard Ned Lebow, "Misconceptions in American Strategic Assessment," *Political Science Quarterly* 97 (Summer 1982), pp. 187–206.
3. Conversations with former Soviet KGB and GRU officers.
4. John Lewis Gaddis, *The United States and the End of the Cold War* (New York: Oxford University Press); Randall B. Woods, "Review Article: Cold War or Cold Peace," International History Review 16, no. 1 (1994), pp. 81–91; Douglas E. Selvage, "Transforming the Soviet Sphere of Influence? U.S.-Soviet Détente and Eastern Europe, 1969–1976," Diplomatic History 33, no. 4 (2009), pp. 671–687.
5. Galal A. Amin, *Egypt in the Era of Hosni Mubarak: 1981–2011* (Cairo: University of Cairo Press, 2011); Efraim Karsh, *Islamic Imperialism* (New Haven: Yale University Press, 2006), pp. 183–84.
6. Calamur, "Nine Notorious Dictators, Nine Shout-Outs From Donald Trump."
7. Shehab Kahn, "Nigel Farage says Donald Trump would be 'very welcome' in the UK," *Independent*, 25 February 2018, https://www.independent.co.uk/news/uk/politics/nigel-farage-donald-trump-state-visit-uk-fox-cpac-a8224266.html; Ben Jacobs, "Nigel Farage gets warm welcome at gathering of US right wing," *Guardian*, 23 February, 2018, https://www.theguardian.com/us-news/2018/feb/23/cpac-nigel-farage-sadiq-khan-us-conservatives; BBC, "Bannon plan for Europe-wide populist 'supergroup' sparks alarm," 23 July 2018, https://www.bbc.co.uk/news/world-europe-44926417 (all accessed 3 November 2018).
8. Jay Croft and Saeed Ahmed, "The Pittsburgh synagogue shooting is believed to be the deadliest attack on Jews in American history, the ADL says," *CNN*, 28 October 2018, https://edition.cnn.com/2018/10/27/us/jewish-hate-crimes-fbi/index.html; Laurie Goodstein, "'There Is Still So Much Evil': Growing Anti-Semitism Stuns American Jews," *New York Times*, 29 October 2018, https://www.nytimes.com/2018/10/29/us/anti-semitism-attacks.htm (both accessed 3 November 2018).
9. Jon Henley, "'Chaos' Dutch PM draws moral for his country," *Guardian*, 18 December 2018, p. 8.

10. Bob Woodward, *Fear* (New York: Simon & Schuster, 2018), p. 320.

11. Ibid.

12. Richard Ned Lebow, *The Rise and Fall of Political Orders* (Cambridge: Cambridge University Press, 2018), ch. 6.

13. For discussion, J. Greenberg and R. L. Cohen, *Equality and Justice in Social Behavior* (New York: Academic Press, 1982); Morton Deutsch, *Distributive Justice* (New Haven: Yale University Press, 1985), evaluated the two principles and "winner takes all" under different conditions.

14. Herbert McCloskey and John Zaller, *The American Ethos: Public Attitudes Toward Capitalism and Democracy* (Cambridge: Harvard University Press, 1984), pp. 154–56.

15. Adam G. Swift, Gordon Marshall, and Carole. Burgoyne, "Which Road to Social Justice?" *Sociology Review* 2 no. 2 (1992), pp. 28–31.

16. G. Jasso and P. H. Rossi, "Distributive Justice and Earned Income," *American Sociological Review* 42, no. 4 (1977), pp. 639–51; W. M. Alves, W. M. and P. H. Rossi, "Who Should Get What? Fairness Judgments of the Distribution of Earnings," *American Journal of Sociology* 84, no. 3 (1978), pp. 541–64; W. M. Alves, "Modelling Distributive Justice Judgments," in Peter H. Rossi and Steven L. Nock, eds., *Measuring Social Judgments* (Beverley Hills, Ca.: Sage, 1982), pp. 205–34; Sidney Verba and Gary R. Orren, *Equality in America: The View from the Top* (Cambridge: Harvard University Press, 1985).

17. Frank Newport, "Americans Still Say Upper-Income Pay Too Little in Taxes," Gallup, 15 April 2016, http://www.gallup.com/poll/190775/americans-say-upper-income-pay-little-taxes.aspx (accessed 22 June 2017).

18. Lebow, *Rise and Fall of Political Orders*, ch. 6 for a quantitative and qualitative analysis of these speeches.

19. Leopold von Ranke, "The Great Powers," in Georg C. Iggers and Konrad von Moltke, eds., The Theory and Practice of History (Indianapolis, Ind.: Bobbs-Merrill, 1973), pp. 65–10; Ian Clark, *Hegemony in International Society* (Oxford: Oxford University Press, 2011); Georges-Henri Soutou, "L'ordre Européen de Versailles à Locarno," in C. Carlier and G-H Soutou, eds., *1918–1925: Comment Faire La Paix?* (Paris: 2001); Richard Ned Lebow, *National Identifications and International Relations* (Cambridge: Cambridge University Press, 2016), ch. 4.

20. Bob Reinalda and Bertjan Verbeek, *Autonomous Policy Making by International Organizations* (London: Routledge, 1998); Nicholas Bayne

and Robert D. Putnam, *Hanging in There: The G7 and G8 Summit in Maturity and Renewal* (Aldershot, Hampshire, England: Ashgate, 2000).

21. Lebow, *National Identities and International Relations*, pp. 67, 85–88, 192, 198.

22. Ibid., pp. 192–97.

23. Miriam Valverde, "Fact-checking Donald Trump's false and misleading claims about immigration, the border wall," *PolitiFact*, 24 January 2019, https://www.politifact.com/truth-o-meter/article/2019/jan/24/fact-checking-donald-trumps-false-and-misleading-c/ (accessed 23 February 2019).

24. Adam Liptak and Michael D. Shear, "Trump's Travel Ban Is Upheld by Supreme Court," *New York Times*, 26 June 2018, https://www.nytimes.com/2018/06/26/us/politics/supreme-court-trump-travel-ban.html (accessed 8 November 2018).

25. Michael D. Shear, "Trump Claims New Power to Bar Asylum for Immigrants Who Arrive Illegally," *New York Times*, 8 November 2018, https://www.nytimes.com/2018/11/08/us/politics/trump-asylum-seekers-executive-order.html?action=click&module=Top%20 Stories&pgtype=Homepage (accessed 9 November 2018).

26. Woodward, *Fear*, prologue, pp. 264–65.

27. Ibid., p. 208.

28. Ibid., p. 218.

29. Glenn Hubbard, "American must reform itself to triumph in the dispute with Beijing," *Financial Times*, 3 November 2018, p. 12.

30. Binyamin Appelbaum, "Their Soybeans Piling Up, Farmers Hope Trade War Ends Before Beans Rot," *New York Times*, 5 November 2018, https://www.nytimes.com/2018/11/05/business/soybeans-farmers-trade-war.html?action=click&module=Top%20Stories&pgtype=Homepage (accessed 5 November 2018).

31. Editorial, "The US gives up writing the global trade book," *Financial Times*, 3 November 2018, p. 10.

32. Jonathan, Freedland, "Why these US elections are so crucial for the rest of the world," *Guardian*, 3 November 2018, p. 3.

33. Julie Hirschfeld Davis and Thomas Gibbons-Neff, "Trump Considers Closing Southern Border to Migrants," *New York Times*, 25 October 2018, https://www.nytimes.com/2018/10/25/us/politics/trump-army-border-mexico.html (accessed 8 November 2018).

34. Michael D. Shear and Thomas Gibbons-Neff, "Trump Sending 5200 Troops to the Border in an Election-Season Response to Migrants," *New York Times*, 29 October 2018, https://www.nytimes.com/2018/10/29/us/politics/border-security-troops-trump.html (accessed 8 November 2018).

35. Fred Chernoff, "Ending the Cold War: The Impact of the US Military Buildup on the Soviet Retreat." *International Affairs* 67, no. 1 (1991), pp. 111–26; Lebow and Stein, *We All Lost the Cold War*, Postscript; Robert D. English, *Russia and the Idea of the West: Gorbachev, Intellectuals and the End of the Cold War* (New York: Columbia University Press, 200); Archie Brown, *The Gorbachev Factor* (Oxford: Oxford University Press, 1996).

36. Kimberley Amadeo, "US Trade Deficit With China and Why It's So High," *The Balance*, World Economy, 7 November 2018, https://www.thebalance.com/u-s-china-trade-deficit-causes-effects-and-solutions-3306277 (accessed 8 November 2018).

37. Daniel Shane, "China is America's biggest foreign creditor. Could it turn off the tap?" *CNN Business*, 11 January 2018, https://money.cnn.com/2018/01/11/investing/china-us-treasury-purchases/index.html (accessed 8 November 2018).

38. Richard Ned Lebow and Janice Gross Stein, *We All Lost the Cold War* (Princeton: Princeton University Press, 1994), ch. 14; Vladislav M. Zubok, *A Failed Empire: The Soviet Union in the Cold War from Stalin to Gorbachev*, 2nd ed. (Chapel Hill, N.C.: University of North Carolina Press, 2009).

39. Mikhail Gorbachev, "Mikhail Gorbachev: A New Nuclear Arms Race Has Begun," *New York Times*, 25 October 2018, https://www.nytimes.com/2018/10/25/opinion/mikhail-gorbachev-inf-treaty-trump-nuclear-arms.html (accessed 20 January 2019).

40. New American, *Terrorism in America After 9/11*, Part II: "Who Are the Terrorists?," 2018, https://www.newamerica.org/in-depth/terrorism-in-america/who-are-terrorists/ (accessed 7 November 2018).

41. Kimberley Amadeo, "War on Terror Facts, Costs, and Timeline," https://www.thebalance.com/war-on-terror-facts-costs-timeline-3306300 (accessed 7 November 2018).

42. Janet Reitman, "US Law Enforcement Failed to See the Threat of White Nationalism. Now They Don't Know How to Stop It," *New York Times*, 3 November 2018, https://www.nytimes.com/2018/11/03/magazine/FBI-charlottesville-white-nationalism-far-right.html (accessed 3 November 2018).

43. Andrew J. Bacevich, "Has the United States Been Fighting the Wrong War in the Middle East?" *Other News*, 26 November 2018, http://www.other-news.info/2018/11/has-the-united-states-been-fighting-the-wrong-war-in-the-middle-east/ (accessed 26 November 2018).

44. Michael E. O'Hanlon, "Our Longest War Is Still an Important War," *New York Times*, 24 January 2019, https://www.nytimes.com/2019/01/24/opinion/our-longest-war-is-still-an-important-war.html?action=click&module=Opinion&pgtype=Homepage (accessed 25 January 2019).

45. NASA, "Scientific consensus: Earth's climate is warming," 2018, https://climate.nasa.gov/scientific-consensus/; John Cook, "The 97% consensus on global warming," *Skeptical Science*, https://www.skepticalscience.com/global-warming-scientific-consensus-intermediate.htm (both accessed 8 November 2018).

46. NASA, "How climate is changing: effects," 2018, https://climate.nasa.gov/effects/; Union of Concerned Scientists, "Climate Change in the United States: The Prohibitive Costs of Inaction," August 2009, https://www.ucsusa.org/sites/default/.../global_warming/climate-costs-of-inaction.pdf (both accessed 8 November 2018).

47. U.S. Global Change Research Program, "Fourth National Climate Assessment," 2017, https://nca2018.globalchange.gov/; Coral Davenport and Kendra Pierre-Louis, "U.S. Climate Report Warns of Damaged Environment and Shrinking Economy," *New York Times*, 23 November 2018, https://www.nytimes.com/2018/11/23/climate/us-climate-report.html?action=click&module=Top%20Stories&pgtype=Homepage (both accessed 24 November 2018).

48. Edward A. Parson, *Protecting the Ozone Layer: Science and Strategy* (Oxford: Oxford University Press, 2003), esp. pp. 53–55.

49. Emily Holden, "Trump races against clock to roll back major Obama-era environment rules," *Guardian*, 3 October 2018, https://www.theguardian.com/environment/2018/oct/03/trump-administration-roll-back-major-obama-era-environment-policies; (all accessed 4 November 2018).

50. Oliver Milman, "'It's a ghost page': EPA site's climate change section may be gone for good," *Guardian*, 1 November 2018, https://www.theguardian.com/us-news/2018/nov/01/epa-website-climate-change-trump-administration (accessed 4 November 2018).

51. Brady Dennis and Griff Witte, "Climate talks at risk of failure as U.S. leaves a leadership void," *Washington Post*, 12 December 2018, https://www.washingtonpost.com/national/health-science/climate-talks-at-

risk-of-failure-as-us-leaves-a-leadership-void/2018/12/12/35151344-fdfd-11e8-862a-b6a6f3ce8199_story.html?noredirect=on&utm_term=.acf3f1c31de4 (accessed 12 December 2018).

52. Chris Mooney and Brady Dennis, "U.S. greenhouse gas emissions spiked in 2018—and it couldn't happen at a worse time," *Other News*, 18 January 2019, https://mail.google.com/mail/u/0/#inbox/FMfcgxwBVMcnGgFZkdFZnFFhSscdzNfl (accessed 18 January 2019).

53. Simon Kuper, "How to Sell Climate Change and Save the Planet," *Financial Times*, Magazine, 5 December 2008.

54. Guy Ruder (Director-General), "We can both create jobs and protect the environment," International Labor Organization, 1 December 2018, https://www.ilo.org/global/about-the-ilo/how-the-ilo-works/ilo-director-general/statements-and-speeches/WCMS_651976/lang%2D%2Den/index.htm (accessed 2 January 2019).

55. Cited in Kuper, "How to Sell Climate Change and Save the Planet."

56. Elke U. Weber, "Climate Change Demands Behavioral Change: What Are the Challenges?," *Social Research* 82, no. 3 (2015), pp. 560–580 and Oxford Cameron Hepburn and Popp Pless, "Encouraging Innovation that Protects Environmental Systems: Five Policy Proposals," *Review of Environmental Economics and Policy* 12, no. 1 (2018), pp. 154–169.

57. Janis and Mann, *Decision Making*, pp. 51–73.

58. Weber, "Climate Change Demands Behavioral Change."

59. Anthony Atkinson, *Inequality: What Can Be Done?* (Cambridge: Harvard University Press, 2015). Also, Robert H. Frank, *Falling Behind: How Rising Inequality Harms the Middle Class* (Berkeley: University of California Press, 2007); Marianne Bertrand and Adiar Morse, "Trickle Down Consumption," National Bureau of Economic Research, Working Paper 1883, March 2013; Thomas Piketty, *Capital in the Twenty-First Century*, trans. Arthur Goldhammer (Cambridge: Harvard University Press, 2014).

60. Thomas Piketty, *The Economics of Inequality* (Cambridge: Harvard University Press, 2015).

61. John Mueller, "An American Global Order? Pax Americans: Has the US Been Necessary?" Prepared for presentation at the ISSS-IS Annual Conference Purdue University, West Lafayette, Indiana, 11 November 2018.

62. Michael Barnett and Raymond Duvall "Power in International Politics," *International Organization* 59, no 1 (2005), pp. 39–75; Ian Manners, "Normative Power Europe: A Contradiction in Terms?" *Journal of Common Market Studies* 40, no. 2 (2002), pp. 235–258.

63. Barnett and Duvall, "Power in International Politics," pp. 56–57.

64. Steven Radelet, "A Primer on Foreign Aid," Working Paper no. 92, Center for Global Development, July 2006, p. 5.

65. Simon Reich, "The Evolution of a Doctrine: The Curious Case of Kofi Annan, George Bush and the Doctrines of Preventative and Preemptive Intervention" in William Keller and Gordon Mitchell, eds., *Hitting First: Preventive Force in US Security Strategy* (Pittsburgh: University of Pittsburgh Press, 2006), pp. 45–69.

66. "Secretary-General Reflects on 'Intervention' in Thirty-Fifth Annual Ditchley Foundation Lecture," UN Press Release, SG/SM/6613, 26 June, 1998, http://www.un.org/News/Press/docs/1998/19980626. sgsm6613.html; Gareth Evans and Mohamed Sahnoun, *The Responsibility to Protect: A Report by the International Commission of Intervention and State Sovereignty* (Ottawa: International Development Research Center, December 2001), http://www.dfait-maeci.gc.ca/iciss-ciise/pdf/ Commission-Report.pdf; Simon Reich, "Power, Institutions and Moral Entrepreneurs," ZEF-Discussion Papers on Development Policy No. 65, Center for Development Research (ZEF), Bonn, March 2003, http:// www.zef.de/publications.html; (all accessed 12 November 2018); Bruce W. Jentleson, "Coercive Prevention: Normative, Political and Policy Dilemmas," *Peaceworks*, no. 35 (Washington, D.C.: United States Institute of Peace, October 2000), p. 20.

67. United Nations General Assembly, "2005 World Summit Outcome," Articles 138 and 139, A/60/L.1, 15 September 2005.

68. *National Security Strategy, May 2010*, p. 48 and also cited on the website of "The International Coalition for the Responsibility to Protect," 28 May 2010, http://www.responsibilitytoprotect.org/index.php/component/content/article/35-r2pcs-topics/2785-white-house-releases-may-2010-national-security-strategy-with-reference-to-rtop (accessed 5 February 2018).

69. In more formal terms these economic functions consist of maintaining an open market for distress goods; providing countercyclical lending; policing a stable system of exchange rates; ensuring the coordination of macroeconomic policies; and acting as a lender of last resort. Charles P. Kindleberger, *The World in Depression, 1929–1939* (Berkeley: University of California Press, 1973), p. 305.

70. G. John Ikenberry, "Grand Strategy as Liberal Order Building," unpublished paper prepared for conference on "After the Bush Doctrine: National Security Strategy for a New Administration," University of Virginia, 7–8 June 2007, p. 3.

71. Joanne Gowa, *Closing the Gold Window: Domestic Politics and the End of Bretton Woods* (Ithaca: Cornell University Press, 1983); Fred Block, *The Origins of International Economic Disorder: A Study of United States International Monetary Policy From World War II to the Present* (Berkeley: University of California Press, 1977), pp. 182–198.

72. Block, *Origins of International Economic Disorder*, pp. 182–198.

73. Statista, "Major foreign holders of US treasury securities, as of June 2018 (in billion US dollars)," October 2018, https://www.statista.com/statistics/246420/major-foreign-holders-of-us-treasury-debt/ (accessed 9 October 2018).

74. Ibid.

75. Ibid.

76. Reich, *Global Norms*, pp. 62–63.

77. Reus-Smit, "Unipolarity and Legitimacy."

78. BBC World Service, Media Centre, "Sharp drop in world views of US, UK: Global poll for BBC World Service," 4 July 2017, https://www.statista.com/statistics/246420/major-foreign-holders-of-us-treasury-debt/ (accessed 9 October 2018).

79. Pew Survey, "Obama More Popular Abroad Than At Home, Global Image of US Continues to Benefit," 17 June 2011, http://www.pewglobal.org/2010/06/17/obama-more-popular-abroad-than-at-home/ (accessed 26 September 2011); Pew Research Global Attitudes Project, "Global Opinion of Obama Slips, International Policies Faulted," 13 June 2012, http://www.pewglobal.org/2012/06/13/global-opinion-of-obama-slips-international-policies-faulted/ (accessed 28 January 2013).

Index[1]

---

[1] Note: Page numbers followed by 'n' refer to notes.

© The Author(s) 2020
R. N. Lebow, *A Democratic Foreign Policy*,
https://doi.org/10.1007/978-3-030-21519-4